# SOCIAL BEHAVIOUR OF CHILDREN

***By the same author***

— Violence and Religion : Cross-Cultural Opinions and Consequences
— Child Space : An Anthropological Exploration of Young peoples Use of Space

---

**About the Author**

**Ralph Tanner** has a B.Sc. and Diploma in Social Anthropology from Oxford University and a D.Phil in Law from Stockholm University. He has done field work in Thailand, the Philippines, Guyana, Zambia, Zimbabwe, Tanzania, Uganda and Kenya as well as in Britain and Eire. He was Chairman of the East African Institute of Social Research and a Lecturer in Comparative Religion in the University of London. He has published books on Murder in Uganda, Witchcraft Killings and Religious Change in Tanzania, the Roman Catholic Mass, contemporary religious change and co-authored two books on the biology of religion, two on the recreation of tribal identity and religious change and another on religion and the environment. He has written numerous articles on the social aspects of religious change, translation and language use, as well as on behavioural theories in the Journal of Modern African Studies, Africa, Journal of Social Sciences, Nordic Journal of African Studies, Anthropos and Studia Missionalia and others. He is currently working on the issues involved in social science field work in developing societies by nationals and non-nationals and the connections between spirituality, well-being and health.

# SOCIAL BEHAVIOUR OF CHILDREN
## A CROSS CULTURAL ASSESSMENT

R.E.S. Tanner

CONCEPT PUBLISHING COMPANY, NEW DELHI-110059

**Cataloging in Publication Data—DK**
*Courtesy:* D.K. Agencies (P) Ltd. <docinfo@dkagencies.com>

**Tanner, R. E. S. (Ralph E. S.),** 1921-
Social behaviour of children : a cross cultural assessment / R.E.S. Tanner.
p. cm.
Includes bibliographical references (p. )
Includes index.
ISBN 8180693848

1. Child psychology—Social aspects—Cross-cultural studies.
2. Interpersonal relations—Cross-cultural studies.
I. Title.

DDC 155.418 22



ISBN : 81-8069-384-8

First Published 2007



*Published and Printed by*
Ashok Kumar Mittal
**Concept Publishing Company**
A/15-16, Commercial Block, Mohan Garden
New Delhi-110059 (India)

*Phones* : 25351460, 25351794
*Fax* : 091-11-25357103
*Email* : publishing@conceptpub.com

*Dedication*

**For Amoret in Gratitude**

# ACKNOWLEDGEMENTS

This study was initiated in discussions with Professor D.K. Behera, the Department of Anthropology, Sambalpur University, Orissa and with C. Pawson, the Department of Psychology, University of East London. I am most grateful for the stimulus which they provided and I regret that pressure of work prevented their continuing association.

My thanks are due to the Librarians of Trinity College, Oxford, the Institute of Social Anthropology, Oxford and the Tadley branch of the Hampshire County Library for providing research resources.

My thanks are also due for my memories of the formative help which I received from Sao Hkun Hkio, Sawbwa of Mongmit and Dashi Yaw, Taungok of the Kodaung Hill Tracts in Myanmar. Also from Ali Farahani of Kilwa, Juma Ndamulo, Nfumo Kabadi and Ntemi Kapongo of the Sukuma, Tanzania and above all from the artist, poet and author Poppy Del who enabled my work to develop over the years.

# Contents

## Chapter-1

# INTRODUCTION

### Aims

Whether within academia media or the cafeteria, modern forums of debate discussing youth culture and the social behaviour of children and adolescents are dominated by examining anti-social rather than pro-social behaviour. Without denying the presence or impact of anti-social behaviour, this study aims to catalyse and redress the balance of debate by presenting a multi-disciplinary and integrated approach to pro-social behaviour with particular reference to the societies of East London, East Africa and East Asia.

### Definition

A dictionary definition of pro-social behaviour remains elusive and cannot simply be viewed as the polar opposite of anti-social activities which are harmful or annoying to others. It is suggested rather than an antonymic definition of anti-social behaviour, pro-social behaviour denotes more than merely harmless or pleasant behaviour to others. It refers instead to behaviour conducive to the nurturing of social interaction and functioning whether on a micro (interpersonal) or macro (social) scale.

There are cautionary aspects to any such definition. The role of pro-social behaviour in nurturing interpersonal and societal interaction and functioning is by no means suggestive of a necessarily conscious or altruistic motivation. Rather pro-social acts such as sharing, help or the provision of comfort are as likely to be sub-conscious as conscious, egocentric as they are altruistic.

In addition there is also the basic problem that the pro-social behaviour of one individual, family or social group; is often likely to be against the interests of other individuals, families and social groups.

The pro-social behaviour of Mafia families and those of Arab and sub-Saharan dictators would be cases in point. Most societies have situations in which one social group is actively hostile to others on survival, tribal, religious or political grounds or have the built-in practice of social duplicity in which individuals cultivate at least neutral relations with their neighbours while acting against them as far as possible in private.

Thus the definition of pro-social behaviour is difficult because it aims at some measure of exactness in interpersonal and societal situations that are endlessly varied and moreover implies social groupings which have some substance. In this the key problem being the suggestion that pro-social behaviour is mainly concerned with the maintenance rather than the formation of bonds and networks.

In such a wide ranging study it is salutary for us to remember Leach's comment that "any system of cross-cultural comparisons which can be used as to make 'the Tikopia' and 'the Chinese' units of comparable type is self-evidently absurd and I do not see that the absurdity is reduced by calling the units 'cultunits' instead of tribes" (Leach, 1964: 299). There can be no overall global pro-asocial behaviour.

The assumption remains to be proved that culture is inevitably dominant in the training and development of children in pro-social behaviour and even more doubtful that there can be any overall humanoid specific characteristics which can account for any social and psychological rigidity in the processes of fitting the growing child into or failing to fit into their surrounding society. In practice this may in terms of time on the ground involvement as being members of the family group and surrounding neighbourhood of shops, school and play ground.

There are certainly cultural traits for any society but it is always a question of to whom do they apply and when. The dominance of the mother's brother over the development of his sister's children in matrilineal societies and the inevitable clash with the biological parent may be a well recorded cultural norm but often there may be no biological male parent and the mother has never had any brothers, so the norm is not practised except possibly in terms of psychological anxiety.

No society even that of hunter-gatherers has ever been or is uniform on demographic, social and economic characteristics alone. There are old and young parents, only children, multiple step parents, the rich and the poor and so on. It is illusionary to expect a so-called traditional society to be any more uniform than a Calcutta or Lima slum, the planned urban housing estate or the Middletown USA (Muncie, Indiana) of sociological fame (Lynd & Lynd, 1929).

The tendency to assume or find uniformities of child training or behaviour is perhaps the inevitable consequence of restricted data and restricted opportunities to find wider and more varied information in terms of the time and money available. Census' are far from accurate and even if accurate represent what people feel to be culturally appropriate at a particular time and does not represent the structure of a family the day before or the day after the census. The Chinese tend to age children from the time of conception not from birth and many cultures do not record babies until they have been formally recognised as social beings.

There is also the factor that any understanding is adult rather than child centred and there is always a research need for as broad a series of categories as possible in order to produce quantifiable data which is often assumed to have greater validity and usefulness.

The factor of cultural variability has also to be recognised in individuals and in the many and varying groups in which they have roles as both adults involved with children and the children themselves. There is always a failure of anything more than nominal coincidence between what is required by a particular cultural environment, the extent to which the people questioned state that they do or might do and what they actually do.

Pro-social behaviour is inevitably a combination of familial realities. The single mother and the step parent are near universal social categories. There is unlikely to be any cross-cultural similarities in how these relationships function and even less in familial and situational variations within a single group whether small or large in numbers. Similarly some families are concentrated geographically in housing or neighbourhoods and others are small in numbers. An Afro-American service woman and mother in Britain listed the 126 relatives which she could visit and perhaps stay the night with when she went on leave to the USA. Her children in terms of pro-social behaviour are likely to see the practical return on such family based behaviour much more readily than the single child of divorced and remarried parents living in neighbourhoods dictated by the career needs of such parents.

Pro-social behaviour may be dictated by understandings of statutory deprivation, the poverty level of particular families dependent on State welfare in Europe or charity in Afghanistan or Ruanda. Then there is always the experience of subjective poverty in which children may not have what others have with whom they associate or see in the mass media. The range of the have-nots is no longer confined to economically-developed western societies but is an international characteristic likely to affect all children in how they play and with what. The cover of a recent number of the British Medical Journal pictured a young Afghan boy holding a crude wooden model of a Kalashnikov machine gun, just as earlier Ugandan children played with stick made models of bicycles and latter mud models of cars.

There are always in every child's life situational necessity factors which influence their growth and understandings of pro-social behaviour. In the poor communities of the expanding cities such as Cairo, Karachi and Ibadan most children will have experienced sudden death, the underemployment of family adults and persistently inadequate food and indeed their lives will be based on their own immediate needs so that the norm of reciprocal assistance in coping with difficulties may be no more than a cultural memory.

Reciprocity does not work either at the opposite end of any social and economic scale. The Kenyan university lecturer with two children in private schools cannot afford to help his relatives who take but have nothing to give in return; if they visit him in Nairobi they are offered the garage to sleep in.

In developed societies their experience of divorce combined with geographical and social movement and even unemployment and bankruptcy may well have equivalent consequences for the mentally developing and growing child. Dependence on relatives or social welfare will have different effects on familial understandings of their existence which will be passed onto children.

There are also situational factors which have become so long standing as to form part of a community's cultural understanding. The prolonged violence in Afghanistan whether from guns or the imposition of extremely restrictive form of social life will have produced forms of childhood understandings for which there is no cultural background or familial support. Similarly the near universal beatings of Palestinian youths by the Israeli police (Peteet, 1994), produce a culture of required adolescent violence to the occupying power and their symbols into which every Arab child grows. The most extreme case of children being brought up without any consideration for pro-social requirements would be the hunter-gathering If of northern Uganda forced by circumstances to become farmers in an unsuitable environment amongst whom every individual is looking after their own interests and their children have to fend for themselves (Turnbull, 1973).

In Maslow's hierarchy of needs (Maslow, 1987) with its five hierarchically ordered types of behaviour there is a useful framework for considering the pro-social behaviour of children. This was created because in his research Maslow found that "good human beings" were rare; indeed he found only one among the three thousand student sampled and only eighteen possible ones among the male "great and good" in historical records.

It is easy to assume that the pro-social behaviour of starving children is likely to be non-existent and that it might only marginally appear as correlating with safety needs which similarly may well dominate their entire needs coalescing into a pack mentality and behavioural pattern of living.

The third level of belongingness and affection need may well involve pro-social behaviour, but then it is always liable to revert to stages one or two under sudden emergency situations of war, famine and disease such as the AIDS epidemic in central and southern Africa which has created far more orphans than the 5 per cent which an average community might be able to absorb or to turn on to the requirements of the fourth stage.

This fourth level of esteem needs will involve children in behavioural changes as their social orbit begins to extend beyond the familial which finally merges into the final self-actualisation stage in which pro-social behaviour is likely to be both selfish and individualistic as in the primary one of physiological survival. A grade of child development from the biological to the psychological via the social and it is in this middle stage that pro-social behavioural are likely to be recognisably of importance.

Finally there is the factor of individual differences. If pre-human hominids have individual characteristics which are clear enough for them to be named, then the range of human individual differences must be just as large and equally diverse. Children in their ability to adjust and the adults with whom they are adjusting are likely to be infinitely variable.

Thus the patterns of pro-social requirements and the resulting behaviours are likely to be immensely varied and similarities are more likely to be coincidental than something which can be assumed to exist in any group of families, communities or societies. The behaviour of children is likely to fluctuate between assumed or observable patterns rather than being sequential and inevitable according to the theories of Piaget.

This approach therefore will be to examine range of societies in which patterns have been deduced by careful research and then to note the variations within them. It is possible that the variations may have greater cross cultural similarity than the traits from which they vary; the step-mother and mother-in-law are sources of tension affecting children may well be a trait common in all patrilineal societies whether in Paris, Porbunder, Port of Spain or Peking. An English mother-in-law joke can be told in Swahili to an East African patrilineal group and be laughed at for the same reasons as in England, but the same joke told to a matrilineal Yao audience falls flat. The typology of variations from cultural norms may well have greater overall validity than any typology of cultural norms.

We can conclude that the pro-social behaviour of children is likely to be based on understandable social reciprocities and psychological needs in which the former probably dominates before the more intrinsically psychological comes into play.

In any social scale altruism can be seen as behaviour enabled by the fulfilment of the earlier needs for food, safety, belongingness and self-esteem; an almost time and motion assessment of what an individual child has time and need to do and as such not likely to be uncommon. Self-sacrifice dedicated to the welfare of others can be found in varying degrees throughout the animal kingdom but even there it can be assessed in evolutionary terms as contributing to the common good in the survival of that community. How these ideas and practices are used and understood becomes a melange of ambivalence, deceit and guilt that continuously troubles the individual mind (Wilson, 1975: 159).

## The Factor of Influences over the Growing Child

There are numerous difficulties with the concept that an individual or circumstances can influence a child. It can be accepted that humans do influence one another but Kipling wrote that "I have five serving men who taught me all I know; how, where, when, who and why," but these are all variables and the primary difficulty is that some have immediate effects and others we can assume are longer lasting. The implications of much research into the ways in which pro-social behaviour is taught to children is that someone rather than something has a long lasting influence on them from the time that they were developing.

The first snag is that this is usually worked backwards from adults who have certain observable characteristics accepted as a permanent and on-going feature of their personality. Further that some individuals have self-acknowledged traits which they attribute to something that has happened in the past. These two aspects may be related to earlier influences but there may be no pragmatic connection between the two as both are in effect creations of contemporary situations.

The only constant influence that can be traced from childhood is some physical influence a birth defect as a physiological fact, an inescapable datum line and which may be diagnosed and controlled chemically. But again even these constants can have their effects altered by various forms of consistent or inconsistent caring over a long period. A man born with fingers damaged at birth was still able to "kill" a German Tiger tank in Normandy in July 1944.

At any time individuals may state with conviction that their current lives have been influenced by what has happened in the past but this is surely a speculative conclusion about something which may or may not have happened; many people include in their current lives what Norman Mailer called "factoids" fictional events which are so near to reality that they might almost have happened.

Certain influences fade and others come in and perhaps there is a cognitive limit to what can be kept in the brain as an influence in any conscious sense. But then influences can occur for which there is no discernable past as happiness from having a good meal in good company which could be assessed as chemical effects.

An influence appears to be such a fluid factor that it has a do-it-yourself element to it as in the historian A.L. Rowse amending his diary to bring it up-to-date in ways which he considered to be appropriate for his current thinking. Most influences are short-lived and some indeed may be carried forward in the adult behaviour of children as in the continuation of marital violence over generations but is this an influence or the persistence of similar social environments.

## The Factor of Randomness in Influences on Children

The persistence of statistics in the evaluation of what may influence the development of children perhaps ignores the fact that each child is not only distinct but the circumstances of their lives are distinct; social science statistics share some of the characteristics of gambling as they are praiseworthy attempts to shorten the odds on a particular pattern of behaviour being repeated.

Randomness is surely the prime factor in all assessments of human behaviour. The fact that certain facts appear more common than others does not mean that they are any less random since their isolation creates particular situational constructions.

If we can static situations then there is perhaps greater assurance that certain events are going to happen, not just likely to happen, but then this is an unreal situation since it is not something likely to happen. As the famous anthropologist Evans-Pritchard once remarked about his professional colleagues that they were all historians and this comment could have been extended to the social sciences in general. This professional "betting" on the reoccurrence of something happening again is an acknowledgement of this randomness.

There is another aspect to randomness whenever some form of quasi-static inter-relationship becomes identifiable such as between mother and child or between siblings. In the assessment of a simple "yes" or "no" factor, the odds are even but with each additional qualifying factor the odds lengthen. So that in any relationship, the complexity of situational factors must mean that the possibility of anything more than crude repetition is infinitesimal. Even then the factors involved are not likely to be repeated so that repetition is likely to be a statistical accident.

Nevertheless the social sciences inevitably aim at achieving some exactness so that in the view of researchers something can be estimated as likely to happen. If we leave the attempts to achieve exactness and discuss the pro-social behaviour of children in terms of spheres of influence, then there may be some understandings of what is affecting the development of children.

We thus approach the analysis of the pro-social behaviour of children within a broad initiative ranging from the biological and ethological to the social and psychological with an interest not so much in the usually unattainable cultural norms, but more in the factors predisposing social units to vary these norms under conditions of social and economic necessity and demographic change. We start by considering the influence of heredity, parents and siblings, family differences, and the influence of peers.

## The Factor of Heredity

It seems obvious enough that much in any human being is inherited from their parents but except for purely physiological traits which cannot be altered so that a static fact has to be accommodated by those involved, psychological characteristics except at their extremes can be assumed to be much more malleable.

Even if we assume that 40-50 per cent of the measured psychological characteristics of adults are due to heredity (Tellegen *et al.,* 1988; Bouchard, 1944; Plomin and Daniels, 1987) working from work on identical twins over a long period (Cohen, 1999), we are not much further forward in assessing the influence of such factors on pro-social socialisation of children since intelligence may and may not be in behaviour which might be pro-social at one level and anti-social at another.

If we examine the five so-called super traits and see them in cross-cultural perspectives, it may be that these characteristics are no more than what those particular societies expect from their children. It is the unilateral assumption that a trait is a constant when the social environment in which it is active can be subject to radical change.

There is of course the fact that these characteristics come from tests and it must remain doubtful whether agreeing to some idealistic conceptions of right behaviour or making correlating choices in hypothetical situations can have any serious validity. A Roman Catholic seminarian faced with a test involving moral questions, refused to answer as both were morally wrong and he would not make an abstract choice without being involved in an actual a social situation, in much the same way that a politician is not happy with "if" hypothetical questions.

Surely a measured psychological characteristic are static and between assessment A and assessment B, there may be a continuation of vaguely similar social environments but not necessarily so and indeed it would be unlikely that any child of five, ten and the adult of twenty or fifty would be living in even an approximation of the same social environments whether in Cairo, Caterham or the Kodaung Hill tracts of Upper Myanmar.

To take the extroversion trait that some people are active and sociable; this was not identifiable in Ugandan school children with high hook worm infections which led to a marked lack of energy. Agreeableness, a tendency to be kind and affectionate must be related to particular people and in no known society can it be a trait which is exercised with those who are hostile to the group in which an adult or child is living. It is just not possible for such a trait to have any pro-social value at all in many societies in which neighbours are rivals and if it is used it might have some functional value as a deceitful but nevertheless valuable ploy.

Then comes conscientiousness, the tendency to be reliable and organised. A Sukuma subsistence farmer would have these characteristics almost as a *sine qua non* for survival and he would run his own reciprocal relationships in a calculating way. It seems likely that only in Western societies with their welfare systems are there disorganised people which are kept alive at the expense of tax-payers or who are disorganised in their personal lives but are kept in some sort of survivable order by their families or friends.

Emotional stability as the tendency to be calm and stable surely can apply mainly in situations which allow this to occur. The emotions expressed in religious services, pop concerts and spirit possession events are both common and sporadic and may well be seen either as the products of culture or particular training.

Finally intellectual openness, the tendency to be insightful and inventive surely is likely to be a characteristic of a certain number of people in any society. Intellectual mutations can and do appear in every society (Tanner, 1997) and the Sukuma and the Japanese have a shared cultural to create "haiku" verses of almost epigramic brevity which require considerable intellectual ingenuity to compose into which listeners weave their own personal and cultural understandings. It may certainly run in families but that is a social environment which is attuned to these types of expectations and therefore may be highly heritable (Lykken & Telligen, 1996; Diener & Diener, 1996).

But is it surprising that individual children develop some at least of the same personality characteristics as their parents, indeed we note often enough when there are striking examples of children who do not. These shared opinions are probably not only those of their parents but of the limited in numbers social contacts in which those families live out their lives. The opinions of others which we know enough about to link it with persons in most cases is probably nearer tens than hundreds and it probably sorts itself out that children are not generally exposed initially to those of whom their parents themselves do not approve, whether they are peasants in Asia, villagers in Bavaria or flat dwellers in central London.

These traits may be hereditable but this is nothing approaching a genetic connection between parents and children since they are indefinable. There may be hereditary factors controlling behaviour at the extreme ends of any behavioural scale such as would occur with Huntington's Chorea, but in what might be called more humdrum situations, the social environment would almost invariably block off or modify an hereditary approach or disposition to a situation requiring behavioural choice.

Alexander Selkirk at his own request was put ashore on the uninhabited island of Juan Fernandez in 1704 and lived alone there-for five years and have become reliable and organised in order to survive such a long period of solitude, but this may have been a new characteristic since earlier he had run away to sea. In the fictional "Lord of the Flies" (Golding, 1954) middle class children are marooned on an island and turn to savagery and one may suspect that this is a commonplace event in situations of war and civil strife in which men with unexceptional family lives turn to violence against both persons and property. Hogarth's pictures of 18th century English life suggest that such behaviour was commonplace and it must be a matter of interpretation as to whether such behaviour now has become rarer or more covert.

Heredity in the context of social behaviour is far too loose a term to have much functional validity to account for specific patterns of pro-social or anti-social behaviour. It would be strange if children did not have some if not many characteristics which they seem to share with their parents, but it is another thing altogether to suggest that anything quite so specific as an identifiable trait has some genetic significance.

For something to have genetic significance it has to be variable enough to have advantages in a very wide variety of situations so that in ways that are independent of human planning or individual success and these five types of behavioural traits are perhaps too exact and even more are tied to specific types of societies. Even if it could be shown to have significance for human societies as a whole, these have been going on in some societies only for a very short period of time and are thus not linked to pro-social necessities as they are likely to be seen cross-culturally.

On the other hand if there is some genetic element that leads to getting on with blood relatives rather than outsiders then there is a behavioural something that is likely to survive in a multitude of different environments because it leads to differential survival rates. It does not suggest or require any particular relationships and any propensity to make it confined to patrilineality, matrilineality or whatever; its vagueness and adjustable utility ensures that it as a genetic trait, it will survive.

If we suggest that a particular child's behaviour is due to heredity, then in fact we are not saying anything of any great importance because it is likely to be confined to a range of families within a particular culture; a form of social "inheritance" which cannot have a biological correlations. If there are hereditable behavioural traits in human children, they would have to be so indefinably wide-ranging so as to fit the circumstances of pygmy children in the Congo, the street children of Brazil and those of the privileged elites in a range of societies and also the impossible requirement that the characteristics would have had similar functions for numerous generations of which perhaps only sexual functional differentiations might fulfil such requirements.

Since the hereditary component cannot foretell its own future, then we have no more than some sort of adjustable human behavioural spanner that fits into as many different social and individual environments as can be brought into consideration which brings us to the possibility that parents do influence their children not only immediately but as a background to possible pro-social behaviour.

## The Influence of Parents

This has become so much a feature of every study of the bringing up of children in the best possible way that it has the characteristics almost of dogma, at least of religious idealism. The weakness of any argument of parental influence on the development of children based on a pattern of familial living which is statistically rare; a family setting in which a father and a mother live together with their children for long and uninterrupted periods.

If we start with the assumption that parents do not have an important effect on the development of the personality and behaviour of their children, then there is supportive evidence that differences among children cannot be convincingly traced to differences in the way that they have been brought up (Maccoby, 1992; Rowe, 1994).

Then there is the commonplace fact that conventional families in any society are a statistical abstraction; of course any society will state that there are ideal family states which the artist Norman Rockwell illustrated so well for white American culture. However conformity to this except in the short-term; the weekend or evenings only husband is commonplace and child care away from the natal mother is a well distributed activity in most societies.

Although the research relates to American families of which many are still composed of mother, father and children, there are and always have been numbers of less conventional arrangements. When the unconventional arrangement is inadvertent—the result of a failed marriage or failure to marry—there is an increased risk that the children will experience failures in their own lives, but when the unconventional arrangements result from a consciously made lifestyle decision no differences in child outcome were found (Weisner, 1986; Flaks *et al.*, 1995).

A cross-cultural examination of family patterns shows that most societies do not have any such close relationships in any time and motion sense once the child has become independent of its mother's breast and has become mobile. It has been estimated that North American fathers perhaps spend 2-3 per cent of their time with their children and mothers 20-25 per cent and that the Aka pygmies father spend 47 per cent (Hewlett, 1991). If influence correlates to time spent in inter-relationships between parents and children, then it has to be some form that is created in the shorter term than the influences that make come from the longer association of children with particular teachers.

Perhaps the most telling argument against any assumption that the parents have a dominant influence over their children is the act that demographically under the most optimum conditions it is a short-term association, certainly important in the earliest years but gradually thinning out and being overlaid by the multitude of new experiences affecting the children in early adolescence and latter.

## The Influence of Siblings

It has often been assumed that the sisters and brothers of any child may perhaps have as much or more influence on the pro-social behaviour of children than their parents. In subsistence agricultural societies children in any time and motion assessment will spend far longer with their siblings than with their mothers and often as negligible amount of time with their fathers. However it has been concluded on the basis of largely American and Chinese research that there are no consistent differences between only children and those with one or two siblings and that this leaves no permanent marks on their characters (Harris, 1998: 52, 61).

In the United States the emergence of large numbers of single child families may be the result of conscious choices by parents determined not have their life styles severely modified by children. However in China the predominance of only children is no longer a matter of personal choice but national policy enforced with some severity by numerous overseers of the birth control practised by married women and so far undesirable consequences in the behaviour of such children has not been identified (Yang *et al.,* 1995; Falbo & Polit, 1986; Falbo & Poston, 1993).

But this issue goes beyond the consequences of being only children since a majority of them are born into sibling relationships and the influences which are brought to bear are likely to reinforce those of their parents which will have already instilled and promoted the values of the surrounding society.

The relationship between siblings are of two patterns; the one in which the first-born runs the lives of the latter-born children because the mother is dead or too involved with subsistence agriculture and the relationships between latter born children. While these relationships may be more constant and immediate than those with parents, the question remains as to how long this influence remains and influential over what aspects of pro-social behaviour.

Even if we presuppose that there is some proto-genetic patterning in the behaviour of every child, then parents have the opportunity to change this which of course they do not except in every exceptional and individual circumstances; whatever influences they will be largely conforming what is socially acceptable already, but can we assume that this is likely to be pro-social in its wider implications?

In most societies it is not a question of sibling influences since daughters marry out and they are ignored in the rivalries of sons. In segmentary societies brothers are brought up in rivalry to succeed their father and in polygynous families the rivalry between the children of different mothers is almost universally expected. While siblings may augment the conformity of children to wider social values, their pro-social influence may be towards the success of their own particular social segment and in this are just as likely as not to be a disruptive influence in the surrounding community.

There is another factor which is shared with their parents. While the relationship may remain until siblings die off, their effective interrelationship may be extremely short-lived. Changes in relative ages are quick and may be broken by attendance at school and by the early marriage of girls. We must conclude that the direct influence of siblings may be a short-term one and as like or not may be one of long lasting and expected rivalry..

## Differences between Families

While it may be correct that every family with children considers itself to be part of a wider society which has some cultural pattern of expected or actual behaviour, there can in fact be no overall similarity between any two families except in the broadest terms of sharing a physical environment, speaking the same language and some understanding of age and sex roles.

Of course there will be clear enough similarities and differences in the ways in which white American, Japanese and Sukuma parents bring up their children but break this down to any section of these societies and differentiating factors make it extremely difficult to find any factor that predominates in more than a few families at most and somewhat tenuously in these.

Then we have to consider the differences which must devolve from individual intelligence, their familial, social and economic network, neighbourhood, school system and the list becomes longer and longer as distinctions become apparent which differentiate even the subsequent families of brothers and sisters who at one time considered themselves to have been exceptionally close; very little is shared; closeness is a subjective evaluation which may not survive the realities of dividing up an inheritance. In all of these considerations only peer groups appear to be a consistent influence on the behaviour of both adults and children and that they adjust all the time to the needs and experiences of every individual.

We have established that in terms of behavioural genetics very little can be laid down as likely to occur rather than as just a probability except with identifiable morbidities. Parenthood in time and motion terms has been shown to be far less influential than idealistic assumptions would suggest and much the same applies to siblings since the relationship may not exist at all. But both these spheres of influence suffer from the disadvantages that they are involuntary roles in which individuals are involved without any choice so that all behaviour starts from this involuntary base of fixed social realities; all children have biological parents and may have biological siblings. Why should experiences with parents and siblings have lasting effects when such relationships do not last all that long in comparison to subsequent relationships and the memorable crises that come latter in the lives of all children.

## Peer Groups and Pro-social Behaviour

The influence of peer groups on children as they might affect pro-social learning and behaviour is significant as the relationships and the groups themselves have no particular inevitability. No child is without some peer group participations and this has none of the constraining inevitability of parental and sibling relationships. They are relating to constantly changing and varied associations including sports teams, gangs, school clubs and hobby groupings.

Since in every child's experience peer groups are universal and far more inevitable than parents and siblings who may not exist at all in any practical inter-relationships, their absence can be expected to have abnormal consequences which are not necessarily adverse. Bertrand Russell in his autobiography describes the loneliness of his childhood and education at home and that when he did get to school he was bullied so that his life was not without peer group experience and to suggest that it did not have some lasting consequences is speculation.

Certainly there are examples of abnormal upbringing in which children do not associate with other children as those who are permanently institutionalised because of severe mental or physical disabilities, the so-called "wild" children allegedly brought up by animals who of course may have been abnormal initially and children brought up or rather sheltered in Nazi concentration camps. (Harris, 1995). It is obvious that whatever pro-social behaviour such children develop it was restricted to very specialised social environments.

Some children may be brought up in relatively isolated social environments such as those born in and form an economically valuable part of a farming family, but these children would still be part of schooling and their upbringing is certainly pro-social to the lives that they may well anticipate living (Parker, 1995).

The age-grading of pastoral tribal societies of Eastern and Sudanese Africa may no longer be functioning as they may have done in pre-colonial times, but the age grading in schools, which must be now by far the commonest experience of children everywhere is a far harsher and compulsory division of juvenile society than anything experienced in a society generally where children have wider choices as to the peer groups which they enter.

Overall there can be little doubt that the experiences of being accepted or rejected by peer groups do have influences on how children subsequently see relationships. High or low status in a peer group or indeed rejection may have lasting effects on the personality of children denied the status to which they aspire (Harris, 1998: 179 and 181). Studying what the child wants and amongst those with whom they feel more comfortable may produce useful understandings of pro-social developments (Kindermann, 1993).

Peer groups are both universal and constantly changing so that the growing child learns to adjust to the pro-social requirements of those who are on their social and demographic level. While their parents may introduce them to the cultural spheres of influence within which they will usually spend most of their lives, it seems likely that the inter-relationships which most children experience in a variety of peer groups has a lasting importance. It is the interplay of cultural spheres of influence and the dominance of peer group relationships which we will later examine for their significance in creating and enabling pro-social behaviour in growing children.

We have seen so far that there are few permanencies in either families or in societies on which cultural and cross-cultural assumptions can be made. Let us now look further at the regularities and irregularities in the socialisation of children.

## Chapter-2

# Irregularity and Indistinct Socialisation

Human physiological and psychological behaviour is a constantly fluctuating dialectic between the consequences of assumed and hopefully anticipated regularity in their experiences and the inevitable disturbing irregularities. Only in time tied societies can there be any exact anticipation of what can be planned and anticipated but this is always modified by human and mechanical failures. It is an imposed restriction on behaviour and one which has very slowly and recently spread socially and economically downwards in a few societies from the watches and clocks of the rich to cheap digital watches, time signals, programme timings and a preoccupation with the time tables of aircraft, buses and trains combined with the social complications of being early, late or on time.

In ethological considerations irregularities are common enough since the higher apes are often faced with disasters and irregularities to which they have always had to adjust as their built-in avoidance of extinction; predators attack, certain trees produce a superabundance of fruit and prolonged droughts causing forest fires that cut back on the environment to which they have for a time become adjusted.

As human beings climb up the evolutionary scale, the regularities would appear to diminish in comparison to the increasing number of irregularities resulting from complex social and geographical environments failing to mesh satisfactorily and the diversities of the individual personality as more and more people are involved in short rather than long-term inter-relationships.

If in fact human behaviour was in the main regular in the sense of having no behavioural alternative to regularity, then they would have failed to function adequately in more than a narrow band of circumstances. In such circumstances socialisation to that form of pro-social behaviour would probably have led to ethological failure and extinction.

It seems likely that the concept of social systems being regular is at least in part the creation of social scientists and political and economic planners who need regularity as part of their professional equipment. It much more difficult to cope with constant irregularity because it goes against the human cognitive wish for regularity and indeed the need to use their brains over concern with their individual and collective futures.

Even the most economically under-developed peasants in environments which may have at one time been untouched by outside social and economic forces, has ways of behaving and thinking which as far as possible mitigate the dire consequences of uncertainty. Any analysis of so-called primitive societies shows that they are as insurance minded as any modern workers with their concerns over the company pension fund.

It seems certain that their understandings of how to live adequately in their harsh environments must have been both pragmatic and practical as they would not have survived socially on the illogicalities of a magical conception as to how the universe worked.

The individual child whether in the slums of Lima or the ordered suburbs of Guildford is faced with different forms of regularity and irregularity as well as different forms of conscious and unconscious anticipation. They will always want to be fed and they will always have some idea of having a party, breaks in the boredom of ongoing life which will provide them with excitement; funerals, fires and fights.

It may be that regularity is some figment of the human imagination which adults attempt to impose on their social environments with very little long-term success. Of course there are school terms and time-tables but attendances will always vary, accidents occur and individual opinions conflict. This is what may happen in a school in Guildford but in a rural environment in Tanzania the possibility of regularity diminishes with geographical distances, as well as social and economic abilities to organise family life to coincide with that of other families and a distant school.

Most subsistence societies appear to function quite well with only a vague idea of regularity tied to the seasons. Ceremonies start when enough of the required people have turned up to make it valid and this validity is more in the mind than in any set procedures; there is no order of service for a sacrifice to propitiate the ancestors and if there is one it is the creation of the anthropologist. Much depends on the appearance of the sun and cloud cover.

Even in the seemingly well-ordered household containing a dozen television sets, watches and clocks the irregularities stand out in the memories of its children; clothes are lost, something is left off the shopping list and someone gets up late while the father's evening train is delayed, and always there is forgetfulness.

Irregularities are so built into the socialisations of children in all societies that only in its extremes are there likely to be emotional reactions for a crisis. Nevertheless they are likely to be constantly influenced by vaguely unexpected events; crossing the road, running to head-off a stray animal, seeing a snake, catching a finger on a thorn, dropping a plate, waiting in a queue and overbalancing with a pot of water on their head. Such minor events all create changes even if they are accepted as a normal part of living.

Any growing child is inevitably faced with irregularities within the hope of regularities and it is the function of socialisation to make children adaptable; mother's fall sick, a meal is delayed, rain upsets sports days, a toy gets broken and they have stomach aches and sibling rivalry comes and goes. Certainly there are anticipated regularities such as the excitements of eating and playing about at night during the holy month of Ramadan when eating is forbidden during day light and the hope of presents at Christmas but there are always disappointments.

Much of the magico-religious life of people whether adults or children at whatever level of economic, social and political development is spent in trying to get the irregularities of life under some sort of control; there are enormous numbers of charms on sale in the markets of Oxford and Orissa and behaviours which function to ensure good luck and to avoid bad luck are virtually universal. Divination, and forms of astrology are a major preoccupation of subsistence societies as well as for large numbers of people in advanced economies.

Regularities as they are now understood in modernising and modernised societies is a necessary part of coordinating human behaviour to ends which have not inevitably been for their advantage. In the main coordination is imposed on individuals and not always appreciated hence Marx's invention of the concept of anomie for work in which the individual gets no profit or personal satisfactions from industrial production.

The fact that there is an official time means that adults and children can be coordinated for certain specific activities. If anything it creates an additional range of anxieties-related to gaps between the irregular realities of day to day living and a scientific abstraction used for a form of social oppression.

Most attempts in modernised societies or in the modernising parts of less developed societies is for the convenience of adults and institutions. There is little in the primary group setting of human behaviour which necessitates exact regularity except in the broad understandings of the agricultural year and the nomadic migrations of herders and hunters. The regularities if any are in terms of graded priorities according to Maslow's Hierarchy of needs.

It would seem therefore that socialisation into pro-social behaviour which acts upon children cannot be in terms of regularities but of social systems within primary groups which copes with irregularities; for children as much as adults it has always been an uncertain world surrounding them. So we would seem to have to accept that what can be defined as pro-social behaviour is likely to be indistinct.

The aim of investigating pro-social behaviour as taught or created for children is seemingly clear since it is surely obvious that any society must want its children to grow up to become socially acceptable adults. Thus functionally there must be educators but does any society have a single model of behaviour towards which the training of children is directed?

There are certainly widespread norms in societies which most people in most cultures overwhelmingly accept probably because the questions related to norms are presented to them in abstract terms; particular people in particular situations are not knitted into these abstractions.

Such widespread norms would be the prohibition of killing and that children should obey their fathers and the five million Súkuma of Tanzania would no doubt agree to these norms that it may be wrong to kill a sibling or parent but relate the situations to an incestuous parent, adulterer, cattle thief, member of a hostile tribe and a witch, then this norm becomes compromised by the situation in which it is invoked. Then the other norm of obedience to the father becomes equally difficult when there is no known father or the grand-father rather than the known biological but not the legal father is the legal parent of the child, apart from chieftainship clans in which descent was matrilineal as opposed to the rest of the people who were patrilineal.

As H.L. Mencken once wrote that we should be thankful that there are only Ten Commandments, so that every child is brought up in situations in which there may be limited ethical values which are part of the prolonged socialisation in which children are involved. Even if there is no deliberate instruction in their social lives all children become aware quite early on that much depends on the situation. Thou shalt not steal but the child may accompany his father to take or is it to steal a Christmas tree from a plantation of which the former is not the owner.

Of course all communities have a norm of the need to get on well with their neighbours based as it must have been in some distant perhaps ethological necessity for their survival but the importance of such a norm to particular children in their own familiar setting will vary for almost any factor. Thus such a norm will become the question which neighbours and under what circumstances. So there appear to be two poles into which contemporary children are socialised; the geographically limited quasi-traditional community often coinciding with the extended family and the family unit surrounded by multi-dimensional alternative cultural units. Children in the Muslim Middle east have been described as living between two cultural ideals and sets of norms, the traditional Islamic-cum-local traditional one which is relatively uni-dimensional and the undefined but invasive one of electronic modernity (Shoufani, 1988).

For the first dimension let us take the Hangaza of north-western Tanzania, high altitude coffee growers and subsistence farmers with a high population density. Their children would be brought up to consider that their own immediate family has priority and that the owners of surrounding highly valued fields are rivals and that boundary disputes are with those who are more distant from them in relational patrilineal, matrilineal and affinal terms. Also because of the shortage of land many of the men are away for most of the year as migrant labourers in Uganda so that in effect children are brought up if not entirely by their mothers with possibly a grandfather somewhere near; most married women for most of the year are performing both male and female roles. This means that the adults in all families have to maintain good relations with their neighbours while at the same time working to undermine such relationships in order to gain more land, and that obedience to the mother does not have the back-up of appeal to the father for most of the year.

So these children are socialised to vague general precepts but which they grow up to recognise as not having any great social immediacy for what goes on around them. Above all that behaviour is governed in the first instance by social realities surrounding the lives of the adults with whom they are living. If this is the case then the pro-social behaviour which is learnt by children does not have any monolineal uniform pattern but is multifaceted by social necessity. They become socialised to the manipulation of values within particular environments.

For perhaps all children there is a confining but negotiable and negotiating social environment in which the more abstract values are quite easy to learn but whose limitations are recognisable from what they see and hear going on around them; a self-regulating system within the precepts of "so far but no further" over social boundaries.

For the second pole in the urban-industrial environment, the required pro-social behaviour pattern which is given to children in much more exact terms in school teaching as to what society expects as good behaviour covering everything from bad language, public cleanliness, good manners while eating and indeed a whole range of required behaviour which is unlikely to have much correlation with what they experience in their own homes and see on television.

What is required of children is given to them by a wide range of other far more impersonal agencies such as the presence of the police, public notices, ticket collectors, time-tables and directions for driving and walking. In practice this environment for children is a rigorously normative one which has none of the ostensibly negotiable and negotiating social environment of a non-literate society and indeed of their own family situations. It is a cultural environment in which children are brought up to avoid these formal controllers of normative behaviour with whom there can be no negotiation because of the social distance between these two social worlds.

The children are still in the same familial environment of rivalry which is split between a limited number of socially acceptable neighbours with whom their adults may have little relationship other than geographical propinquity. Relationships are not seen as related to subsistence except possibly for people who look different to themselves. But their adults may have a more idiosyncratic and individual pattern of behaviour which the children will see as related to what goes on around them and not to any wide range of social patterning.

The control of adults over their children except in the earliest years is only for a proportion of their days if it is seen in time and motion terms and this control is imposed on them by as variety of unconnected agencies, bits and pieces of control which provide no overall normative network which would seem to only exist in communal living such as boarding schools and the communal living of the Hutterites rather more than the more dispersed Amish.

The learning environment of pro-social behaviour is thus more likely to be a family one for only a small proportion of time in which there is direct supervision and if sleeping time is excluded, may only be for a few hours each day and even then they will be under the influence of television or in the requirements of what they have to do for next day's schooling.

There may be some understanding of generalised norms as to what would really get them into trouble, but it is not one which is directly controlling them since much ingenuity goes into avoiding these situations and their consequences. It is a cultural setting in which the pro-social training of children is more one of avoidance than of conformity except where regulations prevent alternatives.

So children in urban industrial settings except in the Muslim world would appear to be made aware of the pro-social requirements of a large number of alternative life styles without any overall normative core. The result of this is that the creation of any relatively stable pro-social code of behaviour for children and for those attempting to provide the teaching to support it, is much more difficult. The young Englishman who became a Sikh explained his conversion in its provision of a set of rules about which there was a comfortable certainty. For most children this is a situation of ethical confusion based on an inevitable social diversity. But how much of this behaviour has a background in ethnology.

## Genetic differences and Pro-social Behaviour

Nature *versus* nurture will probably rumble on indefinitely as the intellectual differences become even more complicated with the increase in available data. There are of course extreme cases in which the genotype may have had extreme negative implications for behaviour as in physical and psychological inabilities to function as a human being at even a minimal level. But only in some cases can we be sure that this is genetic in origin and not the result of some chemical imbalance during pregnancy which might have been avoided or one that can be altered subsequently such as phenylketonuria.

The genotype is only "individually" dominant when it creates situations in which other genes and social environments can have no effect and it would seem that much of our knowledge about inherited behaviour is unambiguously related to extreme and negative characteristics; there is little data of a similar quality on positive ones.

Methodologically in the study of pro-social behaviour of children it is necessary to break away from what may be the prevalent view of genes as being limited in number allied to a pack of cards and that what happens in the human from the moment of conception is the permutations on this limited number of heritable characteristics.

Since there are supposed to be over seventy trillion potential human genotypes the possibility of similarities between individual children even before nurture is considered must be minimal. Each individual is not only different but is subject to differential social environments so that even monozygotic twins will each be subject to different social experiences and much of their similarities may come from the fact that they tend to be brought up in similar environments; staring at someone looking like oneself at the other end of the pram and so on for years on end would surely be an example of nurturing similarities rather than individualities.

A trivial example of such influences of which the researcher might well avoid is the effects of music on the individual child; a single important note in a tune can be played in different ways and presumably have different effects. Three recordings of a single sung word were found to be radically different (Urban, 1996: 201). It is not difficult therefore to presuppose that there can be no single much less influential social environments which would affect children in identical ways.

It would seem then that the categorisations developed by social scientists are possibly no more than rather crude limitations on what children may do pro or anti-socially and no more than a necessity to make the material manageable.

What is one to make of the Bogle family in Oregon, United States of America (*New York Times,* 2002) whose family tree showed that out of thirty-three individuals in three generations only one has no criminal record of imprisonment and even she has two children in prison. The immediate reaction would be that there is a genetic element in this appalling family history leading to such widespread social malfunctions but the one exception is a leader in a religious institution but her children have become criminals. It is difficult to attribute criminality to a single gene as each act for which a Bogle has been imprisoned would have occurred in different social circumstances. It would seem just as likely that these children were nurtured to lie, steal and deceive, but even that tendency may have nevertheless had genetic origins in mutations which worked and survived in the environment of this family in which their children grew up.

**The Level of Influence on Genetic Difference**

A supposed genetic abnormality is not static in the sense that it always has similar overt consequences on individuals living in societies which may or may not have any interest in attempting to alter the consequences of this negative abnormality.

A subsistence culture does not have the resources or indeed the moral imperatives to ensure that an obviously abnormal child survives the peri-natal period. A handicapped child who is kept alive uses up resources in time and materials which a farming family cannot afford to spend on an individual who in the most optimistic evaluation will never be able to contribute to their own survival by performing even minimal farming work. A male child born blind will be killed while a blind girl might survival as her potential fecundity would be socially marketable. There are very few visibly abnormal adolescents among the millions of Sukuma in Tanzania because demographically they would be just numbered among infant mortality totals. No one in authority enquires too closely if a dead baby is found in suspicious circumstances.

Thus the chances of a supposedly abnormal child surviving to adulthood are socially predetermined by factors which are only partially related to the abnormality itself. Once we get beyond the social environmental aspects of minimal survival, there are economic, social and moral factors to consider. This is obvious in the case of children with Down's Syndrome since as recently as thirty years ago it was unusual for them to survive into adulthood. Now their IQs are typically higher and many are employed and leading more self-reliant lives (Lerner *et al.*, 1993).

The state in developed nations or non-governmental charitable organisations may take over the care of abnormal and handicapped children as they have the means and the personnel to do so when the families concerned are mentally and physically unable to do this. It is also more difficult to dispose of such children when they are rarely born in private homes. A village community may be more supportive and generally understanding than those involved who live in an urban tower block with a high residential turnover.

Once there is the economic ability to care, moral factors come into play as well as social ones affecting both parents and siblings. Jews are reported to have a large number of defectives which is noticed in statistics because communities which have a high number of middle class professionals tend to institutionalise their defectives whereas a farming community might more easily find work for such people without losing status.

There is also the factor of whether such families are in fact units capable of such care which is likely to be higher with extended than nuclear families particularly when they are living within walking distance of each other. The ability of a single parent to care is severely limited. So the possibilities of handicapped children receiving attention which might modified their non-social abilities is skewed towards communities and individuals who have the economic means to provide care without damaging their own overall well-being.

## The Timing of Influence Modifying Phenotypic Differences

Whatever the genetic endowment of a child, its ability to absorb the requirements of its social environment must in part depend on timing and the extent of that timing. It can be that a single event may largely modify all the subsequent behaviour of child towards being pro or anti-social, but on the other hand a prolonged environment may have no such comparable effects.

From what we know of psychology the earlier that these socialising events occur the more likely that they are likely to persist into and through adulthood and we can presume that the converse applies. The longer that a particular pattern of socialisation occurs in a child, the longer it is likely to persist in adulthood and the greater the efforts which would have to be put into altering this pattern should outsiders decide that what the child is doing is now anti-social.

There are thus there are "accidental" factors which occur outside the quasi-inevitabilities of genetics and ethology which may affect the developing child or indeed children in a particular social grouping and which might have the characteristics of being social mutations. Facilities may suddenly be provided and in other cases withdrawn and there are always dominant or at least more dominant personalities which may have periodic influences on the development of children. The West Indian doctor in Tanzania who instituted roadside treatment for lepers by the calendar rather than requiring their institutionalisation may have allowed their children to be pro-social in ways approaching local normality.

Chapter-3

# Ethology and Pro-social Behaviour

The behaviour of a primate infant is a combination of presumed genetic enablements or disablements of which little is known except for some hereditary diseases and their personal characteristics and physiological markers.

Then there are long standing relatively simple behavioural patterns which are observable in non-human primates which may be partially genetic but more likely have developed in response to a variety of environmental pressures or events. The fact that Japanese macaques learnt recently to wash potatoes and chimpanzees have now be found to use tools regularly has stimulated an understanding that the dividing line between human and non-human primates is not at all clear.

It is possible that these behavioural patterns in primates have gone on for so long and are so much a part of primate behaviour, that they should be seen as not only the background to human behaviour but should be expected to be observable in their behaviour.

So there is probably a substratum of behavioural patterns in children and their parents or carers which have gone on for hundreds of generations which perhaps in their inevitability could be described as proto-genetic.

Finally there are contemporary behavioural patterns which are imposed on child rearing patterns as part of the macro culture in which they live and its micro-variations.

These may conform to the previous long standing primate behavioural patterns or be divergent from them. These diversions or contemporary cultural conformities may be stressful in the short run in going against these longer standing patterns, although they may be part of a much broader indeterminate evolutionary pattern.

It may well be that there is a constant dialectical process in the rearing of children between proto-genetic patterning and immediate social requirements and obligations. At the same time growing children start with a range of primate behavioural patterns and probably subconscious expectations which are progressively augmented stressfully or benignly as they grow up in contemporary societies which no longer have specific patterns of nurture since all of them are now socially polydimensionable.

There is some suspicion that observations of captive non-human primates may have altered their free-ranging behaviour patterns, but surely it is possible to assume that except for a very few remaining human hunter-gatherers or homeless wandering single hoboes, there are no longer any free ranging humans as all their behaviour is confined by factors outside their control which are social as well as environmental. Methodologically this makes parallels to the behaviour of confined primates somewhat easier to understand and utilise.

Thus human behaviour has always been primarily one in which their behaviour has been conforming to social as well as biological environments over which current and many proceeding generations have had no control or ability to bring about major changes.

It should be born in mind that the first years of human children who are totally dependent on adults for their first years, are in most cases in group environments paralleling primate groups or in more exclusively parental groups for which there are limited primate parallels and thus subject to stresses for which there is no proto-genetic preparation and with which much contemporary patterns of child rearing may conflict.

It must also be born in mind that contemporary forms of child rearing are unlikely to have been going on for as much as a hundred generations and within very varied social and environmental patterns. Nothing like homogeneous patterns of primate societies in which there will have been some behavioural rigidity over thousands of generations.

There may be proto-genetic patterns in non-human primate life which conform to or conflict with the early stages of human primate life and it is these that we must examine to see how they may influence the moral development of children.

- Preference for nuclear social groupings
- Situational hostility to out groups of a similar species
- Hostility and fear of other species
- Sexual distinctions and roles based on this

- Status distinctions; hierarchy
- A male presence not necessarily close biologically, but physically dominant
- A maternal socio-biological connection for a limited period
- Grazing approach to food and eating
- Reproduction
- Non-functional behaviour or play

While these behavioural patterns have been observed in both captive and free range primates may have been part of the background to the contemporary pro-social behaviour of children in modernised societies, there are now other important factors emerging. A number of primatologists have observed more humanlike behaviour in primates admittedly in infrequent instances but significant in that they have been observed at all; food sharing, reciprocity, expectations, conflict resolution as well as empathy, sympathy and consolation which suggest that the primates involved have longer-term memory created interests and expectations beyond the immediacies of the moment (Flack & de Waal, 2000: 9).

Whether these instances of behaviour which some assess as the possible background to human concepts of morality rather than just useful for those individual primates involved or indeed functional necessities for these types of social organisation within which they live, must remain speculation.

Let us look in greater detail at some of these more important ethological factors which may have some bearing on the moral development of children.

We do not see that nature in itself has much to contribute to any understanding of the contemporary development of children cross-culturally except to see it in the context of the infinitely varied social and physical environments in which contemporary people live. Certainly the social sciences categorize human social behaviour in order to have the building blocks for theories, but it would seem likely that an urban community whether in Calcutta or Coventry just as much as rural ones in Kathiawar and Kota Bahru, do have in fact these uniformities. It seems likely that any sample of families however defined would have large numbers of variations in form, function and faith which would similarly be constantly changing. The search for uniformities in the face of such enormous individual and social diversities might seem to have the characteristics of a philosophical and moral need.

Even the more obvious categories of domestic environments between isolated nuclear and extended families, polygynous ones such as the Pakistani taxi driver in Oxford with one English and one Indian wife and the polyandrous families in Long Compton and Beckenham in which one woman lived with two men for decades and those in which grand-parents act as functional parents.

Lump categories may not show functional divisions if the methods of industrial time and motion analysis were applied to human behaviour as with the Zigua child in Tanzania of whose first 60 months of life showed that he had only spent 18 months with his socially accepted married biological parents. Time and motion studies might well shown much the same for the children of working parents in East London apart from the fact that schooling probably accounts for substantial blocks of their time. There are also boarding schools, orphanages and state care institutions in which parents are only involved peripherally if at all.

The social life of humans provides for nothing more than transient uniformities often the creation of outside observers. It is not as if these physical and social environments in which contemporary people live, have any degree of stability since any child is likely to move in any one day between a variety of social environments in home, school and neighbourhoods. These experiences are paralleled by the processes of ageing in both the children and those with whom they live and indeed participate with elsewhere.

It is in fact an evolutionary situation in which an infinite number of variables in nature are seemingly coming together with a much larger number of variables in nurture with consequences at which we can only guess and then try to cut them down to manageable proportions. But there is an intermediate stage between rude nature and hypothetically understandable nurture which we indeed assume to be so since we are able to hold up a mirror our own activities and thus we can scarcely conclude are held in the vice of positivism. Working backwards from a social situation only shows known and supposedly dominant linkages and usually misses out alternatives.

Presupposing that some of our current human behaviour is likely to have some things in common with that of the higher non-human hominids, it is in ethology that we look for overarching similarities in social behaviour which may link largely unknown nature with known nurture.

**Living in Small Groups**

There are few exceptions to the human preference for living in small groups as even under urban conditions, the dormitory areas sub-divide into some sort of family living which is not entirely caused by the design of available housing.

Certainly the grass eating Gelada baboons on the Simian escarpment in Ethiopia graze in large numbers in the daytime in much the same way that the Ford works at Dagenham draws large numbers of humans into a similarly small and specialised environment. Come nightfall the former divide into smaller family groups which harbour for the night on the mountainous cliffs below their feeding areas just as the car workers disperse into their own separate domestic come harbouring areas. The need for grass and cars to assemble does not alter their mutual preference for small groups.

Chacma baboons of the East African savanna move about and live in quite large and independent groups as numbers provide them with greater protection, just as the Sukuma of Tanzania in protecting themselves from Maasai raiding lived in closed up villages with individual houses round small rocky hills but once this danger was removed, they spread out into well dispersed individual households which made them nearer to their food sources and the possibility of protecting them from predators. Nevertheless they all return to small inclusive primary groups for eating, sleeping and copulating.

Livelihood needs may bring humans together but the preference is for smaller groups in which living together provides a wider range of satisfactions, personal and emotional, child care, food sharing rather than its mere production of which very few children can fail to be aware and to benefit from in their daily lives. In the social lives of primates as with humans there is food sharing but whether this is to avoid harassment (Wrangham, 1975), status enhancing (Moore, 1984) or to gain the advantages of reciprocity in varied forms with different species (de Waal, 1987, 1997), all occur within the same small group.

In this nature appears to dominate from as far back as evidence is available and the second set of Lainotil hominid footprints in Tanzania's Maasai highlands showed a small group of upright walking hominids moving together. This preference for small group living is shown in almost every human society and even the dormitory living in boarding schools and the armed forces seems to have been historically transitory in both time and extent.

The variety of forms which this preference for small group living take is based on nurture is extremely varied and children can have no uniform experience of this and indeed will almost certainly know of variations from their own domestic living arrangements in the conditions under which their peers live apart from the people next door. In contemporary London there are three and indeed some four generational groups, a variety of extended families, lodger groups, squatters, sororal or fraternal groups, joint households in which married children lived with the parents of either partner as well as friend and acquaintance convenience groups. In fact the small group form of living is a crude but overwhelmingly popular category which nurture has divided up into many variations. Every child will be aware of it as a personally preferred category of living even if as near-adults they breakaway in order to form a small domestic group of their own choosing. The individuals in a city "squat" are just as much a preferred primary group as any other.

They will also become aware that their own small group has special characteristics which are not shared by others groups which they may have visited or heard about. Apart from speech markers and domestic rituals, their pro-social learning must come in the first instance from these small groups in which they are nurtured. There may also be the problems for children who do not have this small group background and who are brought up or forced into larger groupings but even in the street children of Calcutta and Rio de Janeiro, form themselves into small groups for protection and the raiding of adults.

## Dislike of Out Groups of Similar Characteristics

There can be little doubt that nature guides humans into the obverse of preferring to live in small groups, a dislike of others who may invade and socially and economically menace the groups in which they live. Lethal attacks on strangers has been observed among chimpanzees (Goodall, 1986).

Subsistence farmers everywhere look to the survival of their own families and when land is in short supply success for one family even in such matters as prayers for specific rather than general rain, may well have to be at the expense of their neighbours. Children are brought up to avoid upsetting their neighbours not as a general good but as a cover for the success of their own family. The gods, spirits and ancestors give sectional support and do not have much to do with the general good of the community and mankind in general; there is not much point in praying to a deity who spreads his or her benignity over everyone.

There may be a general good for the community but it is likely to be functionally short-term and usually interpreted in terms of individual and small group advantages to participants. The "not in my backyard" commonplace attitude in most societies has a long ethological background. The tolerance of neighbours is a social necessity more than a moral one in most subsistence communities the Madeirans carrying as sick girl down from the mountains to the Funchal hospital are more likely to be acting reciprocally in the long-term than motivated by any concepts of Christian morality.

This tolerance of neighbours would probably be correlated to the limits of eyesight, the social horizons within which they live which may not include large numbers of people who may have some collective connections with them as belonging to the same lineage, clan or tribe.

In such settings children are brought up to consider that reliable connections with others are not based on some belief in their essential goodness but that they can be relied on because of blood connections cemented by reciprocity when these are not primary ones. The groupings of the higher non-human hominids in which the males cannot know which are their own offspring seem to be held together at least in part by reciprocal grooming and sharing of food when there is a surplus.

In an urban housing estate neighbours may not be all that close because of the fear of unreciprocated demands for goods and services in communities which do not have a long social history of togetherness. In rural villages in Britain it may take a decade for a newcomer to be accepted although in the United States which has a population movement of something like 20 per cent per year, well above the British rate, newcomers are accepted more readily since American culture has a migrant mentality and often have welcoming arrangements for newcomers.

It is not quite an active dislike of outsiders of ostensibly the same sort as oneself, but children are brought up in social environments in which they are trained to avoid commitments to their neighbours unless there are perceived advantages in doing so and this has a very long history indeed; a hesitation in a urban housing estate to borrow some sugar from the family next-door as it is not known when and what they might ask for in return.

## Hostility and Fear of Other Species

It is not just hostility to those outside the close personalised groupings of people who are ostensibly the same as themselves but who may be and indeed will almost certainly be in competition with their own group for certain goods, land and a place in the list for preferred housing, which are part of every child's socialisation and moral understandings. The fear of losing an advantage coalesces around obvious differences in appearance.

Non-human hominids are usually wary of species who look dissimilar to themselves and this in part accounts for racialism in which there is a distrust of people who look dissimilar to themselves even if it may not be a noticeable feature of artificial and ephemeral communities such as schools in which each social generation may only last some three years.

A pre-industrial community usually adopts similar costumes or graded appearances but modern complex pluralistic societies make this dislike of outsider species extremely easy to perpetuate by having innumerable groups which deliberately make themselves look different. In almost all modern societies which are structurally segmented, children see a social system of numerous sub-cultures which overlap but which are often in competition. This is not just as question of Orthodox Jews and fundamentalist Muslims with beards and shrouded women. There are police, railway staff, nurses, doctors, lawyers, nuns, prostitutes, clergy, school children and so on who look different for the good reason of desired recognition which aids various forms of pro and anti-bias. The symbolism of opposing sports clubs is flaunted and no child in Northern Ireland can grow up without being aware of what is in effect almost hereditary sub-cultural hostility. All these make these other "species" out groups easily disliked and certainly suspect.

Nurture takes over these dislikes making them much more explicit in specifically encouraging dislike of certain biological characteristics, socially constructed appearances and areas which should be avoided; social distance however interpreted has a nervousness provoking anxiety in every individual and is often explicitly dangerous which is certainly part of the environment in which urban children develop.

## Sexual Distinctions

Children grow up in a social world in which males are taller, heavier and have greater muscle power and that women have to conform to this so that even in the more dysfunctional families most violence is male initiated as it is the non-human hominid world. They become aware early on that women defer to men and that it is to their advantage to do so; it is a rare modern family without substantial economic independence that has men and women functionally equal or locking themselves into long-term interdependence.

While it is not impossible that there are non-human hominids with homosexual and lesbian tendencies, there is not likely to be any pay-offs within their social groups for such animals. Certainly such a male can survive on the periphery of male dominated groups but the female whenever she comes into oestrus, must inevitably be the object of male breeding aggressions. The primate female as much as the human woman is able to negotiate for personal advantages before allowing herself be sexually used.

Children grow up in social groups where there is a sexual division of labour which if it does not exist in single parent families will be visible to them in other types of family groups in which there are adults of both sexes. Some non-human hominids share child care as do some human families but it is likely to be heavily skewed towards the women if only because men are away for most of the day whether hunting or working in offices and factories. Most subsistence agricultural communities have the women working in the fields with their youngest children tied on their backs.

Some small cultures do have a much more equal division of child care duties and division of labour as the Lahu of south-west China who have an ideology of gender complementarity which dominates virtually all of their social life (Du, 2003), which even managed to clash with the Chinese Communist Party's top-down ideology of sexual equality as being too extensive for their state ideology to cope with.

As with non-human hominids children grow up visually knowing the physical differences between the two sexes and in addition their differences in facial and body ornamentation. Commonplace cross-dressing by modern Western women rather than men is not likely to alter this basic identification that men and women are separate. If children see transvestite males they are likely to be objects of contagious social ridicule, but not the Western office-working female.

Children thus grow up in modern editions of non-human hominid life in which there are the rudiments of a division of labour not only in the care of children but in such matters as males hunting among some chimpanzee groups. The expectation must be that children grow up to see themselves as either male or female and the different forms of nurture have developed along this polarity for individuals of being socially acceptable for most activities as being one or the other.

The unmarried presumably homosexual Sukuma is ridiculed not for his homosexuality which may occur often enough in institutionalised and accepted male groups but because in order to survive he has to publicly perform the female functions of cooking and water crying.

## Male Physical Dominance

In every non-human hominid group it is visually obvious that males are larger than the females and no juvenile there or human child grows up unaware that this is a basic fact of their lives. Non-human hominid males are ostentatiously violent if not quite so physically so in forms of behaviour which can be allied to machismo practices present in many societies. Popular sport is almost exclusively male and violent and where women have excelled it is in individual competitive segregated athletics.

Thus it would seem that children grow up in societies in which men overtly dominate perhaps in part as a ethological inheritance from their size, but that it leads girls to an awareness of covert ways in which they can work round this physical dominance. They must grow up aware of this bilateralism which not only involves different ways of behaving but different ways of manipulating the social situations in which they find themselves embedded. Calculated reciprocity would appear to have a long anthropoid history (de Waal, 1989).

## Hierarchies

In non-human hominid social life there appears to be little evidence which suggests that equality is either aimed at or functionally acceptable; the baby monkey grows up in micro-societies in which dominance is important and to either dominate or be dominated is part of leading an adequate and indeed life. Social lives moreover in which individual dominance is always being both achieved and contested. It was Bernard Shaw who said that if three strange men were put together in a very short space of time one would dominate the other two and of course George Orwell who wrote in Animal

Farm that "all the animals were equal but some were more equal than others."

Every human child grow up from the start being aware that their social lives are run on hierarchical realities although they may be taught much latter in school and church that there are political and religious ideologies stating that inequality which is not functionally accepted is morally wrong. Older families will have had children in succession giving the older ones authority from birth order and in their peer groups there will be an early sorting out into leaders and followers, schools have teachers in authority as well as form prefects and team captains. They cannot avoid learning that it is an hierarchically ordered society in which there are familial or institutionalised ranks.

They will also learn just as in the non-human hominid groups, that males dominate, that there are ways round this and that in their own families male dominance is not total and that the women have their own ways round this totality. In both Indian and Chinese societies there are mother-in-law dominances in which the wife is subjected to prolonged subordination (Wolf, 1975) which may account for the suicides of some women (Shah, 1959) and the particular Hindu ideas of the proper religiously subordinate roles of women (Meer, 1976) even to the popular support for widows who kill themselves on the funeral pyres of their husbands.

There are also age-sets or age-grades in some Nilo-Hamitic societies in which men move up in status at irregular but predetermined intervals and formal and informal initiation rituals in many societies by which both girls and boys become social adults, not necessarily coinciding with the menarche. As well there are the grading ceremonies which children go through in order to be accepted in to such organisations as the scouts or guides apart from all schools in which there is strict age grading far more rigid and wide-ranging than that of Maasai society in eastern Africa since it involves everyday physical segregations. It seems likely that all juvenile gangs have initiation procedures often of a stressful nature as do the hazing procedures in American universities.

No child grows up unaware that ageing is a continuous process and that it is marked off by legal and social boundaries and by group affiliations and that in any age grouping of people there will be hierarchies of dominance.

## Matrilateral Preferences

Children have a preference for their mothers and this is as obvious in modern societies as it is among non-human hominids. Most societies are patrilineal and patrilocal tracing their names through the male parent and often property as well; the male side of the family dominates.

However in such situations children and the adults into which they develop have a choice between preferring the families of their fathers to that of their mothers which may not have ethological correlates but which is a development from the obvious biological foundations. In modern societies the male side continues to be more disciplinarian and the mother's side more kindly and supportive. Whether in Birmingham, Banaras or Bamako, if a choice is possible people will prefer to associate with the mother's side of their families. In African patrilineal societies the mother's brothers are the preferred relatives and it is a title applied to what in western societies would be called friends just as the fictional titles of uncle and aunt are applied in English families by children to long standing friends of their parents. A room full of single men in Mombasa, Kenya referred to each other as mother's brothers.

Of course the minority of matrilineal societies would have these preferences in reverse with the mother's brother having many responsibilities for his sister's children and the relations of her husband who has no direct responsibilities for the care of the children, would be seen as the kinder people. It is still nurture dominating over nature.

But this is to separate the structure of societies created by humans from the basic ethological factor that people prefer their mothers to their fathers if they have to make a choice. This is shown clearly in the visitors to convicts in Kenyan prisons which are predominantly mothers and in the answers to questions put to Tanzanian and European Roman Catholic seminarians as to who they would save in a boating accident, if they could save only one person chose to save their mothers over their wives. Both groups held to the view that mothers were irreplaceable while wives could easily be replaced. There would appear to be a straightforward follow through from non-human hominid ways of living.

## Grazing as Opposed to Formal Eating

In this nurture clearly opposes nature in which all the higher hominids and indeed all animals eat intermittently and continuously. The chimpanzee eats whenever opportunity allows just as their babies are fed on demand and in most subsistence cultures babies are fed on demand, while in western societies the potato crisps packet is similarly demand grazing. It is often given familial moral overtones that if children graze, then they will not be able to appreciate and eat the food which has been specially prepared for them by their mothers. This has no anthropoid parallels as non-human primates do not cook.

It would seem that the use of the clock rather than the complexities of cooking as well as the fact that often members of the family only are in their home at fixed times, means that modern societies are imposing a pattern of social eating and breast feeding at fixed times for which there are no parallels in non-human hominid life. Clearly much of what goes on in human societies have no parallels in primate life but could not be said just on these grounds to be going against nature, whereas imposed meal times is doing just this, overloading the stomach at regular intervals for social reasons. However carnivores do over load at irregular intervals as do humans at their seasonal and rites of passage feasts.

## Concern for Reproduction

The genetic requirement to reproduce among hominids has a presumed history of millions of years and centre round the oestrus cycle which makes the female only sexually receptive at regular intervals. The change to the menstrual cycle making the female potentially receptive at all times to sexual advances must have occurred latter in evolutionary history but still correlated to millions of years and the ways in which this is approached through the different processes introduced by different systems of nurture would appear to be only a few millennia old.

Nature and nurture have allied themselves in having reproduction dominating human activity and children must realise this in the ways in which their families and society in general interests themselves in it nurture in providing for various forms of birth control would appear to be acting against nature. Much human sexual activity which has reproductive potential is undertaken without reproductive aims, which presumably is the case also with non-human primates. Even homosexual and lesbian couples can share the desire to reproduce through adopting children and in the case of lesbians undergo artificial insemination or virtually anonymous sexual intercourse with a donor.

## Play

The young of all non-human hominids seem to play for the pleasure of such activities as Sri Lankhan monkeys jumping repeatedly into puddles of temporary water and to suggest that it is functionally useful as leading to muscle coordination and development perhaps forgets that it has no functions other than play; in the first instance this is physical activity and that it is interdependent with adult encouragement.

## Having a Home Environment

Whether primate and human territoriality have similar correlates is still no more than speculation but both have preferred localities although the former would appear to have a sense of home on the lines of wherever they happen to be resting; it is a mobile circle of social distance which may relate to food sources.

This marks off personal and small group territories in distinct ways which are not as distinctly nature as the scent marking off of territories but both children and adults mark off their personal areas in distinct ways.

The higher primates may not have homes since they do not require protection from the weather but they certainly have preferred and recognisable neighbourhoods which they occupy, expanding and contracting with their numbers and needs and moving with the group as with the defensible space round a warship.

For the human child there is always the home area which is ostensibly safe developing from the mothers' arms and gradually expanding into a preferred and not particularly large preferred neighbourhood. This sense of a nominally friendly neighbourhood does not expand indefinitely and would not include the work place unless this is the same as the home; the male study and the female kitchen are examples of exclusivities as do the preference for divides uses of lavatories wherever possible in houses.

Children of Pakistani origin living in London with a majority of their relatives living in Pakistan does not have an expanded sense of neighbourhood and indeed their sense of home neighbourhood may be smaller than that of a Caucasian child born there; they are likely to see the outside social world as more generally hostile. Their preferences for one or the other may vary with time and aged based needs; Pakistan in the summer heat and dust may not be liked but the exuberance of Muslim festivals there may be much more exciting than comparable activities in London; there will always be fluctuating comparisons and needs.

There can be no doubt that the human child has evolved from a genetic background which has included living in a preferred neighbourhood and to have a specific home as in a cave and latter in something specially constructed, comes from nurture and it is only then that there are specific boundaries. This would certainly add a further dimension to the wariness of human children over both the ends of their own acceptable space and other people outside these nurtured limits. Children may go out for a variety of reasons but they usually prefer to come back into a neighbourhood which is seen by youth gangs and peer groups as necessarily defensible and more specifically to a section of this which is seen as narrowly and definably home.

In conclusion we can see that ethology provides a number of pointers to the ways in which children are likely to develop without being specifically taught. Further that much that nurture brings into their required understandings are very likely to run up against these natural dispositions and thus become a source of tension when children under the conditions of modern urban living are required to spend most of their lives with people and in places that their "instincts" and nurture tell them should be mistrusted and if possible avoided.

This is not to go so far as to agree with Huxley's biological functionalism (Huxley, 1894) who wrote "I account for morality as an accidental capability produced, in its boundless stupidity, by a biological process that is normally opposed to the expression of such a capability". Nor indeed to share Dawkins optimism in the way that human can adapt "Be warned that if you wish, as I do, to build a society in which individuals cooperate generously and unselfishly towards a common good, you can expect little help from biological nature. Let us try to teach generosity and altruism, because we are born selfish" (Dawkins, 1976: 3). We are still left with primate behaviour pointers as to how the pro-social behaviour is likely to be formed.

## Chapter-4

# ANTHROPOLOGY AND PRO-SOCIAL BEHAVIOUR

Anthropology is the study of people who are assumed to be different to the culture of the researcher, an assumption of difference and there is not usually an assumption of any identity of interests; they are not one of us except in the most general terms that there are relationships between the two parties and that almost certainly they are consciously or unconsciously mutually influential.

This field of study certainly started with extreme differences between cultures that were assumed to be civilised by their own definitions and those which were not; it was a looking down at these other cultures from outside with an assumption of superiority according to a wide range of factors which were often not only cultural but related to education, age and sex.

These studies gradually turned from a less obvious "us" and "them" approach to the contemporary less culturally biased one which attempts to understand not only the intrinsic functional logic of their social structures but how these people came to see and now experienced their societies in these particular and inevitably different ways. An acceptance of difference within some measure of equality.

The problem now is that there can be few communities or individuals which have not been and are currently being influenced by social and economic factors which are part of the researchers own social experience. It is now a paradigm which to some extent is shared and not just existentially divided.

Whereas ethology is clearly based on attempts to observe and understand animal behaviour to which the objects of research do not consciously contribute, anthropology has human researchers working to understand other humans which is a far more difficult process with adults and even more so with children.

Anthropologists are inevitably biased by the illusion of their own scientific detachment and the nature of their own socialisations. A cross-section of any graduate body of anthropologists shows their differences and indeed some study the work of their published predecessors and reach diametrically different conclusions. It is certain that the psychological and demographic characteristics of every anthropologist differ from some hypothetical norm.

To study the behaviour and understandings of children of another culture is doubly difficult as these cultural differences may well start at the boundaries of their own cultural environments. The natal languages of observer and the observed are usually different and even within a single language there are likely to be linguistic codes and semantic differences which are inclusive to groups of neighbourhood children. The fact that the observer is older and of higher education makes for barriers against understanding.

In the study of the pro-social behaviour of children there are two divergent approaches, the supposedly detached and the supposedly personally involved which each have problems of methodology apart from their correlation to the personal choices and aptitudes of the researchers which at any time in a research project unconsciously may guide both method and choice.

In all research projects since the social sciences aspire to scientific rectitude, workers are lured to if not hypnotised by the existence of statistical data. There is firstly the problem of their accuracy for recording variations in the behaviour and attainments of children; an element of falsification is probably built into all the statistics produced by organisation concerning their own practices which is magnified by the arrival in them of a decimal point.

Then since one has to accept that there are few if any characteristics of children which break down their individuality and in their years of development they are almost certainly changing rapidly, statistics block off the children into categories which leave the growing child and adolescent segmented rather than elided along a continuous process of individual change. Social and biological change may not coincide, and figures regarding school attendance, test results, religious affiliation and so on all beg the question of what these terms mean for individual children.

Even in economically developed states with allegedly efficient national and regional official and voluntary welfare systems and schemes, there are numerous patches of extreme difference. Statistics away from a bureaucracy committed to their necessary creation are doubly suspected for they are the justification for their work and the size of their staffs and budgets.

So overall anthropological studies may be using whatever statistics they can find because they fill gaps about which the researcher has no other means of obtaining data; the homes of children when the concept of an address and permanency may not be a cultural requirement; a child may spend most of her/his time away from their biological parents not because any marriage may have been dissolved but because this form of togetherness may not be seen as a cultural necessity. The numbers on the school roles and does attendance mean arriving at a set time or just some time during the school day. The lassitude of children in Uganda schools was found not to be due to their laziness or cultural ineptitude but to high levels of intestinal parasites and consequential anaemia. Statistics must remain suspect as a serious contribution to the understandings of child development which has to be observed and evaluated as far as possible in individual rather than block category terms; overlapping ranges of behaviour.

The other approach involves various degrees of participant observation. It is a mute point whether any researcher can become a fully involved member of a community in which he is not a "natural" member without gross and horrendous personal costs to those who undertake such research roles and further it must seem likely that by such absorption into another society, researchers loose their detachment and become biased in favour of the ideas and practices of the communities which have accepted them. The framework of thought becomes rather more "my special children" rather than "those whom I have chosen to study".

Thus most anthropologists are observers of different societies or sections of societies different to their own in which to some extent they have been accepted as socially licensed intruders. Moreover they see these societies either through the eyes of those who see it is to their advantage to attach themselves to these outsiders or through their own free ranging observations by just sitting and looking; the Malinowski approach to anything which he saw that was of interest when he walked about; not too difficult in the totally alien environment of the Trobriand Islands.

In most cases the anthropologists are able to develop some sort of useful relationships with at least some members of their host society. However this usually results in a relatively extensive knowledge of a few and watered down understandings of everyone else about whom most knowledge is obtained second hand. A published work on the religion of "the" five million Sukuma was the result of close personal relations with perhaps no more than a dozen men (Tanner, 1967).

So something can usually be got out of any research situation into which researchers come for short periods and then go; few if any live in their research areas beyond the support range of their grants, even if it is just in another part of the town in which they have a teaching position. The mind and the incentives to continue research in a particular area of study is usually muted by changing interests, the physical processes of ageing and personal commitments; partners and children do not mix well with long absences.

It can thus be relatively easy to study adults who if they are not hostile are usually quite indulgent to the behaviour of socially alien adults, but with children the problems of study are compounded by the accentuation of almost all differentiating factors. It is not only the problem of strangers about whom all societies socialise their children to be suspicious as coming into the general classification of avoidable or should be avoided adults. All adults are large and loom over children and adolescents with various forms of physical, familial and social dominances.

This leaves anthropologists with difficult problems of access which compound those of research with adults which are usually uni-sexually biased anyway. They cannot participate in any activity which involves children for which they do not have predetermined interests. So they must remain observers and this is both time consuming and restricting not only by the range of vision to the small numbers who can be observed, but by the periods over which observation can be carried out.

Then there is the perennial problem of how far does the presence of an obvious stranger, moreover one who stays for some time and there is no known social role for or understanding of a lodger much less a researcher, alter the asocial situation in which they are participating. American Indians and the Todas of the Indian Nilgiri Hills are conversant with anthropological interests and even the terminology used in their studies.

How far indeed is the study of children done through the eyes and minds of adults. A thorough study of Sukuma children (Varkevisser, 1973) brings together all these difficulties without mentioning that they exist when her introduction thanks three men and three women and particularly the family of one woman. In this admirable work we have a study of Sukuma childhood which is in fact the study of three families near to Lake Victoria out of possibly a million Sukuma families which have children.

Few anthropologists have studied children no doubt because it underlines the outsider status of the researcher. While in less urban and perhaps unfortunate climatic conditions in which people live most of their lives indoors so that little can be observed and studying indoor life inevitably means the study of a single family and modifications of their behaviour because of the researcher taking up space in a housing unit which is already overcrowded. The best that can be done in this situation is the study of a family over a number of years and in many different locations such as "The Children of Sanchez" series (Lewis, 1961). The "Sanchez" series involved the writer in a prolonged personal involvement and despite the vivid nature of what was recorded there is the difficulty over the value of impressionistic writing over which there can be no more than similarly impressionistic comments. Most such studies cover the lives of children as adjuncts to the lives of their superintending adults and almost always in terms of their socialisation ideals.

It would seem therefore that social science approaches could best be through observation in which they are not all that present in the minds of the children so that the children are the initiators of the behaviour which is observed rather than responding to initiatives put into their minds by adults. The use of security cameras over playgrounds and areas in which children congregate would provide data on the behaviour and composition of groups. The contents of essays in explanation of behaviour and in fact the use of data in which the researcher has not specifically initiated a matter of interest such as use of school libraries, visiting the school nurse, who picks them up from school, the composition and longevity of friendship, what children object to in the behaviour of other children, body language, form of language used when adults are not present.

It would seem therefore that the anthropological world-view has become so substantially modified by change shared with that of the researchers, that it has in fact merged into the more general studies under the heading of sociology. The "us" has become merged into the "them" in complex inter-relationships which are no longer methodologically separable except in terms of social and geographical distance.

What then is the value of studies made by researchers who classify themselves as anthropologists. Their value may lie in their accentuation of difference which is indeed valuable in cross-cultural understandings. There is also the fact that much of this data such as Chagga Childhood (Raum, 1940) is so far back in social time that it has aspects that verge on both the historical and ethological.

In virtually every classifiable situation in what might be called traditional societies in Malekula, Chin hills, Azandeland and Siwa oasis has become so changed that it is not difficult to find in the contemporary lives of their children much more of the modern than the relics of traditionalism.

In virtually every part of a modern child's life there have been major modifications in comparison to the lives of their parents much less those of their grandparents. The control of mass diseases except for AIDS, the lengthening of life so that the elderly are a frequent social reality. The dominance of electricity, the love-hate relationship of the developing world for Western society, the pervasiveness of the mass media. The continual and widening presence of education as a basic bureaucratic process with its parallels to the factory and office. The awareness if not the actual experience of social disturbances from inflation, corruption, crime and violent political instability.

Thus it is to this newer world that we have to turn for any understanding of contemporary childhood since we can assume that the practices surrounding radical change has raised new issues of which their parents have had little experience. With this the main methodological problems may be within the social and geographical distances between which the children are socialised towards pro-social behaviour.

## The Factor of Social Distance

Personal understanding of relationships must depend in part on knowing who they are not just as fellow human beings but as particular ones who are different. This comes early into a child's consciousness; they learn kinship terms which are tied to known faces to which are attached elements of taste, sight, hearing touch and smell and whether they are biologically connected or not, they learn that certain people are not socially related to them by so-called natural processes of exclusion. Researcher can only have an "ordered intuition" (Steiner, 1989: 174) about what this connection may mean to the individual child within their own culture and immeasurably more so over cultural boundaries.

This understanding comes early into an infant's performance and "between 7 and 9 months a Kung Bushman baby, like their western counterparts who formerly played happily with anyone, develop a discriminating uneasiness in the presence of people they don't know" (Konner, 1972).

While this cannot be the result of any conscious learning, it would seem to have some ethological backing since it correlates to the infant's use of all five senses to discriminate between those on whom it may depend for survival and those who are not. This has the adaptive function of removing the infant from generalised danger from outsider humans and further that whatever its possible ethological background, it is promoted if not taught by the mother or whoever is the primary carer (Ainsworth & Wittig, 1969; Morgan & Ricciuti, 1969).

There are few if any societies in which children do not learn to distinguish those who are acceptably insiders within the group as in open-door societies of subsistence farmers or villagers and those who are socially distant and outsiders, even though those who are acceptable may be quite numerous as being known by face and more distantly by sight.

In closed door communities the growing children are taught to be nervous of all people outside the front door whom they do not specifically learn to be benign, but there are in-between groups. A gypsy/travellers encampment in a road-side lay-bye in England will have few visitors and that their children will learn early that these are either actively hostile; such as inspectors of one sort or another who are expected to find fault or the occasional benignly curious of whom they can take advantage. Much the same would apply to a Bushman encampment with an even longer experience of lethal and predatory contacts with outsider Africans and Europeans.

Western social thinking has tended to consider that exclusive minimal relationships are essential for the well-being of young children and indeed they have usually acted as if it was the norm at which they should aim. A study of 186 non-industrial societies (Smith, 1879) showed that in only five was there a single exclusive caretaker for a child. In a Hausa village 6 to 14 month old children had an average of 3.8 caretakers each and we have already mentioned the Zigua child in Tanzania who had only spent 18 of the first 60 months of his life with his parents.

It is astonishing that the need for one continuous carer for young children should ever have been thought of as essential for their subsequent mental health and social well-being. A study of the development of children in residential nurseries in Athens showed that young children over a six month period had an average of 29 caretakers with "mothering" from six different nurses in a full day and 13 different ones in a week. A parallel study of a London home found that children in care for 4 ½ years averaged 50 caretakers worked out on the basis of an individual having worked with a child for at least a week. Indeed it was a staff policy to discourage close attachments as any such continuity could not be maintained because of staff turnover. A follow up study of these children at eight years found that most were regarded by their teachers has having severe problems as excessively attention seeking, restless, unpopular and anti-social.

This is by no means exceptional as those visiting such local authority homes with a special interest in a particular child might well be told that this was the particular carer's day off or rest-period. On the other hand in a home run by resident nuns the nature of the care received from this small group with very little turnover of women was continuous.

The conclusion must be that children in almost all societies except those in closed door contemporary urban ones, are regularly cared for by several people but not too many and indeed the main attachments of the children may not be the mother who are and is likely to be a variety of relatives and neighbours. Evidence seems to suggest from non-industrial communities which have of course preceded urban ones by many millennia that five caretakers for a child is not so much adequate as normal but that fifty is not.

The children in subsistence societies all have working mothers from whom they are rarely detached but industrial societies with large numbers of working mothers who are detached from their children, and it is this detachment which may correlate with later problems. This is avoided if alternative care-taking arrangements are made which are difficult to organise in closed door communities in which contemporary small families are well dispersed. This problem is easy to see when in a developed society only 3 per cent of 6 to 10 year olds lived in exclusive groups of relatives while 67 per cent did in Kenya (Whiting & Edwards, 1988).

There can be little doubt that most children grow up in social environments which teach them that there is safety and satisfactions in associating with those who are not social distant. However this is not some abrupt distinction since where there are physical distinctions they will prefer that form of ethnicity throughout their lives and in subsistence societies there will also be reciprocal feelings of closeness with people of the same lineage and clan which are still to be seen today in the vague feelings of affinity between dispersed members of Scottish clans.

The child also learns that there are usable affinities in shared membership of religious groupings particularly when such groups form small exclusive open-door colonies such as the Amish and Hutterites. However social distance is not just a question of the child learning the pro-social differences between insiders and outsiders, there are issues of class and caste and in many cases it correlates with geographical factors.

## Geographical Distance Factors

Theoretically there is in everyone's mind and certainly in those of children a geographical circle of personally assessed safety within which there is some sense of reciprocal interpersonal obligation. This circle of assumed safety and obligation expands with age, but it is ultimately terminated by coming up against the socially defended space of other institutions, social groups and the unassailable anonymity of densely populated towns and cities. It probably returns to the same sized primary group from which the child originally developed.

Individuals and their children coming from open door communities in which there are very limited concepts of trespass beyond personal private space, come up against gross limitations on their social movements when they enter closed door societies. Barbed wire round the houses of important people, and the extraordinary notices telling such people not to walk on what is obviously public and ownerless grassed spaces in city centres.

Whereas in open-door communities safety is related to the limits of sight, in which children are within sight of responsible adults and also see them, in locked door communities, children's anxieties have a narrow geographical range; this loss of security often corresponds to the world outside their windows augmented to some extent by the frightening world seen on television.

It is only in long standing communities within high density cities such as parts of Liverpool and London undamaged by bombing in World War II that there were neighbourhoods more open than closed in which children grew up with close relatives nearby. One study (Wilmot and Young, 1957) stated that the average distance between the houses of bride and groom was 200 metres. Even in such communities there will be a range of acceptable strangers; football pools payment collectors, insurance and rent men and of course the postman. Such communities have disappeared with the provision of improved housing in which acceptance of new socially distant accommodation took no regard to retaining kinship groupings.

An attempt was made in Manila to retain these configuration in a slum clearance scheme run by an overseas charity in which the planning was done with models of houses, not just plans which on which few could visualise what was being organised on their behalf and over a long period of negotiation the people who agreed to move there had chosen the house type they preferred and its location.

In entirely locked door communities as in urban housing estates the degree of fears of the outside is augmented by the fact that most front-doors have multiple locks and security chains. In these locations the turn-over is high and although relatives may be near rather than far away, this radius is likely to be some 25 miles and it requires a phone or special expeditions to keep in touch. In the actual housing estate the alley ways, the tunnels, sub-level garages and elevators are usually dirty, graffiti covered and known to be dangerous.

There is thus a cumulative dislike of the people outside the front-door which the child senses as much as taught which is augmented by the mass media with its concentration on crime and periodic if not persistent national scares about paedophiles and campaigns against any known sex offenders being housed anywhere.

It is possible to over-estimate the amount of travelling done by adults and children in all societies and the effects which this may have of their pro-social understandings. For most adults there is commuting between the poles of home and work which in non-industrial societies involves adults and children moving to their fields in the morning and back again in the afternoon prior to the main meal of the day.

There would be similar but less frequent visits to markets and religious festivals mostly on foot but also by cart and bus. In these different movements the children become aware of the continuity of certain social contacts and the touch and go social world outside the home neighbourhood in which there are excitements of seen and heard alternatives but none of the social understandings which goes with closer social distances.

In highland Myanmar the hill woman and their children come down to the every five day markets in the nearby small towns in which the outside world is brought into their mutual consciousness on a regular basis. Their growing children brought up in particular forms of pro-social behaviour becomes increasingly aware that what they have been brought up to believe is right, becomes attenuated with geographical distance form their homes.

In industrial societies the daily commuting of adults is either the man and woman going off alone to work or the mother dropping off the children at school which at least initially is experienced by their children as a form of desertion and then as a form of organised separation from family life.

The range of movement of such women and their children as a combination of time and distance is probably not much different to that of subsistence farming women, except that non-conformity to what they believe to be right conduct and which they impart directly or indirectly to their children, can be measured in metres rather than kilometres. We can thus see that this system of living is potentially much more disruptive of the learning and practising of any system of pro-social behaviour based on social closeness of human relationships.

There are however other aspects of social and geographical distances which come early into the understandings of children and that is class and caste. In most communities in which the housing is likely to outlast the occupancies of those who currently live there, there are sharp social divisions; social boundaries over which children are taught not to go or are told that they would be unwelcome there. A striking example of this was the Garsington wall in which the owners of houses in a private housing estate built a wall across their privately owned road which had allowed access to and from the local government housing estate next door; this wall lasted for some thirty years.

Any English village and certainly even the smallest town will show differences in class occupancy maintained by correlated differences in accents, costume, both inside and outside property, political affiliation, sport preferences and how their gardens are organised. There is little association over these boundaries described colloquially as "being on one side or the other of the tracks" except on such neutral ground as the flower show, harvest festival, village decoration and local sports. There are no social exchanges except for domestic employment. It is a socially segmented social world into which the child is socialised.

In a number of societies in which there are religious divisions children grow up in religious ghettoes into which their parents have moved for greater protection and social comfort. In such situations children will grow associating both in and out of school with children of the same faith while at the same time being socialised into a violent antipathy to the opposing faith. In Belfast, the capital of Northern Ireland, 70 per cent of the population live in religious ghettoes of their own choosing after decades of harassment (O'Malley, 1983). This segregation by religion for protection is a feature of living in Israel and in Indian cities where Hindu-Muslim tension is endemic.

In Hindu India where the commonplace class divisions are augmented by the concepts of religious pollution which are fundamental to that faith which has resulted in geographical-cum-social divisions in even the smallest community. These complications create a religious socialisation for children which not so much pervades their understandings as regulates their lives.

Since the caste or more particularly the sub-caste of everyone in a village community is known by a combination of residence, occupation, temple affiliation. Segregation is a religious necessity since the presence there of anyone from an inferior sub-caste would pollute the whole building, and general appearance. In many villages there is a ban on untouchables using public wells and in their use of the village reservoir they have an area reserved for them opposite to the part used by caste Hindus (Deliege, 1999).

So in Hindu communities children grow-up in a complex system of segregations to which their pro-social behaviour and obligations are attached. These complex separations can even involve pollution from the casting of a personal shadow, the avoidance of any touching, sharing of utensils and certainly no inter-dinning. A marriage ceremony in a village in which the guests came from different castes would have them feeding separately with their food cooked by people acceptable as religiously clean by their own sub-caste.

It is not surprising therefore that Hindu children grow up not only with a sense of their own exclusiveness in their particular sub-caste socio-religious practices but also their superiority to certain other sub-castes and their inferiority to others.

Western social reformers are often disturbed by the extent of divisive pro-social behaviour into which Hindu children are socialised in India without recognising its usefulness or indeed recognising the extent of social segmentation in their own societies. There is the limited usefulness of any theory of equality when people have no wish to share similar patterns of social behaviour.

It would seem to be the case that except in the generalised moral teachings of religions and schools, children grow up almost universally in environments which require pro-social behaviour to a limited number of people and to exclude from this the enormous numbers of others with whom they are likely to come into contact with in their lives.

Let us finally look at the divisions between communities which may provide a typology of social environments within which children are socialised.

Chapter-5

# SOCIAL ENVIRONMENTS : A TYPOLOGY

The pro-social socialisation of children is dictated not only by the extremes of the geographical environments in which they live or the everyday requirements of culture and the individualities of the parents and children involved, but also by the realities of social life over which those involved have little control beyond conformity.

At one end of this behavioural range children have to contribute to the survival and ordered well-being of their families and care-providers; the dominance in such situations whether in Bengal or Bamako that the latter get a return on their expenditure for raising children or consider their children as factors in the reciprocities involved in survival from year to year.

At the other extreme there is the plain fact that children are a drain on their caretakers standards of living; materially there is no return on the expenditures of breeding and maintaining children until they leave home. A group of peri-urban Zigua women who were talked to about the merits of birth-control were immune to arguments about the advantages of fewer children in terms of their own lives. However when these women with low standards of living worked out on the blackboard the cost of a child from birth to puberty in their own experience, they were amazed at how much money they would be spending for which they would get no return unless the child worked for their families to the limits of their physical and mental capacities from as earlier age as possible.

The move from one dimension to another is occasioned or has been occasioned not so much by any change in the ideologies concerning childhood and child care which almost certainly came after socio-economic changes but by industrialisation and urbanisation. This process has been caused by the individualisation of work and the construction of societies around the need for the mobility of labour in which the families of workers are a handicap to the efficient and profitable use of machinery, however disguised it may be by the varying ideologies of capitalism and socialism.

Children have no part in this type of society as all contemporary societies as far as they are institutionally and politically able, have legislated them out of any economic opportunities to contribute to the living standards of their families or to the immediate economic needs of the societies in which they live. All contemporary societies have legislated for a lengthening period of dependent childhood with no necessary return to their parents or the providing society at the end of it. Education in itself is held to be a good investment even if there is no reasonable possibility of getting employment comparable to the standard of education which has been so expensively obtained in the use of the children's own resources and the national economies.

If children do have a part in contributing to their families standard of living or more likely their marginal survival as in carpet making in Pakistan or brick-making and match production in India, it contravenes national legislation and incurs derogatory international comment. The societies concerned ignore these contraventions because of the economic and social realities in which their families live as marginal to urban society and there are few rural subsistence opportunities available for either children or adults in such fringe landless families.

Where the worth of the child as an individual is a matter of national ideological importance, it is very largely a question of the care-givers being able to act on this against their own immediate interests or in its wider implications the society itself can afford to do this because of its high national income and the support which this has in national politics of various types of absolutism and from democratic voting support elsewhere.

Whatever ideologies are involved and whether they preceded or came after the realities of economic and social change, children have been seen largely in economic terms; parents pay, schools have budgets, universities have subsidies and education has to compete nationally with other ministries and political needs. Educating and providing for handicapped children may be a moral necessity but it remains an expensive expenditure.

Even in economically well developed societies the expansion of education and the seemingly pro-social framework surrounding this, may have been occasioned at least in part by their exclusion from opportunities to earn along with women in order to protect male employment. Education may have contributed to keeping them off the streets and becoming a visible source of social distress and disorder. A visitor on coming to a secondary modern school to give a talk to the top form was told that he could talk as long as he liked as it would fill in the time of these boys who were only waiting to leave. The same visitor in a comparable Kenyan school was asked by the boys if the topic was part of the examination syllabus which would get them employment in replacing expatriates in the early years of political independence.

It is perhaps necessary first to remove from detailed consideration the relatively isolated small societies which have been studied by anthropologists in the past Margaret Mead (Mead, 1963) describes three small New Guinea societies. The Tchambuli in which the men acted according to Western stereotypes for women preoccupied with gossiping, arrangements of their hair and going shopping, while the women were energetic, managerial and unadorned, the Arapesh in which both men and women behaved more or less as westerners would expect them to behave in their sex roles and the Mundugomor in which the women acted ion a fierce initiatory fashion.

Leaving aside the question as to whether the focus of her research rested rather arbitrarily on the differences in sex role behaviour which caught her anthropological eye, women were an important source of conflict in all three societies whatever the overall sex roles may have been.

The lesson for us here is that there may have been but probably no longer are numerically small societies such as these New Guinea ones with unusual behavioural norms. All they do is to show that humans have the capacity to develop very varied forms of social life. However these forms were too specialised in their own ecological and social niche to be copied by or developed by other societies which did not apparently fit into the same pattern.

Next there are micro societies which are surrounded geographically and socially by a different macro society which tolerates their different way of living because they are not a threat to the majority and do not actively attempt to recruit outsiders since with their high birth rate they breed their own continuance. The examples of this are the Amish and Hutterites in north America who have existed successfully for more than a century and have brought up their children in a distinctive pro-social pattern.

Then there are the monastic systems of Christianity and Buddhism and to a lesser extent Hinduism in which children are educated residentially into a particular pattern of pro-social behaviour. Whether these specialised systems of socialising children have any wider significance as models for the wider macro-society or are just influential for the children involved; they are small specialised units within much larger social patterns and influences.

The macro social systems must be our main concern however varied they may be internally when subject to careful analysis. Very large numbers of people numbered in millions living under broadly similar conditions of varied forms of social, economic and psychological insecurity in towns, suburbs and villages.

These enormous demographic groupings of Chinese, Indians, Indonesians, White Russians and Western Europeans and others, each have much in common and each is different culturally from the others, all within a major difference between Easterners and Westerners as to how they view themselves and others (Cohen & Gunz, 2002).

While from a humane perspective we may try to and stress that children are individuals and individualised units within each and every social setting, it is this macro-matrix which surrounds them and channels them into particular forms of pro-social behaviour. It is this matrix composed of large populations and bound together by clocks, electricity, printing, petrol and material wants that dictates to a large extent how children should behave and how adults should behave towards them; further this occurs without any need for agreement or even dialogue.

There would thus appear to be a typology in which pro-social requirements and socialisation are correlated to the unwritten social patterning of the surrounding cultures :

(1) Subsistence families and groups in rural environments working as farmers or herdsmen in which the children are socialised to understand that pro-social behaviour is working with other family members as an ongoing contribution to their family's well-being. Further that individualism which overtly handicaps this is bad, however much it may be practised and tolerated covertly.

(2) Peri-urban and urban high density families and groups Redfield's 'culture of poverty' in which families and individuals are attracted to cities by rural poverty and

landlessness but form part of the septic fringe of contemporary developing societies. In this environment children move between urban and rural relatives according to their understanding of the better chances of survival but which society cannot adequately sustain in either situation. Children in this situation form a scavenging element, the street children of Brazilian cities and the child prostitutes of Bangkok and Nairobi. In this situation pro-social socialisation is no more than the street requirements for survival in which there is overall a time span of a day at a time.

(3) The half-way situation in which the state makes a determined effort to develop society and the future of children but is forced by the absence of revenue and large-scale development to discriminate against the practices of equality of opportunity. Pro-social behaviour begins to individualise opportunities for children so that they can leave rural and urban subsistence existences to the detriment of their existing families. Even primary education is a substantial handicap for the families of the children who attend when it is combined with the time taken to walk to and from school in rural areas, so that it shows a bias for town-living families who do not need the work of their children. Such states while having a wholesale primary education policy, for higher grades impose smaller and smaller quotas for places. In such a situation the rural families are required to teach the pro-social ideas and practices of economic and political development, which may only benefit the minority of permanently urbanised families with regular employment who will often if they can afford it prefer their children to be privately educated. A situation in which pro-social socialisation will be split between the practices of the past and the realities of the present. Family members will still expect the reciprocities built into subsistence cultures where there is some equality in the standards of living of all but which cannot possibly apply when some are well-off and others are poor. The example given was the Kenyan university lecturer who states that if his relatives come to Nairobi from the countryside, they can sleep in the garage as he cannot afford to feed and subsidise them when he has his own children as individuals to consider.

(4) Finally societies in which irrespective of parental wishes, status or economic standing there is an overall and quite successful centring on the child as an individual whose personal abilities must be developed. This is carried out without much specific attention to what the society as a whole needs or the parents might perhaps wish. Pro-social socialisation is directed towards what the child needs to be a member of an abstract depersonalised society. This avoids the teaching of anything more than short-term transitory obligations to their families whose social maintenance is now the obligation of the state's welfare and private pension schemes.

This typology is not a sequential one since all four types can exist in a section of a community and people can move or be moved from one type to another as in the mass movements of Chinese in the people's Republic of China in fulfilment of Maoist ideological programmes and the resettling of many millions as a consequence of the completion of the Yangtse High dam.

Most children even in the most hypothetically traditional society, will grow up with an understanding that there are people over the geographical and social horizon who are different to themselves. More recently the commonest and most widespread change in children's perceptions will not be the growth of cities and the regimentation of life required by such concentrations of population. It is the perception of material differences introduced into their minds by the varied and omnipresent mass media. Thirdly in all societies and at all social levels the intrusion of strangers into their lives; teachers, ticket inspectors, rent collectors and shop-keepers and even more extensively and intrusively in more quasi-traditional less developed communities the presence of tourists, missionaries for a variety of different spiritual, social and public health systems as well as itinerant musicians. It is the overwhelming confinement of the surrounding social systems into which children are socialised which must be our major concern.

Chapter-6

# Methodology : The Difficulties of Data Collection

We can make endless hypotheses about the vicissitudes of child development in various social environments and make seemingly parallel experimental studies with caged primates and groups of children but it seems likely that the correlations are largely in the minds of those holding such views. There are two serious methodological difficulties over experimental studies whether with primates or human children.

We cannot assume that primates or humans used in such experiments are what might be called free range. The monkeys are caged in and the children are similarly caged in by the school environment and indeed the experimental situation with even the most benign involved adult is restricted.

The fifty chimpanzees in the Budongo forest in Uganda have at least twenty five square miles in which to move. Other monkeys move freely until their group comes up against seemingly impassable barriers such as rivers on which there are floating islands of vegetation which they can use to float over. Even the monkeys co-inhabiting with humans in Indian cities or Thai monasteries are in fact more or less free range with the former seemingly treating the whole city as a food source. Children released from a teaching period rush out into the playground and celebrate their own interpretation of free range with vocal and physical exuberance.

The second restriction on proving any point related to child development is no human group could ever be subjected to the restrictions imposed on primates in experiments. Indeed experiments with humans are severely restricted by ethical standards which prevent anything approaching the range of situational factors experienced by most children being tested.

We can observe children but while social scientists may hope that the observed group is left as isolated as possible, it is usually the case that when some behaviour oversteps acceptable boundaries, other adults will step in and impose solutions. Apart from the fact that much is unknown about the backgrounds of children involved in experiments, it is usually and perhaps inevitably a situation that the children are being tested in situations in which there are adults somewhere in the background.

There is also a tendency to use data from situations which are either extremely abnormal or accepted as socially undesirable. Alternatively social scientists can use severe cases of deprivation to illustrate the consequences of what must certainly have been abnormal social environments. The two girls who were brought up in extreme isolation and apart from other socio-biological inadequacies when they were found, neither could speak. One died at 10 years with a mental age of 2 ½ years, while the other became normal (Davis K. 1947).

We also tend to assess children sleeping on the streets or engaging in quasi-criminal and illegal activities as failures of the political and social systems of Brazil and Nepal rather than as inevitable patterns of adaptation. The ways in which the human species has been able to survive over millennia in many different physical and social environments.

So we can see that the theoretical aspects of child development go forward handicapped on the one hand by the necessities of common decency restricting comparative research and on the other deliberate primate studies handicapped in other ways by being either caged or free range and thus often out of sight.

## The Wider Viewpoint : Methodological Issues

There would seem to be certain problems within the existing patterns of experimental and field work research over the development of children which make for difficulties in evaluating their results in all cultural settings.

Firstly much work has been done on children which in effect separates them from their environments as individuals not only at the time of the observations but also before and after; preceding factors and consequences of what is recorded at a particular time. This would apply just as much to the six cultures study of children of the Whitings

(Whiting & Whiting, 1975) which despite their thoroughness left the children suspended within the small sectors of time within which they were observed. Certainly such studies see their children as individuals but not as part of particularised environments who are more or less stuck in a special social and economic slot.

A second difficulty is that pro-social behaviour is seemingly seen as some overriding almost "moral" good for the benefit of society as a whole; it has almost the same characteristics as a religious injunction. If social is taken to mean any activity which involves more than single individuals, then any consideration of what an individual child does alone or in various group contexts is going to be differently evaluated. Pro-social behaviour is thus likely to be no more and no less than what fits into the demands of the primary group with whom the children spend most of their time. Whether the ideas of what is pro-social behaviour for this group are likely to be the same as those of outsider groups may well be a matter of accident rather than design and indeed they may often conflict in relatively homogeneous societies much less those in which there are enclaves of extremely different sub-cultures.

So there are going to be layers of pro-social behaviour in descending order of social closeness and with this the ability of various large and small sub-cultures to further particular patterns of pro-social behaviour in their children. Of course there are variations in the ability of such sub-cultures to contribute to and control pro-social behaviour of their children in such situations as the Amish and Hutterite communities. Even in such closely knit communities of a particular family are likely to be and perhaps inevitably will be in some respects different to those of their surrounding community within which they are so closely integrated almost every level.

Not only are there layers of pro-social behaviour but it is inevitable that what is considered as pro-social and personal at one level will often be seen as anti-social and impersonal at another. It is often been found that the children brought up in the Kibbutz style of Jewish living have many pro-social behaviour patterns, but it is unlikely that this is extended to their neighbouring Palestinians.

All children will be brought up within this layered approach to pro-social behaviour in which they are brought up within a combination of multi-layered and multi-lateral requirements which are not often the result of rational considerations for the benefits of the larger scale society within which they are brought up.

While this is certainly important if not of overriding importance for children to recognise the existence of these social dilemmas as they grow into adulthood, it is not a dominant feature of research into child development. The 'common good' seems to be a foundation theme.

Thirdly there is the difficulty as to whether children in terms of the social realities within which the majority will have to live, can ever be considered in isolation from their usefulness to the society to which they belong. In crude terms societies are functional in the sense that their parts have to contribute in some way to the functioning of the whole and if this is not so, they are costed out of its workings. To work on the assumption that the child as an individual value to be assessed away from the society in which they live, may well be unreal as the basis for evaluation as would be concentrating on the need for "happiness".

In anthropological studies of subsistence communities in which their "isolation" is predefined, children are integral contributing parts which gives them a credit rating in any functional assessments. However in studies of urban-industrial communities, the same functional assessments of children are not only not made but are positively avoided. Of course this is got round by ignoring the fact that children in such communities are social and economic handicaps and suggesting that they provide emotional pleasure to their parents and represent useful future parts of the larger society surrounding them.

It would seem that research into modern communities involving children is skewed against the issues which are in the forefront of the considerations of most quasi-traditional subsistence families and communities and indeed in the minds of modern families and communities; a balanced assessment that would deal with worry that for most modern parents children are not worth the effort.

A fourth issue may be the need for research to concentrate on how their present condition fits into their whole anticipated life pattern. It is reasonable to see life as a series of confrontations between what is needed to survive and the left-over elements which give some reasonable even pleasurable return to the individual.

So to study altruism, indeed to give it an important place in what children are taught or acquire, is no doubt important for any understanding of moral philosophy. As an activating factor in the lives of almost all people of any age and any culture, it may be an ideal, but as an actual determining impulse in the lives of any individual, it must be a very small part of their social lives and a serious economic handicap.

It would seem that much research is based on an implicit assumption of the possible "goodness" and improvability of man. Even if it is not stated or implied as such much research into the pro-social behaviour of children is based on a "moral" conception not only of how societies function but how they should function.

There are possibly two ways in which theoretical development can at least coincide with scientific requirements in which social scientists work with children in groups or individually under various contrived conditions or the uncontrolled free form observations of children without the stranger observer being directly involved at all.

## Experimental Work with Children

Parents with children often ask them questions and even in replying to those with whom they are living without ostensible or prolonged tensions, the answers may only be both comprehensive and accurate in their replies to simple "yes" or "no" on the level of a bag of crisps or what they want to watch on television. In such long-term culturally distinct situations the known may be questioning the known about the known; it is a form of reality not summoning up the experimentally unknown.

There is no reason to suppose that children as adults do not have their own private ways of thinking about the surrounding adult world. It seems unlikely that they do not have their own ways of only partially exposing themselves to such intrusive outsiders.

The presence of an outsider, however benignly disposed and widely accepted as not coming into the framework of someone to be avoided, still comes within the category of adults about whom it is sub-consciously as much as consciously and sensibly prudent. The interrelationship becomes triangular and to want to see answers being produced for a wider range of activities and thoughts, would involve waiting around for very long periods in the hope of getting a valuable gem from some non-experimental reality.

For the majority of questions and answers within stable family groups much will depend upon the moods of both parties. The questions may be innocuous in terms of the adults asking but the body language and tone with which the questions are spoken may well carry different messages that could be disclosed by the words themselves. The minds of the children asked are interpreting what has been said faster and on a different level to that of the questioners. An example of this was questioning Ganda children in their responses to certain key words; European children can be expected to reply "father" very quickly to the word "mother", whereas these children tended to reply "plantains" which form the basic food source provided by whichever woman is doing the cooking. Is this answer a reflection of the absence of known fathers or a more basic concern for food? So in addition to interpersonal reactions, there are likely to be cultural differences not so much in respect of reality but also from what the children expect to be acceptable answers.

There is also the assumption of a stable family environment as a datum line for research understanding which is a particularly Western concept. A high proportion of northern Benin are fostered out and there appears to be strong social pressures for mothers not to have close personal contacts with even their new-born and infant children (Alber, 2003). This is not just instability but something so alien to the Western principle of the necessity of parental care for pro-social socialisation as to be classed by most western educated researchers into the framework of socio-psychological pathology.

The stability of any family group may be a legal concept but in practice it is virtually non-existent in all childhoods considered over the years with the absence of one or the other of their biological and social parents combined with an inevitable series of domestic tensions and disasters.

Social scientists want to know much more about child development and its correlations than can perhaps be found out in experimental situations however ingeniously constructed in which children are tested with hypothetical situations rather than real ones. There is also the fact that whatever the results they cannot be tested against another group which has not been tested in this way; the results fall down on the absence of this uncontaminated control group.

There are also problems over conditional thinking and the extent to which the thinking in language copes with "if" which is easier to deal with in English than in Mandarin Chinese in which the same question asked in both these languages gets different answers even from those who are to all intents and purposes bilingual. What of the Bangladeshi child who speaks Bengali at home, learns about Islam in Arabic and prefers to read the magazine "Hello" when not at school where an English linguistic code is taught which has little common place use in the Tower Hamlets of East London. Thus "if" semantically may be worked through in terms of who is asking the questions so that an Asian-British possibly a woman social scientist asking the questions might well get different answers to the same questions from an Anglo-British male one.

Apart from the semantics of different languages which may make it difficult to have certain types of thinking such as those which have only two tenses the "present" and the "not present" in which the past and future have to be denoted by the accompanying sentences or the languages which have no indefinite future so that any question of "if" might have to be related to a specific "when". There is also the fact that few adults live in a socio-psychological environment in which "if" is more than an infrequent part of their thinking and possibly modern at that and related to "luck" and lotteries.

Even if the children can cope with the difficulties of imagining a social situation with which they may or may not have ever been confronted, such questions and answers can never be correlated to what the children might actually do should they at a latter date be confronted with situations which the social scientist considers to be similar; this in itself is an ideological imposition, almost a leap of faith.

Built into such questioning will always be some split which is present in every behavioural issue confronting adults; what the rule is, what usually happens within their understandings of what goes on in their community and what they themselves have done when faced with such a need to make a decision. It is theoretically possible for these three facets to coincide but it would seem to be rare as they are in reality three behavioural discs which overlap to varying extents depending on the social environment and personality.

These children in such questionings are being faced with complex issues of which they cannot be aware just as may be the case with adults who are not reflective moral philosophers with impeccable private lives. They may well know what a rule is in relation to their own near relatives but the fluctuations in this might only be raised in their minds by direct questioning. Children in an English village would agree that stealing is wrong but nevertheless accompany their fathers to take Christmas trees from the local forestry plantation. It may well be a functional impossibility to apply an overall rule against stealing, the taking of property with the intention of depriving its owners, when this can be applied to souvenirs, stationary and not paying a railway fare.

The intricacies of theft are one of the easiest moral issues to understand because there are no adults anywhere who have not stolen something in their lives, if not to have done so frequently within the literal meaning of the law, but which do not raise moral issues in their thinking. Questioning about violence is much more difficult because it is either imaginary and media correlated or too personal to be easily made overt.

Then there is the issue of questioning. Outside domestic necessities such as "have you washed your hands" and more rarely "what happened at a school today", it is not a common form of interrelationship. The first question may be common enough but the second is likely to be rare after the first few days at a new school. It may even be a form which is generally seen as hostile and might even be a new semantic form which is part of contemporary life which comes from schooling and economics and is related to social status.

Certainly in many cultures perhaps even well developed western ones, direct questions are often seen as personally intrusive, pushy and bad manners and overall getting to the point too quickly. In less economically developed societies, information is obtained in round about ways rather than being elicited by the baldness of a question. In such societies the sophistication of conversation obtains information with the circuitous skill of the planning of a chess game; they are not in a hurry.

So deliberate questioning more especially done by those marked by obvious social distance, the outsiders who assume themselves to be viewed as benign because they have personally assumed that role, has some almost automatic tension creating elements. Adults are taking the lead and this to most if not all children is a mixed blessing. In the minds of many children, adolescents and adults questioning by social scientists is not much different to the behaviour of intrusive civil servants.

## Field-work Approaches

The details of field-work and working with children in school or home show repeatedly that however carefully the social scientists into the community in which they are aiming to work, they are always more "outsider" than "insider" and to think that their academic professionalism and what can only be their theoretical detachment is naïve. The same or "other" ethnicity of the researcher may not make much difference either way when this is augmented by differences in costume, accent, smell and indeed every differentiating factor.

We know that to get accepted in an English village after moving there is often a matter of years and the social scientist in a school is not a permanent member of staff and certainly less part of its social environment than the cleaners or kitchen staff. They are people who come and go regularly for short periods of time over some months and even if they eat with the children they are still outsiders by age, size, dress and language.

We know that all children are taught to be wary of outsiders and this is certainly not new but is an almost ethological component of all social life and the questioning of children by a known and well liked teacher is acceptable, but it is role related to the school environment and the teacher is not a child. Children even if they were not conscious of this wariness, would not extend to visiting social scientists the partial and qualified openness that they would give to teachers, their parents and their peers.

A selection of questioned children who come from a single school and the group environment of a form, cannot be assumed to be uniform except for the fact that a child is being asked questions by an adult. The standard background variations are always there and for each of these there are even more numerous sub-divisions; sex, biological/ social age, real educational status rather than form, religion, ethnicity, class, occupation of parents, marital status of known parents, neighbourhood, languages spoken at home and with peers and to what standard, biological handicaps and so on. It seems likely that the social scientists may not have much more information on the background to the children questioned than might be available for getting a job as a shelf-stacker in a super market.

On the other hand a child or adolescent on probation after conviction for some petty crime, would have a bulky file on their current and past behaviour and details of every interview collated by an adult directly responsible for influencing them.

## The Dubious Value of Questioning Children

To conclude it seems likely that children would accept questions which have an immediate relevancy about what they want from the school lunch menu, relatively easy to answer because there are no more than three choices. Experience with foster children showed that they can cope with issues involving limited choices but not complex ones. But the questions asked by social scientists parallel those offered on an a la carte menu in a restaurant which certainly lead to a lot of dithering by adults or the choice of a T-shirt when there are dozens on offer puts the child into a situation of comprehensive uncertainty.

Questions asked by ostensibly benign outsiders are not as simple as choosing a toy in a shop since the range of possibly answers has no boundaries. To the child being questioned a question requires an answer and there is no "don't know" category which they could provide.

One suspects that even the most accurately designed experimental work on the development of children, must remain what it is "experimental" and thus out of social context and without any possibility of comparative "real-life" parallels to test the validity of any conclusions against the background of what the children probably experience as the comprehensive anxieties of their own personal lives. A question is either a rare or a circumstantially common place event and in the latter case the children are both unprepared and wary. It would be interesting to see to what extent the Judges Rules on the interrogation of suspects in police custody would allow the questioning of children on matters concerning moral development, particularly as it is always assumed that they have to be protected by the presence of a parent or some legally entitled social welfare representative. Are there alternatives to experimental studies of children which are bedevilled with a permanent range of methodological drawbacks? Are teachers in any better position to evaluate the social and psychological development of the children whom they teach?

## Teachers Criteria for Assessment

In considering the public and professional roles of teachers it is prudent to remember the distinction between on stage and off stage behaviour (Goffman, 1969: 129). It is not so much the criteria which are important and even allowing for cultural differences, the objectives of teaching may be shared largely by all teachers. The key to the assessment of criteria is the extent of mutual exposure which teachers and pupils share.

There is the time-table regularity of teachers on duty. But the teacher is an abstract concept in the context of many schools with large numbers of pupils. For how long is a specific teacher in contact with a specific child and what is the nature of these contacts. The ideal of career teachers spending the whole of their professional working lives in one school so that whole school generations lasting perhaps five years pass under their assessing eyes needs to be examined. Above primary schools form teachers, pupils will go to different teachers for each subject in different parts of the school.

If the period of assessment is 5-7 school years, then we need to know what proportion of term times a teacher has been in a position to assess any child; the exposure to how many periods per week and how many children were in the classes taught; a class of twelve and one of 24 are totally different in what the teacher may get to know about a child as an individual.

Then there is the factor of the type of teacher activity in which assessments are made. There are differences in the interrelationships of teacher-pupil in arithmetic, English and art which may only have in common the fact that both are confined regularly to a class-room for set periods. In this setting there are different types of assessments between those related to the subject which is impersonal in mathematics and science and more personal in art in which there are no exact standards of excellence.

The teacher is the focus of class-room work and each will make spot judgements on the degree to which the children are paying attention and responding to the teacher's efforts. This is certainly a personal judgement in which a number of shared biases are involved; certain pupils will have reputation shared among staff members and pupils will have nick-names which show that they are generally liked or disliked and will be passed on by overlapping generations of pupils. This comes down to assessments based on a known number of periods but is very much a two sided equation.

How teachers may view individual pupils will vary between the idealism of first appointments and relationship to the reputation of the school; many will apply for jobs in rural schools while only a few will seek to become teachers in inner-city schools regardless of their reputations. Then there are teachers near to retirement, those that want no more than supply jobs in which they have no long-term commitment to either school or pupils and teachers returning to teaching after bringing up children; the overall differences between teachers who view teaching as "the" job or just as "a" job.

The type of teacher-pupil contact is important in such assessments. The observations in class are confined; it is an exact universe and special behaviour is required from all those involved as they are on stage. Then there is corridor, playground and canteen activity in which only certain types of forbidden or attention seeking behaviour will catch the eyes of teachers who happen to be looking.

Finally there is the teachers involvements with so-called out of school voluntary activities in which the pupils are there because they have chosen for their own reasons to be part of these special groups. Extra time which children spend in activities of their own choosing will contribute to positive assessments of those children; disruptive behaviour is less likely to occur apart from the fact that there is a closer supervisory role for the teacher in team sport than in overlooking larger numbers of children in playgrounds, corridors and canteens.

The criteria themselves for overall assessments of children may be the ones provided in the abstract by the examination requirements for further progress within the educational system. More prominently it will be the degree of observable conformity to the disciplinary code of the school set out in hand-outs and on notice boards as well as in the tone set by each headmaster or headmistress. In general there may be little difference in what is expected in all types of schools. These all tend to share most of the characteristics of ideal bureaucracies; a clear-cut hierarchy of authority, written rules, a full time staff under whose administration the transient generations of pupils pass and there is a clear distinction between what happens in the school and life outside (Weber, 1978: 956-63). Thus the assessments of teachers of their pupils may be one of the latter's degree of conformity to the requirements bureaucratic institutions dominating all complex societies.

However within this there is the question of the individualities of teachers and children and the amount of information which is available to teachers about the whole lives of the children they are assessing. Teachers will vary with their personalities, age, sex and social and geographical backgrounds while the pupils will be much more uniform by age and the cultural watershed from which they are drawn. It seems likely that teachers will be assessing children on a variety of scales such as their own ideas of the appropriateness in terms of different cultural and family backgrounds.

Whether teachers admit it or not they have become members of the middle class with expectations of middle class behaviour shared with the behavioural codes of the schools so there is a preference for the quite and well behaved child, the conformist without more positive characteristics.

There is little reason for any teacher to know much about the social backgrounds of any child because they have so many children under their periodic supervision. Only when something goes wrong is their vision widened without being able to do much about it other than to hand the problem over to specialists. The speech therapist working with a "gipsy" boy who is uncommunicative and when he does speak is either unintelligible or speaking Romany knows that their relationship will end when his caravan moves on.

Except in the sense of moral behaviour such a teacher is more or less filling time and unlikely to have any long-term effect on such children however much they may try. On the other hand the missionary priest in Tanzania who spends eighteen months getting a single autistic child to be able to say "good morning" may well have achieved something of value for the child and himself; perhaps it comes down to time and motion factors as to whether child in school can be treated and evaluated on individual terms.

The teacher belongs to a definite culture and yet may be faced with a multi-cultural class who would speak one language in class and another one at home. Even if there is a shared assumption of English, it is likely that for most of schools which do not have a largely middle class intake of pupils, there will be the "elaborated" code spoken in the school and the "restricted" one at home (Bernstein, 1975). The body language shown in schools may be the ones appropriate to the home culture and relate to sex differences in which boys and women teachers may clash culturally with misunderstandings over the use of hands and eye-contacts.

When it comes to writing assessments there is a tendency to use written ones on work done during the term and above all to remember recent events, even though the contact may have been over a long period; what does one write about a child who appears to have little individuality or indeed an abrasive personality when the teacher has little time to delve deeper into what makes the child have these characteristics.

There is also a tendency when evaluating individual children to assess them in relation to the classes to which they belong; comparative standards on either side of the grey area of conformity to acceptable standards; those at the "good" and "bad" ends of the scale of behaviour are likely to be more accurately reported on. For others there are their showing of some unusual characteristics which are either approved or disapproved of. It is an anecdotal process relying on rather unreliable episodic memories.

If these evaluations are not just opinions and are correlated on a score sheet, then other factors come into play. Too many low marks and disorderly conduct remarks reflect on the teacher's abilities to teach and keep order and too many comments on unusual behaviour might raise questions of bias. Also if similar assessments are made of individual children by different teachers then there is the possibility of informal collusion. There is also very little follow up in subsequent behaviour to see whether assessments were more or less correct.

There is also the important factor that teacher assessments are made on the basis of "on stage" behaviour without much knowledge of how the individual child carries on in the children's "off-stage" social system which runs independently and parallel to the official system. However much the teachers may know about this system it is a subversive one with its own linguistic and behavioural code adaptively reacting to the system of the school.

So to see teachers assessments of children in terms of their pro-social behaviour, it is bound to be one that relates to the institutional demands of the surrounding society; how successful have they been in making school children fit into what is likely to happen to them. As with all institutions attention is more likely to be paid to the successful promotionable ones and to the administrative expulsion of the failures.

## The Paradox of Exactitude

We know that human behaviour is not only immensely varied but is varying all the time that it is being observed and categorized but this data is often worked out to three or more places of decimals. We are bound to ask who is convincing whom in such mathematical presentations-because decision-making is unlikely to notice of such exact numerically expressed data. Let us examine some such studies.

Some methodological issues arise in all careful studies which isolate particular child centred dyads as in the study of "Mutually Responsive Orientation" between mothers and their young children (Kochanska, 2002). This thorough research concludes that a mutually satisfactory relationship between mothers and children leads to the development in the latter of conscience as they become eager to embrace parental values and standards of behaviour.

This is indeed what one might expect from the standpoint of generally accepted western behaviour, but there are drawbacks to even this most through study of more than 200 mother-child dyads. Of course there are the usual queries as to how these dyads were chosen in Iowa, USA, which like any other social frame must have had its own particular characteristics and the absence of any control group.

But there are other difficulties in referring to conscience which surely involve a wide ranging structure of behavioural understandings and some moral correlations ranging from everyday admonitions to blinding flash influences of particular incidents. Were the relationships all so uniform and was the concentration of mutual understandings between mothers and their children so much "sweetness and light".

Certainly young children may and indeed almost certainly will be imprinted with some at least of their mothers' values whatever they might be for which there will be widespread cultural variations. To what extent do these correspond to general overt community ones and specific more covert ones over what might be wrong in their particular personal circumstances. There is much difference between being imprinted with the moral values of not stealing and being kind to others and having these acts related to others who happen to be ethnically different and the property of strangers, railway companies or government departments.

What is missing from such assessments are the time and motion correlations of the mothers' relationships with their children; how long is this a separated one and not shared with a parental partner, passers by in the street and fellow shoppers in the supermarket and other children in adult supervised play-school. Is the partner a weekend and night-time parent, use of baby sitters or grandmothers, presence of other children and mothers' absence in part-time work.

Even when there are detailed studies of children, they are either of particular families or of observation of children for a limited number of periods which are not seen as a behavioural section taken out of their lives experienced as a socio-psychological whole. This is not so much a reflection on such careful research work but of the impossibility of bringing into consideration all the factors required for the assessment of individual children much less their group characteristics.

These conclusions and many like them are valid because the design of their field-work makes them valid but must surely be defective in terms of other varieties of relationship; the urban slum family in New York, Cairo and Rio de Janiero, the Amish and Hutterites, single parent and the common polygynous and rarer polyandrous families. Perhaps such studies could be more safely entitled as restricted evaluations of self-selected dyads in particular dominant cultural environments.

## Freeform Observation of Children

One suspects that the verbal world has come into its current complex social realities much latter in evolutionary time than physical interrelationships. Words enable and restrict and are often ambiguous and require social embroidery for them to be understood in context. Much of this is based on eye-sight and body language rather than the range of sound or indeed print.

Although they have some verbal abilities, it is primarily with physical actions that children demonstrate important feelings; they do things rather than speak about them. Their screeching and yelling has hominid parallels in which the latter may be making a much wider range of intra-species social activities understandable that had been previously thought. Any school playground is a bedlam of sound and forms of physical interrelationships which are difficult to quantify.

Much hominid life under natural conditions can be observed continuously with cameras and binoculars which bring their distant activities into close observation when they are in view; the restrictions on the information gathered may no longer be due to the obduracy of these primates to having their privacies intruded upon and the physical difficulties of getting close to them on regular basis. It is now curtailed by the sheer quantity of the information gathered and the difficulties which researchers have in processing multiple factors involving several primates at the same time; perhaps even the time which researchers have to devote to such tasks may now be the main handicapping factor.

Since we now know that we can reach this standard of observation with wild primates there is still the drawback of presenting data in numerical form rather than as summaries of what has been seen such as copulation of chimpanzees has not been seen and only rarely between siblings. The point has been made without bringing in numbers of observations made by various and varying observers and drawing upon such figures the criticisms that come with all statistics of socially variable behaviour.

In attempting to understand the pro-social development of children it might be appropriate to abandon the experimental approach so much more convenient for social scientists and use the methods that are used to examine the behaviour of primates in the wild and to see how children in the equivalent of "wild" conditions where any controlling factors are not those provided by the circumstances of the experiments themselves. Continuous camera and sound recordings of their behaviour when the social settings are not entirely controlled by adults.

An important restraint on primate study in the wild is the costs of setting up research and without doubt it is extremely expensive in both personnel and materials and the using up of time in isolation. Modern societies are increasingly photographing places whether occupied or not by people for preventive security and this must include many areas regularly occupied by children and adolescents. These sources of information available for long periods have yet to be used for systematic analysis yet those seen on screen are more easily identifiable than unclothed primates.

While the data from experiments is restricted by design, the data from such continuous recordings is the reverse and must always contain the possibilities of new aspects of behaviour becoming recorded rather than the percentage facets of experimental data.

Thus the problem is not the difficulty of getting data on the public interpersonal behaviour of children but its quantity even when restricted to playground behaviour of a known number of children in a single school which can of course be correlated to the school records of everyone seen on the films.

Even accepting the possibilities of developing Parallel Distributive Processing or Connectionism to social behaviour in general as a potential way of handling massive quantities of data and it has so far only had qualified success with relatively simple human activities, the problem is still the quantity of data. Science has yet to develop a satisfactory way of coping with multiple variables constantly varying from sources which are also varying. We are then back again to the biases of social scientists picking and choosing what they wish to analyse but there is however the important fact that the data itself is not experimentally controlled.

There is also the difficulty that the facts may be clear enough but the fact that certain children hit others or do something out of expected statistical proportions leads to interpretations which are almost certainly biased and to have such assessments done through a committee adds greatly to costs. The recordings remain hard data and it is their quantity which might well become the major drawback to their use.

But to have such recordings available which are out of the control of any social scientists means that this impersonal data is available at latter dates for reassessment as would be the school and other records of those identified.

## The Dimensions of Explanation and Memory

Historically formal instruction has always been confined to specialised literate minorities rather more involved in administration than religion and most teaching was confined to copying during long apprenticeships just as it is now in subsistence cultures when someone wants to become a herbalist diviner. General formal instruction into the pro-social and religious requirements of a society may only have occurred in Islamic ones for many past centuries in the learning of the Koran by rote.

With universal primary education religion has come to be taught as a specific subject by specially trained persons who nowadays are more likely to be Muslim than Christian in Western societies and as a basic school subject in Islamic societies usually taught by secular teachers. Pro-social behaviour is more likely to be part of the general school ethos of helping others than as something that can be taught as a subject.

It is probable that the contents of such teaching are no more remembered in its specifics than any other subject unless the child develops a special interest in religion. It is only recently that religious instruction for Christians has gone beyond stereotyped questions and answers. The standard explanation for any ritual which has not been stabilised in print, is that this is what we have always done.

It seems likely that children do not distinguish between the requirements of everyday social living and behaviour that has a specifically pro-social or religious backing. A sponge like absorption of the requirements for everyday behaviour in which no theme is separated from any other.

While it may be possible to correlate the current behaviour of children to the presence or absence of religious or secular ideas and practices, such possible influences must be largely seen in retrospect; what is done now and how it relates to past influences. Indeed these recollections and explanations overall are likely to focus on either past repetitive activities or singular events which were not repeated or repeatable.

What young people and older people may give as reasons for certain behaviours cannot have a high degree of reliability except in the sense that they have been asked to recollect and have provided answers in this form. There are innumerable factors which may have influenced these replies to take the form recorded which would include the whole biological, social and psychological biographies and environments of those replying.

A direct question may be a form of behaviour which is particularly Western and moreover authoritarian in format. The child who is questioned is always inferior to the questioner in age, size and is likely to be dressed differently and whatever language is used is not likely to be in the format which they hear at home and certainly not the one which they use amongst themselves.

Beyond this unnoticed absorption of general behavioural requirements, children are likely to remember behaviour which occurs at special events which initiate ideas and behavioural changes. These might be related to cyclical and linear rites of passage and secondly around what happens about the inevitable crises of death, disease and disaster. It is perhaps the striking unusualness of these seemingly one-off events which imprints them into the child's mind as pro-social requirements; what should be done by those involved who want to feel at home within a particular primary group during peak events.

Thus there are two suggested alternatives to the gaining of knowledge, regular behaviour such as that seen in repetitive religious and social rituals which have gradually become implicit knowledge through their repeated practical application about which there is no need to have any understanding (Anderson, 1983), except that they occur and are memorable breaks in the day to day routines to which the child is accustomed. From this comes procedural knowledge of such rituals from repeated application becomes consciously accessible and influential (Karmiloff-Smith, 1992). A Muslim child learns the procedural movements required for daily prayer, the Hindu child how to decorate images and the right behaviour for "puja" prayers and the Roman Catholic ones how to cross themselves and genuflect before the altar with its special hanging sidelight.

These rituals mark off time either because they are linear, their sisters and brothers only get married once for the first time and the birthdays of Christ and the Prophet Mohammad mean special food and presents. Since in most societies religion and secular behaviour are inseparable in the ways that children participate, it is these occasions which become significant parts of their memories. They are accepted as likely to be accurate by those who want to know what children remember from their childhoods and since they are remembered that they have been in some ways influential.

We can also consider that these rituals are correlated to particular patterns of behaviour which extend into social life and thus have a moral influence on what they do; avoiding the use of the left hand, there are special times and places in which everyone behaves in a different way and that men are usually dominant on these special occasions.

However cognition and the ability to remember and explain to further the understandings of outsiders of pro-social behaviour created for and by children probably relates to two different types of religious ritual (Whitehouse, 2002) which is applicable to other aspects of social behaviour.

Firstly knowledge and memories of frequently repeated rituals, the Mass for Roman Catholics, "puja" for Hindus and Jains and the five daily prayer sessions for Muslims. But then most children are involved in a wide range of social rituals which are repeated day after day, feeding domestic animals, the regularities of schooling, the place and timing of excreting and getting dressed; indeed the lives of children however disorganised it might appear to outsiders are filled with repetitive regularities.

The analyses of what children do repeatedly may take several forms; the autopilot repetitions of behaviour, eating, sleeping and excreting which will always occur and take further cultural forms. In religious rituals what is expected of participants of all ages is so repetitive that they all cued in to what they should do at any point without having to be led in by anything more than a word or gesture.

Then there are explanations for unintended innovations in the behaviour of children and verbally transmitted explanations for common behaviour which is likely to be in stereotyped phrases such as "a good child is one who behaves well", which are likely to be linked in to special occasions. It might even be suggested that tautological reasoning is the basis and maintainer of pro-social behaviour.

There are also explanations for repetitive behaviour; the Jains in their theology (Humphrey & Laidlaw, 1994) have no place for daily "puja" worship which preoccupies faithful Hindus but which they regard as "empty" ritual although it is widely performed by the devout in all religions who provide themselves with their own parallel wide and personal explanations.

Lastly there are the quasi-official explanations of experts who exist in all communities, the knowledgeable and talkative apart from more official explanations of what is taught to children which are widely publicised in print and probably little known outside professional circles. Insofar as these are likely to be remembered by children as reactions to charismatic individuals and their story telling, as well as the reminiscences of the old.

Then there are memories and explanations of rituals that are climactic either from their rareness as they are related to crises, the death of a mother or sibling or because they are related to a rite of passage. In which the individual can only participate once. No child is likely to forget their own circumcision and that because of this painful experience they have a new status; they are treated differently. They have been central figures in these events whatever the political, social, religious or economic reasons may be.

If pro-social behaviour is standardised at all, it must be through print but this does not mean and indeed cannot mean that it is continues to be so in the minds and practices of those to whom the printed versions are taught and indeed learned by heart. Print may imprint itself on the ways in which institutions function, but not necessarily imprint its instructions onto the minds of children; too much is printed. The Prophet Mohammad is thought to have simplified the religious requirements for his new followers, because he did not consider that the average Bedu capable of remembering anything more complicated than the simplest of procedures.

If social behaviour had not become standardised in this way, it is more likely that children will tie pro-social correct behaviour to what they remember either from repetition or from singular events. It seems likely that the memories of children, the realities of their pasts and the guides to their current pro-social behaviour, are tied to small capsules of events which carry within them their own reasons for them to be remembered. The why or the how is no part of their necessary understandings but imbedded in the semantics of speech.

## Pro-social Behaviour and the Diffusion of Language

Although the principle family unit in economically developed societies has been described as the isolated nuclear family, consisting of mother, father and children, it has been found to be not nearly so isolated as the phrase would suggest. Public transport, cars, the mobile telephone and television have meant that there is little cognitive isolation apart from the fact that relatives tend to cluster within a twenty-five mile radius of any family's residence.

Nevertheless most children spend their formative years talking to the same people principally mother-child and child to child while talking also to an equally high proportion of outsiders such as school teachers and shop assistants; they grow up within a basic social and linguistic dyad. It seems likely that the higher up the social scale the family is situated, the greater the time spend in this semantic dyad.

The unit for any understanding of the development of children in economically developed and developing societies must surely be this division between children's experience of the in-group and the out-group distinguishable by almost every aspect of their social and psychological lives.

Not only is there this dyadic understanding of the children's interrelationships, but the family aspects are always boxed in within the walls of their housing restricting access to and from outsiders; the closed door as a special social barrier limiting contacts. A shift in the persons with whom a child communicates requires an abrupt shift in the physical setting (Schieffelin & Ochs, 1986: 176-7).

There is also the factor of declining fertility so that the only child is becoming a common feature of many family forms not only in the Western world but in China as well. Thus within the home the child may be talking to only two types of adult; the more permanently present mother and the intermittently present father. So the characteristics which used to mark off the first-born from their subsequent siblings may extend to a life-long and increasing isolation from the comfort of relatives.

So it is not surprising that the shift of the child into formal schooling and the presence there of what they may well feel to be functionally strangers-cum-siblings, making for the bilingualism of linguistic codes which they use. There are the contrasts between these outsider roles which they have to learn to acquire and keep going and the limited ascribed relationships which operate within the home (Anderson, 1984).

In addition to this understanding of sub-cultural linguistic codes, there are in addition children who grow up bilingually and even trilingually in which they have more than one natal language. Steiner states that he was polyglot with an equal knowledge of French, German and English, it was an habitual and unnoticed practice for my mother to start a sentence in one language and finish it in another (Steiner, 1975: 116). The children in the tribally intermingled areas of northern Myanmar may have a knowledge of several languages from which they switch from one to another without much noticing that this has happened.

The modern situation may be entirely different with children in China and India starting to learn English early on in their schools and English children learning French and other European languages at a similar early stage. A sequential process in which the acquired knowledge of the new language and its ideas overlays the ascribed knowledge of their natal dyadic linguistic codes.

The most important aspects of children's lives with which research methodology has to work must be the extent to which children absorb various cultural understandings through variations of natal and learned linguistic codes. This may be even more confining in bilingual environments when combined with regimentation of schooling which has no replication in social life except in the households of the 19th century rich.

We have seen that most methodologies suffer from the restrictions of emulating the exact inorganic sciences or provide so much data as to make analysis almost impossible even with adequate funds and many researchers working in concert over long periods. Perhaps in the end we are left with "ordered intuition" as the best that can be done (Steiner, 1989: 174). Let us now look at the linguistic background to the development of children in greater detail.

## Chapter-7

# Language and Pro-social Development

### The Primacy of Language

To think of human behaviour as involving some identifiable basic units except in the senses of some relatively simplistic biological categories, is a crude abstraction of little use in identifying the pro-social requirements for the training and behaviour of children in particular societies. If we accept that it is the complexities of language rather than communicating sound, which distinguishes humans from animals, then language is an important basis for identifying what pro-social behaviour is required of children in any society.

Whether language induces particular types of behaviour or *vice-versa* is irrelevant. There are several thousand different languages and each one alters and restricts the behaviour of all those who speak each one. There can be no uniformity in what a child learns to say and how it is said by one child as opposed to another; these varied basic structures of speech in each language are quite distinct and cannot be used for intercommunication. "The fact of the matter is that the 'real world' is to a large extent unconsciously built up on the language habits of the group. No two languages are ever sufficiently similar to be considered as representing the same social reality. The worlds in which different societies live are distinct worlds, not merely the same world with different labels attached" (Sapir, 1949).

This is apart from the fact that all intercommunication except for a very limited range of circumstances, are translations in which each party interprets what the other is trying to communicate over the barriers of dialect and the differences of understandings which relate to sex, age, occupation, status, religion and education, leaving aside personal appearances and appraisals of personality differences of those who just do not or do like each other. The young girl will learn very early in her life that her correct way of speaking as a woman will be different to that of her brother and indeed that it will often be quite distinct as in Japanese.

It is a moot point whether anyone can think in terms which cannot be expressed in their language but children are not likely to be in that area of creative thought on the boundaries of their culture; they listen and learn and their fantasy talk is going to be within the language structures which they have learnt. Children learn ways to express themselves which are exclusive to the language and culture in which they live.

Children first learn to talk not in the abstract but to certain persons in their primary group and to see others as outside this communicating relationship. So it is kinship terminology which first enters their understanding and in many cultures their mothers and fathers are referred to as the daughter or son of someone else; even married couples may not refer to each other by any personal names. This will be one of the first factors which make children aware of their position in a network of kin.

A Sukuma child in Tanzania will hear their elders greeting visitors with whom marriage can be contracted as "lugishi" and those who cannot as "lwimbo". Both sons and daughters will refer to their elder siblings as "nkulu" and younger ones as "nzana". A paternal uncle is "baba", another father, with the same demonstrative adjectives as are used for siblings because he is older or younger than their father; he will inherit the widow of his brother if she has nowhere else to go as her family will not want to look after her as it might involve renegotiations over the return of bridewealth cattle payments. The paternal aunt "sengi" is known to be especially powerful as she can curse children with the same effectiveness as their own mothers and fathers and their paternal grandparents; her children and her brother's children are in competition over the inheritance of their father. Maternal uncles and aunts are "mami" and "mayu" respectively from whom no tensions can be anticipated. So children in most societies grow in contact with other people to whom specific labels are attached, even to the extent of attaching kinship labels to the fringes of known relationships with classificatory kinship terms.

In Swahili speaking societies the mother's brother "mjomba" is the most preferred relation who is not involved in squabbles over property, so that virtual strangers with whom a relationship is needed in a town where it is necessary to share lodgings will be referred to as a mother's brother. The five residents of a single room in Mombasa all belonged to the same tribe and were all called mother's brother. Even in contemporary England where there are uncles and aunts through both mother and father without distinguishing titles, the former will tend to be preferred.

We can assume that children are fixed very early into a pattern of language use which controls much thought and that this may be distinguished from thinking; deviations from this would not be something that children are involved in. Burmese children learn very early that there are personal pronouns which distinguish relationships as to whether the speaker is equal to, inferior to or superior to the person with whom they are talking. The accidental use of the wrong pronoun would soon be corrected as wrong. In all these distinctions which are made in language between one person and another, the children will be told that this is the way that they should talk, reasons are not given because they are not needed even if they could be known there would be little point in wasting time telling children the reasons for how they should speak in order to be accepted as reasonable members of their already existing society. This is the way to speak and that's it.

They will pick up the special vocabularies of the culture in which they are living, not the vocabularies of specialists. Lap and Massai children will soon learn to distinguish reindeer and cattle by their horn shape, just as the Najaho distinguish the subtle shades of earth and rock colour in their environment.

So we can appreciate that children grow up as speakers of natal languages which not only have specific kinship terms but rich vocabularies which their families use regularly. Almost before they can walk they know kinship terms and their connection with status since it will be linked to what they see going on in their homes; who eats first and what. Meat eating is rare in most societies because cattle are rarely killed just for food and the children will notice that certain parts of a slaughtered animal go to certain patrilineal, matrilineal and affinal relatives as well as to village officials. (Stevenson, 1943: 132,140) Perhaps the same thing goes on in Western families of the Thanks giving and Christmas turkeys and in what societies at what social status level to women eat before men.

While it may be possible to read too much into the structures of the languages which children learn, the tenses of verbs which they will learn to use correctly through the accidents of socialisation. The language of the five million Sukuma has eighteen tenses, so in this it is richer than English. These tenses are grouped by their relationships to time which treat the past as nine forms of completed actions and three for the forms of the future; very sophisticated gradations. Also in the process of language socialisation they will learn without knowing that they are learning that Sukuma has five tones; high, normal, low, descending and rising (Batibo, 1985).

The Kamba child will not learn that their language has no indefinite future tense but that the future is expressed and thus thought of in terms of immediacy, not so near and possibly in a year or so. It is not that they are blocked off from the open ended future which continues as it were out of sight, but the framework for thinking in such terms has to be worked round as in the concept of saving for the future which such children might well think of in terms of the agricultural year, and the breeding cycle of livestock.

Children in such cultures may only become aware of time as something external to themselves when they encounter the school time-table and year the time being given on their national wireless programmes. Many will grow up in subsistence agricultural communities in which time is seasonal and judged by the visibility of the sun. How early in life do Ssonjo children learn to tell night time by the movements of the stars which their adults use to govern the flow of shared scarce water into their small bean plots.

Children also learn about the importance of place in many languages in which nouns cannot be used except by locating them in terms of nearness and distance in the Swahili enclitics "mo", "po" and "ko". This will be related soon enough into the proper places to excrete in which amongst the Ssonjo the women go uphill behind the village and on the East African coast along the beach to the left of the village.

Children also learn in Malysian and Bantu languages that nouns are grouped so that each one has to go into its appropriate group to which are attached the correct enclitics for personal pronouns for use in adjectives and verbs. These are sophisticated systems of social and material classification which are absent from Western languages.

Thus we have to conclude that the most important inputs into the behaviour of children which they cannot avoid are absorbed through their immensely varied natal languages. Western thinkers who have worked within languages which have an enormous syntax and through which they have avoided the expression of most scientific thought, have difficulty in recognising that other cultures have their children growing up within different patterns of thinking at least partially constrained by their natal language learning. There is also the factor that many languages do have their syntax tied to literate rigidities, and so are always in a process of change since natal languages are not taught as anyone who has attempted to learn an unwritten language finds out that no one knows its grammar.

## Children Absorbing Natal Languages

The influence of language upon the development of children is one of absorption rather than of learning. No child learns their natal language as would be the case of a second language deliberately taught in school or one that is learnt because of a relationship over a linguistic divide making the learning of a new language a social and emotional necessity.

In the process of absorbing a natal language, children take into their cognitive processes ways of thinking and understanding which dictate certain attitudes. The first Hutterite word learnt by the small 2½ year old son of a sociologist working in a Canadian Hutterite settlement was 'kiss' because he had learned that if you immediately kiss the toddler he had hit, punishment from the supervising adults was avoided (Hostetler and Huntington, 1970). In much the same way as children of long-term British residents in Asia whose young children were largely brought up by their Asian nurses often spoke Urdu or Mandarin as well as English. Kaye in her autobiography describes how until she was sent to England, she was probably more fluent in Urdu than English (Kaye, 2002).

The ideas which children absorb consciously or unconsciously in this process would be extremely hard to break free from latter in life when these may no longer fit into the politically and socially correct forms of behaviour in to which they have come to live as adults.

While it can be assumed that there may be some biological similarities between human beings in environments which may have similar subsistence needs, it cannot be assumed that their processes of thought will be similar or indeed that similar words will have similar meanings.

Children brought up in the highly subtle distinctions in the Japanese use of the English word 'yes' and the more than ten Chinese terms for "reason" have become attuned to particular cultural complexities related to pro-social behaviour.

A Japanese child learning the word "sunao" takes in a range of attitudes for which there is no adequate English translation since it implies "naturalness, naivete, straight-forwardness, simplicity, frankness, open-mindedness, mildness and compliance" (Murase, 1974). Further that these meanings imply subordination and lack of self-determination and that this word assumes co-operation to be acts affirming self (Kumagai, 1981). It is stated that there are no less than sixteen ways of saying "no" in Japanese in which the use of social contexts avoids the loss of face (Ueda, K. 1974). In comparison English has an unsophisticated abruptness.

So it can be seen that in learning Japanese as their natal language children become absorbed into the complexities of social behaviour particularly forms of circumscribed individualism which would not be the learning experience of children learning English. We must conclude that children in absorbing a distinct language, learn to label certain perspectives as reality opposed to certain other actions, encourages them to extend their repertoire of cognitive schema in language specific ways. The language which these children have absorbed defines for them that a particular schema which gives direction to their thoughts (Bloom, 1981: 83), and thus inevitably to their behaviour then and latter in adulthood.

## Language and Child Development

It is not simply a question of how soon children learn to speak or understand what is being spoken to them and there can be little doubt that most children moving from one cultural setting to another can learn a new language relatively quickly. It seems likely that their patterns of thinking will vary with the language being spoken even though the natal language is likely to be more integrated into that social system.

Thus children brought up within a certain language will have learnt to express personal relationships in that idiom so that in some societies a child may have several fathers and mothers and no aunts and uncles and in matrilineal cultures such as the Yao of southern Tanzania authority over their behaviour will rest with their mothers' brothers. So that any new language which children learn may well conflict with the paradigms of thinking that were learnt originally in infancy.

People learning a new language cannot say something clashes with the views to which they are now morally and emotionally committed and break the grammar of the language in order to do this. Few languages support the political ideology of equality. It is not possible in Burmese for anyone who has not been ordained to treat a Buddhist monk with the egalitarian spirit which is a feature of Christian ideology. To do so would testify to the uncouthness of the speaker and not to their presentation of a radically new idea into Burmese Buddhist practice. Revolutionary egalitarianism is much more difficult to promote when there are no linguistic provisions for such views. Europeans with some democratic ideas enabled by the structures of their own languages, may well feel uncomfortable with the inequalities of the personal pronouns which have to be used in speaking Burmese. In the same way that an English child may not recognise the importance of bowing as part of correct Japanese behaviour.

In most non-industrial agrarian communities children are brought up into hierarchically organised families in which they are socialised by the constant attention of their siblings and their relationship with their parents is on the lines of silence and obedience. On the other hand the children of Western middle class families is either segregated from their parents or actively involved with them. The use of language and what is learnt is heavily correlated to community expectations. Pro-social behaviour expectations in white American society have children being encouraged to express themselves in every possible social occasion. This would be seen as bad mannered and ill-disciplined in African and Asian social settings.

We know that language constrains pasterns of thinking just as it enables certain social behaviours but even to speak of a language as having specific and accepted overall and binding characteristics in a culture is almost certainly a new development associated not only with printing but with widespread even universal schooling in which a particular language dominates. This follows the centralisation of education and the political need for nation states to attempt to have a single language for both administrative and business purposes.

It is this "official" language which children learn in schools which is often used in research and which in practice varies substantially from what the children use outside school in the status related linguistic codes of their families and in the communal languages of their societies which do not have sufficient population to make them politically significant and their languages to be recognised politically. So almost all children are brought up in communities in which the language of education, politics and economics is different in both major and minor respects from the languages which they use at home.

Children will soon notice not only that language varies with the social groups into which they fit themselves or are fitted whether at home, at school or in peer groups, but that they fit in with varied patterns of required codes of pro-social behaviour. Children in some cultures will not learn to say "thank you" for which there may not be an equivalent to the English phrase, because they would see any act as part of an ongoing network of reciprocities and "thank you" terminates an event. On the other hand "thank you" in English speaking societies is expected of children because interpersonal relationships are not usually thought of in terms of ongoing reciprocities.

The variations from a single linguistic form which influence how children learn to think in particular ways are numerous and of varying importance. There are limits to the amount of linguistic knowledge that a child can absorb and it may only be as an adult and a loquacious one at that who can use the thirty or more tenses in the Bantu kiSukuma language. Most children even an intellectually clever adolescent verging on adulthood will only know a percentage of the standardised vocabulary but possibly have a greater knowledge of specialised words and usages in their families and communities (Burton & Kirk, 1979).

In English we talk about pro-social behaviour as if it were a linguistically unitary concept. Children learn that required behaviour is a complex of various words and phrases which are correlated to situations rather than to overall generalities. The kiSwahili learnt in markets by Sukuma children will be deficit in grammatical niceties.

Firstly there are language universals which are known to all members of a culture as well as those on the fringes where cultures meet. Even the crudest learning of a second language by children on the social fringes of their natal languages, will involve them in certain words and sequences such a political slogans, a advertising jingles and abusive language. Egyptian children overload tourists of unknown nationality with deluges of "good mornings" and "how are you".

Political slogans remain just that until they are hooked onto to some social activity which pays off. The appeal to children of self-help slogans faded in the Tanzanian compulsory villagisation campaign when their government failed to provide the new villages with the facilities which were promised as part of the disruption caused by this collectivisation.

Then children pick up the language codes of small groups of people with special interests which may not have a wide social range of use. Sukuma children from agricultural families pick up the local names for plants and soils just as Western children pick up the names of footballers and pop-stars; the difference is that this specialised knowledge for the latter does not link into any reasonable possibilities of employment. The Indian and Afro-Guyanese have differential mathematical abilities which is correlated to a combination of culture and business as the former are into shop-keeping and trading at an early age.

There are also more specialised linguistic codes of small groups of people with interests and knowledge which does not extend beyond small localised groups and finally personal linguistic idiosyncrasies which are picked up by children from particular well-remembered people such as teachers, parents or mass media figured personalities which in India have an enormous following. Chance events will influence language as well as personal friendships.

Formal schooling takes up a smallish proportion of children's waking time so that the learning of a language and its influence on their lives has a time and spatial correlation; they learn from those whom they meet regularly in society or in their memories; often a particular popular entertainer has a time and emotional influence on a child at least equal to that of a language teacher. We do not know the extent to which such figures on the fringes of children's awareness of the harsher realities of life, may or may not have long-term influence on their general behaviour.

The language which is learnt by children is not static despite the fact that it may be encoded in dictionaries, grammars and systematic teaching. All children learn new words and meanings from popular songs and in the schools of mixed minorities children, almost certainly a proportion of imported words. Even today in Britain the grand-children of soldiers will hear their father using a number of Urdu words surviving from the fact that nearly half of the pre-1947 army served some time in India and which are still used in the contemporary British army.

Finally there are always intellectual-cum-biological restrictions on what any child can learn since their mental capacities in any population will vary; there will always be some whose mental capacities are on the fringes of sub-normality and brilliance quite independent of literacy. Universal compulsory education makes children aware through the medium of language of their superiority and inferiority to others. Colour blindness excludes a number of children from a range of understandings apart from the fact that some languages do not recognise some colours. A child in the family of a diviner is likely to be exposed to the stimulations from hearing and seeing the range of people in trouble seeking the help of their father or mother, while other children in families on the fringes of subsistence survival will have different stimuli.

More importantly there are constraints and enablements which come with any language and which the child absorbs, like it or not. Early on they will learn the linguistic correlations to female and male roles and possibly from this an understanding of binary oppositions and at least in this respect an either-or constriction on social realities. There are always rewards for conformity and anticipated rather than real punishments for speaking out of turn and using the wrong idioms.

The child learns early in his or her life to speak as a particular person and this will always relate to their social position which will see them primarily as members of groups over the membership of which they have no choice; however much they and their parents consider them to be individuals, they are always in relationships marked out by language. Overall the thought and behaviour of children are found in and remain within the structures of their natal languages.

## The Divisiveness of Language

Since the phrase pro-social is generally accepted as a term which is not socially divisive, the knowledge of a specific language through socialisation is inevitably tied to basic social distinctions. This is our language which is the centre of our understandings and gives meaning to all that we do and you who speak another language do not have this key to this very special reality. The more disparate the languages, the greater will be the feeling of emotional and social differences which prevent the development of any moral and social affinity; the speakers of Pushtu and Pukhtoo may have some elements of affinity as might the speakers of French and English but between these two groups of speakers of totally different languages which have nothing in common there can be no automatic affinity within the brotherhood of man.

Whatever other factors which make for the ungovernability of Afghanistan as a unitary country, these language differences must be a major factor. Belgium as a country is divided into almost equal numbers of French and Walloon speakers with only the federal territory around Bruxelles having a national character.

In some cases as in the mixture of tribes in the northern Myanmar highlands a child may zigzag between languages on almost a daily basis as when Kachin and Palaung villages occupy the same mountain ridge with only a few hundred metres dividing them.

Elsewhere in India and Nigeria the disparity of languages has enforced a complex, divisive and a tendency to create a federal system with its disadvantageous antipathies to national progress. People want to be socially and politically allied with speakers of the same often officially promoted language even when they use different languages almost all the time in their daily lives.

Similarly as we have already discussed no language grammatically accepts any such equality as there are age, sex and status distinctions and discriminations. If language is influential, then there can be little expectation that it might be the vehicle for any political programme of equality.

Children who are brought up in village communities or neighbourhood clusters have linguistic relationships with a wide variety of people both relations and neighbours. Many communities in a geographical sense are socially and economically open-door so that other adults wander in and out just as children often do the same with or without adults accompanying them in the company of their peers and siblings.

Such children then would have direct experience of talking not only to blood relatives but also to affinal ones of different ages and kin and social status but also with classificatory relatives. It may even be that a child can grow up in a village such as the one near Kipumbwi on the Tanzanian coast in which thirty-three households were related to the occupiers of every house accept one. Nevertheless this village was on an all-weather road and they would have been in touch with a wide range of passers-by.

Children brought up in such environments will learn early in life that everyone talks in different ways to different people according to their relationship to them and also because they have special roles which are not based on kinship. Such communities may have specialists but their in-house nature may not provide for linguistic distinctions which are not dominated by family relationships, age and sex.

So children even those who are socialised within a single language learn that it socially divides by reason of its grammar which is absorbed rather than scholastically learnt but they are also socialised into the intricacies of the uses of their own languages. They learn that there are linguistic codes which have a wider coverage than their own immediate social environments. Even before they enter primary school or kindergartens they will have some knowledge of other codes that the ones that they learned in their homes which are spoken by social strangers. The linguistic codes of bureaucracy, political speech, the medical and legal worlds and that of trading.

No child in fact learns their language as a single uniform grammatical controlled way of speaking, thus their linguistic socialisation will always be socially discriminatory. With these linguistic codifications come alignments which are socially divisive as they are used in practice if they do not actually define to whom pro-social behaviour is expected, make clear enough what is expected even if it is subconscious.

Language supports the satisfactions and values of particular social groups and societies, even cultures, whether it is in the grammar, dialects or linguistic codes into which children are socialised. Optimistically language unifies as in the linguistic codes of science and theology but these are no more than veneers which in the lives of their users are never applied to the social lives of their speakers outside these specialised worlds.

Whether languages reinforce the discriminatory nature of social life or creates the situations in which it occurs, there can be little doubt that languages except within an ideological framework are the tools much more for discrimination than for enabling any generalities of pro-social behaviour with its narrower needs of social obligation.

## Language and the Learning of Pro-social Behaviour

It is certainly correct that behaviour can be learnt by imitation but this would be restricted to a limited range of behaviour and could not be related to the intricacies of inter-relationships. Once we are considering more than the behaviour of non-human primates language becomes the main and perhaps even the essential medium for any complex social training and its social expression.

While languages can be classified and used in certain societies in identifiable ways, there can be no assumption that particular parts of any language are going to be used socially in narrow and specific ways; any abstract word can be used in the ways that a particular society wants which will not be transferable to another society.

Through their languages an Indian is going to learn that his most important role is with his mother, a Chinese with his father and an American with his spouse (Hsu, 1971). Pawnee children from Oklahoma are going to learn that the same word is used for mother's brother's wife, ego's wife and the sisters of ego's wife and that those men and women are allowed to have sexual relations beyond the boundaries of what the western culture understands as the obligations and entitlements of monogamy (Triandis, 1994: 94). So language and morality are culturally tied in together.

So we can appreciate that it is language use as much as the language itself which is tied into morality and more specifically even within a single culture, society or community pro-social language of one segment may not be the pro-social behaviour of another; father, mother and siblings may be speaking different languages in regard to the morality for which they are carrying meanings.

Children do not learn a natal language and the word learn has scholastic overtones which may only apply to the process of acquiring second and third languages. They are absorbed into using the same language as their carers and in the micro-social environment in which they start their lives.

Later in school they may learn additional usages of their natal languages in linguistic codes in which the language of the school may be that of the professional classes in to which they have been born or different ones (Bernstein, 1975); a situation which is as likely to occur in Beijing, Banaras as Birmingham.

For many children going to school will involve the learning of a national lingua franca and possibly in addition yet another language which would be useful in their subsequent working lives. It seems likely that even if there are no confusions between the meanings of these different languages of which there will be very many, their ideas may stay within their natal languages.

A Tanzanian Roman Catholic priest, one of the first to be ordained there, learnt a succession of languages after absorbing his natal language kiHangaza,; then kiSwahili in his primary school, English in secondary school, Latin in the first half of his seminary training and then French for his final years of training in a North African seminary. The first languages are Bantu and have the same grammatical constructions while the remaining three have Romance language foundations. We can presuppose that this man will have become trained to think in two different ways. A Ruandan bishop to whom it was suggested that he was not telling the truth, replied that such duplicity which was part of his natal language and he would have avoided this if the questions had been asked in French.

There is considerable data from research to show that answers to questions will depend very much on the language which is used. A test in Hong Kong (Bond & Cheung, 1984) provided different answers according to the language in which the test was structured which suggested to the subjects who was interested in the results. Mandarin Chinese suggested Beijing authorities, Cantonese Chinese suggested Hong Kong political authorities and English the British colonial authorities.

This is not the place to go into any discussion as to whether it is possible to have a thought which is not provided for in the language involved in thinking since it would be difficult to structure the necessary experiments. "From a historical point of view languages are much more the products of their culture than determinants of them. What one can or cannot express distinctly in any particular language at any particular time in its development is the aggregate result of the totality of social, political, environmental and intellectual influences that have from generation to generation affected its speakers lives" (Bloom, 1981: 59).

Individual children have to absorb the language "as is" in the forms used by their carers; it is a restricted context however much it is and may be in the processes of change and these changes are likely to be microscopic in terms of their total language understandings and essentially passive. Speakers are unlikely to be aware that within their life-times there have been changes in the form and meanings in the languages they use everyday.

Language restricts its users to express themselves in certain ways and for children to do otherwise would be to expose them to constant criticism and sanctions because it would be inappropriate. The child for its first years grows up in a linguistic set of railway lines from which it would be virtually impossible for them to divert.

## Language and Family Relationships

Every language has a vocabulary for personal relationships which any child learns almost as soon as they start to speak and recognise those with whom they are in contact. But the relationships which are recognised in one language are not always those that are recognised in others.

Currently English does not distinguish between matrilineal and patrilineal relations so that children do not grow up learning that the two sorts of uncles and aunts are different not only in their titles but in the way that they can be expected to behave towards them. Similarly English docs not distinguish between the two sets of grandparents.

However kiSwahili does distinguish between the two sorts of uncles and aunts and the brothers and sisters of their fathers are expected to be more disciplinarian while those of the mother are expected to be more sympathetic towards the problems and behaviour of their sisters children. Indeed the father's brothers are referred to as fathers while the mother's brothers are felt to be significantly helpful. This must have been the case not so long ago in England since most children if given the available choice between going to the mothers or fathers siblings prefer the former. There is no difference in the expected behaviour of either sets of grandparents amongst either the Swahili or the English as both societies share the benignity of the alternate generations.

But this may be starting at the wrong end of this issue by using the word "family" which in western cultures is certainly a single word loaded with benign assumptions and more specifically related to the nuclear family of father, mother and immature children living with them. It has a somewhat empty connotation when applied to people who are rarely in contact and then probably only for rites of passage particularly marriages and funerals when there are perhaps material as well as emotional factors involved.

In kiSwahili family is translated by five words; "jamaa" which can also mean society, company, assembly, gathering and meeting; "ukoo" kinship, affinity and ancestry; "ndugu" which can mean relative but can also refer to fellow citizen, tribesman and countryman; "ahali" similarly meaning kinsman and "ufungu" relationship and connection.

So there is in that language a strong kinship element in words which do not refer to any close relationship and in many cultures it would be quite correct to refer to uncles and aunts as mothers and fathers. In societies in which there are few other institutions with which individuals can be associated, it is kinship which defines and is used to define most of the people with whom children would become associated even if they are not even distant relatives.

Relationships marked out linguistically as correlated to various types of expected behaviour can be extended rationally in so-called classificatory relationships by which almost all their inter-relationships can be slotted. Newcomers to urban living in Kenya who need some support there may create a fictional mother's brother relationship so that there would be some benign feelings between them. Important friends of parents in Britain are often introduced to their respective children as aunts and uncles as they would not understand the word "friend" or "business partner"; they would know how to behave towards uncles and aunts and what to expect from them.

Thus it would seem that pro-social behaviour in the sense that it is tied to English linguistic terms has become tied to the so-called isolated nuclear family in a somewhat idealistic framework of thinking, whereas in many other cultures it remains the principal means of either identifying relationships or creating them. In such cultures in the absence of long-standing, recognised and efficient institutions as in China the assumption of some even tenuous kinship connection is a reason for getting preference.

Children soon learn the relationship between kinship terms, people and pro-social behaviour involving reciprocities. A family tree for a well-to-do Tanzanian Swahili showed that the material out-goings over a year more or less accurately mirrored incomings. For this man his family was not some socially tenuous group meeting occasionally for rites of passage and religious festivals, but a network combining social and economic needs; his relatives got nothing without payment. A child in such a cultural environment that people linguistically classified as relatives, have advantages for them which would have to be kept alive by pro-social behaviour.

A child is brought up linguistically to see certain individuals as permanent features of their social landscapes and that there are benefits from these linked relationships. Pro-social behaviour patterns are in the first instance are learned as related principally to a range of kinship terms which are most functionally efficient when related to a small range of not too exclusive relatives. So we can conclude that language provides a network of potential relationships about which in proportion to social distance children learn the fundamentals of pro-social behaviour.

## Language and Exclusiveness

No language provides any form of equality for its users in its grammar which distinguishes various forms of inequality. The exceptions to this are in religion and politics in which there are often nouns and personal pronouns which suggest ideological equality which never conforms to the other social forms of the languages which are used in those societies. Such exceptions takes on political significance and becomes part of the "quasi-official" language taught in schools, religious classes and used in the official documents of religious organisations and governments in their official document. But even this "official" equality does not disguise the fact that although those inside those social groupings are defined as equal, those outside are unequal to them; the slogan "our brothers and sisters in Christ" or indeed in Islam is a statement of ideological inequality between believers and outsiders.

All children are brought up within the language of their principal carers and is certainly a linguistic code which may vary from the grammatical language which will be taught to them in schools and will vary again to that of the people with whom they work. Thus the earliest language learning is likely to be highly varied particularly when the carers and the parents are both involved part-time with their children. In all cultures the children of the well-to-do and socially prominent will be cared for by employees or servants of a different social strata to that of the children; sometimes these carers are also from other cultures and give to the children in their care a knowledge of another language so that they may have some understanding of kiSwahili, Swedish, Urdu and Mandarin Chinese before they have attained any competence in the languages of their parents.

It is important to recognise that children are the passive receivers of the social messages which are implicit in the languages into which they grow. They have no choice in this and latter in life it would probably be virtually impossible to eradicate these presuppositions of social behaviour carried by language.

There is first of all the exclusiveness of the individual's own language which they will always feel to have superior qualities to the languages of foreigners. Of course latter in life any individual may recognise the superior elements in other languages which may be absent in their own but this is an uncommon intellectual attainment. The child grows up within this feeling of exclusiveness and social superiority; even their nursery rhymes are linguistically nationalistic.

Some languages provide for distinctive and ineradicable inequalities. English is not the only language to have the personal pronouns "he" and "she" and equality can only be inferred by moving into the plural "we". Burmese has personal pronouns which vary between the relationships of the speaker to the spoken to who may be equal, inferior or superior.

In the languages which are predominantly used by pre-industrial societies it seems that "we" as a personal pronoun predominates and that the wife of a family member might be referred to as "our wife" without any suggestion of physically sharing her beyond her cultivating and animal care work.

In the urban industrial world "I" is the common personal expression which is used and even the personal "thou" in English had lapsed which would seem to suggest that the language in which a child grows up may well show in many contemporary societies that thinking and acting in communal terms is no longer so important.

The children will correlate pro-social behaviour to the languages within which they have grown up. This is apart from the linguistic codes which they will become aware of from watching television, attending sports matches, gang membership and schools and which will be attached to variant forms of pro-social behaviour. But these linguistic codes are important and ever changing signs of exclusivities which children as much as adults find important for social and psychological protection; languages are personal but what is entailed is impersonally controlled by their grammatical structures even if personally provided.

## Language and Sexual Equality

It must be obvious enough to any child that there are differences in the work that men and women do domestically and in the world outside the home and that power rests largely in the hands of men who are proportionately physically stronger than women. On the other hand they will also see that men do not have the same power inside the house which they demonstrate outside. These inequalities are often shown in languages into which children are socialised so that the forms of speech which they learn to employ to men and women both relatives and outsiders provide a linguistic background for these inequalities.

In considering the functions of language in the socialisation of children, it is useful to remember that these years have been divided between educational processes of deliberately planned learning in schools and language socialisation for all that is learned in the home and other social contexts before attending school (LeVine, 2003: 2).

But not all languages give grammatical support for sexual inequality. English and even more so Finnish, make no distinction between men and women except for personal pronouns and nouns which are tied to sexual roles. So it is reasonable to speculate that the movement for women's emancipation and the growth of opportunities for women outside traditional domestic ones does correlate with English speaking societies; it could be said to have started and to have spread along the lines of English speaking expansion.

No child in any culture can fail to become aware very early in their lives that there is a sexual division of labour as for a start woman feed others and men are fed first. It also seems likely that few if any boys and girls see this as inequality but merely the way that their society is "naturally" organised.

An important point may be that sexual equality as a pro-social requirement taught to children in western economically developed societies is a recent ideological imposition. This has to make headway against social practices which are usually supported by both language grammar and linguistic codes. However successful it may be to teach equality as a moral requirement, there is always the deeply implanted pattern of language which children absorb from their earliest days which suggests otherwise in almost every sentence which they hear or speak in many Asian languages.

The ideology of gender categorisations is usually enacted in the languages of such societies and it is through language that the individual child's cultural understandings of gender categories are learned and their coordination achieved (Foley, 1997: 289). It is notable that the Chinese and Japanese ideograms for "noisy" and "talkative" consist of three small characters meaning "woman" (Iwao, 1993: 99), and there is no way round this characterisation.

Each child grows up within a particular linguistic code appropriate to sexual and social status in the community in which they live. Exceptions to this where there are women prime ministers, doctors, writers and heads of schools will do little to alter the structure and uses of a language which they learn from their mothers, siblings and fathers.

This linguistic distinction which children learn does not mean that the sexes are linguistically isolated but that in communication between men and women they talk in a ways that are tied to the sexes of those that are talking to each other. In a status structured language like Japanese the head mistress and the headmaster would probably be sensitive to the anomalies latent in the ways by which the former addresses male subordinates. In such situations linguistic patterning makes female-male status changes more difficult when the women's social status is underlined by Japanese which does not happen in English. Of course in some societies the post-menopausal woman gains some of the social characteristics of sexual neutrality and is thus able to gain greater standing in inter-sexual relationships.

Of course it could be argued that these sexual differences in how women talk to men or are talked to is not discriminatory but language use does not occur in a social vacuum and so would be correlated in the minds of children to what they experience as the power structure of their own families.

## Language and Social Equality

Both political and religious ideologies have on occasions had doctrines of equality and it is often assumed that these worthy hopes are defeated by a combination of human weaknesses and the insidious powers of capitalism and the hostility of non-believers. It may be more appropriate to see these failures to put believe into social practice in terms of the effectiveness of the pro-social behaviour taught to children but above all to the languages in which they are socialised.

Swahili speaking politicians at a public meeting might well use "jamaa" the term for family in respect of those attending but no one would think that its social use would go beyond the political needs of the moment.

It would seem that besides the languages in which they are socialised which must to varying extents channel behaviour, there are always social exclusivities which make it very unlikely that any child is going to grow up with any serious understanding of equality in any of the social activities in which they are likely to be involved.

The concept of "us" whatever the word used is always socially exclusive even when used in nationalistic contexts, varies in two ways. Firstly social distance in which even relatives are graded in terms of diminishing importance for their value in ongoing or anticipated reciprocities. Secondly in a graded range of crises in which the children and their caretakers will see a wider circle of people as important for their survival.

The widely expressed hostility of Muslim children in Bahrain and Iran to Israeli aggressiveness in Palestine and Pakistani ones for the freeing of largely Muslim Kashmir from Indian control is expressed in language in which these children are socialised. It may well be that language is the main medium for expressing both open and partially suppressed hostilities and inequalities simply because it is there in the heads of children from the time that they cease to be infants.

Apart from the children's understandings of the tensions in which they and their families are involved since few English speaking ones from the poorer sections of their societies would not know of or refer to the police as "pigs", most languages have inequalities built into their grammars and speech.

Languages such as Burmese and Japanese are structured round the social status of the individual speaking and that of the person to whom they are speaking. This makes for disparity in the powers which individuals may have to influence the pro-social behaviour of children; in fact the impossibility of any equality involving language. Of course there are a range of equal relationships in which children may be talking to other children but even in this there will be distinctions of status expressed linguistically.

A young men's football team in Kampala, Uganda had enormous numbers of sub-managers who were in change of particular aspects of the team not just in terms of their responsibilities; membership of the club was no more than a means obtain some status within the group and towards outsiders in general. Similarly the Legio Maria, a Roman Catholic breakaway independent Church in east Africa, had designated officials in charge of washing the altar cloth and so on. It seems very doubtful if any children grow up into situations in which linguistic equality has much validity. In Burmese such distinctions are grammatical whereas in Japanese they would be classed as etiquette in which individuals would be reluctant to speak until they know or can reasonably guess at the status of the person to whom they are speaking; hence the importance of visiting cards which show the status of their owners.

Such children or perhaps all children are brought up to express inequalities in their behaviour which includes their languages. Religious invocations to equality may well be heard as part of the mnemonics of religious membership rather than being a constituent and practical element of faith.

A majority of faiths Christian, Jewish and Muslim have men and women separated for worship so that children there will see sexual inequality demonstrated and even in the mosque where worshippers pray in lines according to their arrival have preferential places for the most important worshippers. Such congregations break into inequalities as soon as they leave their places of worship and of course they see as they go home other places of worship for different faiths and so it is that these geographically distinct places of religious differences are often the objects of deliberate collective violence.

It may be that one of the functions of the pro-social behaviour of children is to reduce these potentials for confrontation. This is socially unrealistic when all societies whether they express it or not, have feelings of superiority over those who are not committed to their concepts of secular and religious truth. It seems more likely that pro-social behaviour training is directed at reducing disruption within the group and that in general it has little concern for reducing the disruptions of abstract hostility to outsiders.

The age-set and age-grade systems of Nilo-Hamitic tribes in which young men entering manhood are grouped in a class for a number of years until pressure from another group of younger men forces the creation of a new group and the promotion of the existing one to a more senior grade has faded in many societies with economic, political and social change typified by the objections of young men to gerontocratic rule (Abbink, 2000). These age-set and age-grades would have distinctive names which were not repeated so that throughout their lives these young men would know each other by the name of the group within which they were nominally equal; they have set positions involving almost statutory inequality.

However this has been replaced or rather appeared independently of any knowledge of such traditional systems, by the universal system of education in which age-set differences are institutionalised into overall inequalities. Most countries aim at and often virtually achieve comprehensive universal primary education for both boys and girls usually from about the age of five years; a rigid system indeed.

This results in almost all children being incorporated into an age-set based on neighbourhoods under some degree of official and parental pressure under legal compulsion. This is occurring at younger ages than any traditional social system had seen any social need to group children and to recognise their social distinctiveness as a useful way of looking at and using children. Thus this would appear to have given children a legal status as pupils independent of the economic needs of subsistence families, indeed to make parents liable for penalties should they keep children away from school on the grounds that they are needed at home as part of the family's manpower for survival.

In the school children are placed in an age-set form by year of enrolment by which process they are ignored and looked down on by the previous year's age-sets and in turn handing out the same behaviour to those who are enrolled in subsequent years by giving them a term stigmatising their socially institutionalised inferiority.

Only at the upper-end of the educational system are there sparsely provided wide-ranging benefits for the years of segregation and moreover the educational age-set system closes down in early adulthood or late adolescence whereas in traditional systems it was just beginning to pay-off in increased social benefits as a return on the years of inferiority which they had endured.

So long before there is any question of a pay-off for their long years of education largely in a linguistic code which is not that of their own communities or families, children are forced into a comprehensive system of rigid inequalities which have to be justified to the children in terms for which they have no social experience or indeed linguistic comprehension. For most children it is a prolonged period of filling in time until they can do their own thing for which they have long been biologically prepared. Furthermore this system of inequalities is not integrated into the social needs of families except for relieving them of the obligations of child care or socialisation for prolonged periods. The medium for this guarantee of prolonged status inequality is the learning of a combined official and social linguistic code.

In this age-set educational system children are taught theoretical pro-social behaviour hopefully to become part of their outside lives and a system of discipline necessary for the running of complex school institutions which inadvertently prepare them for the monotony of urban and industrial employment.

## Language and the Envisaging of Alternatives

Western scientific and philosophical thought has developed along the lines of 'either-or'; a logical construction in which the identifiable components must be one thing or the other and the conviction that nothing can have more than one meaning at a time. This is understandable when the components of what is being discussed are inorganic but when the elements involve human behaviour which at the best are related to specific environmental factors and time locked, there are serious difficulties in entertaining such a defined approach to child development.

This line of thinking culminating in its expansion following the Enlightenment is very recent in human developmental time and would seem even now to apply to a very small proportion of adult thinking and decision-making which is more likely to be used in accountancy than in human inter-relationships. It has conspicuously failed in law which is perhaps no more exact than in traditionally oral decision-making on customary issues.

It may be that a more usual pattern of thought is not monochromic (Hall, 1966) in which the brain socially copes with one thing at a time but polychromic in which several activities are carried on at the same time as in Arab social and business relationships in which the Westerner is trying to deal with a point at a time.

Even Turner's exemplary exposition of binary alternatives (Turner, 1967: 79-81), could be said to have been a typology imposed on the Ndembu's understandings and which has contributed to an outsider comprehension of African rituals. It may be that in theory they would agree that white cannot be black but that in the gradations of colour it seems likely that in social practice nothing is either pure white or pure black, as in the Sukuma seeing blue as a lighter shade of black named after a commercial ingredient "Reckitts Blue" bought for making clothes whiter in the wash and which is also used as a facial decoration for Ikoma men when dancing.

It would seem therefore that without literacy there can be little exactness and that even then it is related to a narrow range of factors which are of limited use in the leaning and maintaining of inter-relationships.

One can speculate whether children do think in such exact terms of either "this" or "that" in their understandings and relationships except in experimental situations. A child in a toy shop when asked to choose one, will dither almost indefinitely until the choice is restricted by the donor.

On the other hand some languages require nouns to be classified into certain categories so that pronouns and adjectives can be grammatically allied to them so kiSwahili has categories for humans, trees and plants and then a number of classes in which nouns can only be put by learning that this is their proper grammatical place; there is no logical core (Loogman, 1965). Other languages have varieties of placing which appear to have some exactness which in practice become socially negotiable. In French the speaker has to learn which nouns are male or female which outside the obviously tied ones, the child has to learn by rote.

Japanese goes much further in the absence of such classifiers as "the" or "a" and nouns are expressed as "five persons of carpenters" and "two cylinders of pencil". This language has large numbers of classifiers for human beings, animals, long slender objects, books and magazines, flat things like paper, coins or clothing, full cups, pairs, slices of meat or cake and items used generally; the complications of Japanese are endless (Bleiler, 1963: 124).

When there is multi-dimensional scaling of what ideas go together among the Cree Indians of Canada (Berry and Bennett, 1992), "living like a white" came close to "stupid" and "crazy" and "cunning" and "wise" went with "thinking carefully" and "is respectful". Some Kpelle farmers of Liberia who were asked to sort some objects by colour or association (Glick, 1968), failed to do so and yet they had been considered intelligent by Western psychologists. So the exasperated psychologist asked them to sort the objects "the stupid way" and they then sorted them in ways that western psychologists considered to be "intelligent".

So while children have to make quite specific choices in the language which they use and in their social activities, these are always socially circumscribed. It may be that this does not extend to thinking in matters involving reasoning in which an almost indefinite number of factors are hypothetically involved. The choice of words to explain or illustrate choice is perhaps only a terminal part of linguistic activity and children may feel that in certain situations, the alternatives are more numerous than they can express. Should there be an element of pro-social behaviour which transcends the restrictions of language and environmental factors it must surely remain a philosophical abstraction.

## Children with Bilingual Backgrounds

Some children may become proficient in a second language while being in school but this may not have much affect on their personal understandings and behaviour even though they may have considerable knowledge of the culture behind the second language from both school learning and exchange visits which are quite common between children in economically developed western countries.

Children are subject to bilingual influences in two situations. Their parents may have married foreign partners so that either the mother or father is living in a culture of which they have had no previous thorough experience. This was common enough in the early period of British domination of India when it was thought politically and socially advantageous for upper class Indian women to marry British administrators and senior soldiers. The children of such unions were culturally divided with the boys learning English and often being educated in Britain and the girls remaining in India within the language culture of their mothers. There was considerable debate in correspondence from the fathers of such children as to which culture it would be best to bring up their children but in fact it always seems to have ended up in the problems of divided cultural loyalties of which those children must have been well aware (Dalrymple, 2002).

In latter years long-serving army men married or cohabited with women of lower status in India and their children came to form the Anglo-Indian community from which latter they continued to marry women who already spoke English; in effect these people became a sub-caste maintained by endogamy.

After World War Two the continuing presence of the British Army in Germany during the Cold War meant that many men married German women. In these marriages the women used English at home rather than their husbands learning German with the children having a quasi-bilingual upbringing.

As the British withdrew from overseas military commitments, their presence was replaced by United States defence personnel who married foreign nationals in large numbers so that an air force base in England would have married women clubs for those who were of Korean, Japanese or Vietnamese origin. One suspects that the language spoken to their children would in most cases be that of the mother as few men would have bothered or seen the need to learn the language of their wives once they had left the countries in which they had married and as speaking their languages would not have helped their military careers.

Subsequently there has been a considerable movement of Asian women to Britain in arranged marriages to men who found getting wives in their own country difficult and thought that such women would fit in better to their ideas of male domestic superiority. The mothers would make every effort to bring up their children as British since they would see no advantages in maintaining an Asian cultural connection as they had no practical intentions of returning there.

Perhaps the most tragic of all bilingual situations will have been the very large numbers of women abducted during the Partition of

India into two countries in which because of their contamination by forced sexual relations with men of another faith, they would not have been able to return to their families even if they were enabled to do so. It seems unlikely that the children of such forced marriages would have been brought up in any practical way in the cultures of their mothers despite their psychological distress. So we see that in these cross-cultural marriages there is always a dominant culture and that if the decision is not made for them children will be brought up or adhere to that culture. While they may retain some quasi-romantic illusions about the non-European culture of which they may genetically have been a part, it does not amount to the creation of subordinate sub-cultures.

However the fact that these children come into families which are overtly or covertly culturally divided makes for difficulties in their pro-social upbringing and indeed a possible factor in their psychological and social difficulties in adolescence as into which sub-community do they "pass".

It is also prudent to remember that the distribution of blood groups shows that there has always been a considerable amount of cross-cultural breeding and that women rather than men have always a negotiable asset for use over cultural barriers and that throughout history children in very large numbers will have been brought up in families in which their parents come from different cultures; it might almost be seen as a dialectical situation contributing to social changes. Conquering peoples with exogamous religious mating rules have always married local women. Such marriages would have often been within linguistic similar groups so that the learning of a Bantu language from either mother or father would have not been very difficult as the basic grammar and many of the phonemes are similar but this is not so with languages within the Romance group.

The other type of bilingualism into which children may be born and brought up is in the families of immigrants in which the culture of the home country is maintained domestically in food, costume, festivals, rites of passage and language. These families are often self-contained with the man working in the host community's social and economic world and speaking English or German while their women stay in the home and do not learn the host language. So that as far as possible the two social worlds are kept apart with very limited contacts between them and of course few which lead to marriage.

The children of such families are forced into cross-cultural learning by the fact of compulsory education and street life in which they have to practice two different systems of social behaviour in which their parents are trying to live a form of living which is no longer possible and which was formed in parts of Bangladesh, India and Pakistan to which they will never return and will only visit from time to time when they have earned enough money to do so.

An east London child born to Bengali parents will almost certainly learn and value Bengali not only from their mothers but from their grandparents and as a partial antidote to the feeling of discrimination which they are likely to experience in their outside lives. With that language will come a pattern of thinking maintained by the fact that it is the language of their home environments. This natal language is likely to develop a local linguistic code into which some English terms and words will be added.

Such children are learning Bengali and English in parallel but sequential social environments and while there may be some learning of English through television programmes even in that there will be a preference for Hindi films and videos. English will be learnt rather than absorbed as a second language and through this there will be divergent cognitive processes. Children who spoke languages with greater gender loadings such a Hebrew developed gender identities sooner than those speaking languages with little or no gender loading such as English and Finnish (Guiora, 1985).

The natal languages of immigrant or self-sustaining minorities whether they be Hebrew, Mandarin Chinese, Turkish or Gujarati will always be in the process of being overlaid by the dominant local languages in the surrounding culture and at the same time it is always being resisted by the needs of these micro-communities.

It may also be that the learning of the dominant language will vary with the social and economic status of their families; professional ones will stress this learning of the dominant language while the semi-skilled will only learn as much as their economic needs require. Learning of a second language will vary with sex; boys go out more and will learn more of the dominant language from these out of school activities, while girls as adolescents will be allowed fewer of these.

The difficulty for children who are to any extent bilingual is not whether they can conduct simple inter-relationships across a divide which is both cultural and linguistic but that in an enormous range of word forms which can be used, few are exactly comparable. A word in English, Gujarati or Japanese can have divergent meanings for which there are no equivalences in another language.

It is not a question of whether one language is superior or inferior to another which will obviously be the case within each culture for which its use can be said to be culturally designed. When any language is taken out of the particular contexts in which it is at home, it will be functionally out of place and often the English translations are clearly inadequate.

The Garo language of North-East India has no general word for "carry" but uses a series of terms referring to the different techniques of carrying and in using English a Garo speaker would feel the inadequacy of the English term "carry" and uncomfortable without adding subordinate explanatory terms.

The Palaungs of northern Myanmar use eleven different personal pronouns and eight forms of plurals so that in speaking English they would feel that that its simple three part singular and plural personal pronouns not only would appear rather crude but leave a lot unexplained about the persons with whom they are speaking. Such feelings of social discomfort must always be the experience of children and adolescents with any sequential language learning.

## Language and the Morality of Time

There is little doubt that keeping to cultural understandings of time has a moral tone and that in western urban-industrial socialisation pro-social behaviour is related to punctuality and by this the child is guided towards a socially acceptable and normal social life. A test with various aspects of time in Zambia found that primary school boys coming from a township environment were better able to remember time than their rural counterparts but there were no differences in their recall of non-temporal concepts; even the recall of digits is not independent of their significance… and such significance is culturally determined (Deregowski, 1970).

As we have already pointed out English has an indefinite future tense, while a number of other languages not only do not have such a tense which would allow considerable latitude in how the future is foreseen, but have tenses which relate to specific time periods. For such languages the conceivable future may be no more than the annual cycle of subsistence agriculture or daily employment.

There are parallels to the understandings of children about their own needs which are tied to the immediacy of demand feeding for the very young and the time regulated meal times of older children in most families and inevitably in schools.

Similarly there may be no indefinite past so that historical or indeed prehistoric time in kiSwahili "zamani sana" by which a teacher is trying to explain the past, may end up in a child's mind as when their grandparents were alive or born or at the most when British and German colonial power came into their countries. The past in such languages is telescoped into knowledge of particular persons or the undifferentiated mass of ancestors.

It might seem therefore that the pro-social learning of the children in such natal languages will be brought up to an understanding of immediacy, indeed to have inherited this in some ethological sense from the needs of their proto-hominid ancestors. Further that clock-time is imposed on the growing child because of the needs of the institutions in which they are involved; they would much rather "graze" for food as their stomachs dictate than sit down to time spaced out meals for which their primary needs are not considered. The immediacy of time in most subsistence societies is dictated by the sun and cloud cover so that no social activities have an isolated temporal fix. Such an approach could be typified by the Sukuma who had a fixed dial plastic watch who remarked rightly enough that it gave the correct time twice a day.

The Sonjo of Tanzania who irrigate their plots of beans from springs in the mountain wall behind their villages by dividing the day into four six-hour periods but how the division actually occurs is dictated daily by a combination of crop needs and social status rather than time (Gray, 1963), so that for these people time is not fixed but constantly negotiable by those involved being actually there at the places where water can be divided. There is also a difference in the ideas of time which come from how it is filled; the Nuer thought that time was slower in the dry season when there was less work and faster in the wet season and indeed different levels of timing according to physical, ecological and social "rhythms" (Evans-Pritchard, 1939). Perhaps time is slower when it always has to be walked and to hurry up has no social correlates.

But how does time enter a child's understandings beyond the needs of their stomachs for food and their minds for comfort. Uncertain seasonality when the rain is either too much or too little but more closely its connection with lunar time since the moon changes its shape for a whole night whereas the sun just moves unchangingly across the sky. The certainties of time may come to the child from the night sky.

But time in its modern senses has to be taught to children by a combination of literacy and mechanics and its provision by the broadcasting of time through the many transistor radios. The child needs time to understand and become incorporated in institutions over which they have no control; all schools are controlled by clocks and bells.

Children also become aware of the connection between time and morality even in subsistence societies when they are born into Christian families. Even in a community in which there may be few literates, the times of services are posted on the notice boards of all churches. More importantly conversion to Christianity provides the families of such children with a day off every week but its calendar has no correlation to nature but is socially imposed from the northern hemisphere so that the rebirth theme of Easter does not coincide with their agricultural year.

Islam has prayers to be said at specific times and their children would see the clocks which are prominent in many mosques as underlining the proper times for worship. Moreover Islam is a religion based on the lunar calendar and thus not tied to any cultural area or understandings, which means that its festivals change by ten days every year and have only occasional connections with the agricultural calendars of farmers.

Children universally are tied into mechanically understood time whenever they leave home and move into social environments in which they are not primarily thought of as individuals. This is an enforcement onto behaviour which in terms of inherited ways of behaving is very new. It has no ethological correlations in which time is tied to day and night sequences, the lunar months. To be accused of unpunctuality is probably one of the first clashes which they have with the outside world.

Chapter-8

# Change and the Pro-social Behaviour of the Growing Child

Such a title contrasts change with the social behaviour of children suggests a somewhat static approach to any understanding. Although it may be attached to identifiable codes and principles, it is always and inevitably extremely variable. Indeed if it was static then the child would not be able to survive the inevitable different situations with which they would be confronted. The children change at the same time as their surroundings change.

Thus change is an important aspect of all children's lives as they biologically and psychologically develop and their surroundings change almost on a minute by minute basis; the whole concept of any children having a stable life is an illusion unless stability is defined in some way that is incorrect.

While functionally to do or not do something may appear to cover a range of situations, in human behaviour this would only be correct for particular situations; of course it may be related to what has gone before in children's understandings, but there is never an exact fit.

## Change and the Growing Child

The stable society exists only as an illusion in the minds of those involved or as a result of some system of categorisation that manages to exclude from consideration much that has gone on in even the smallest social group on a regular basis as changes affect any child that come into five categories. Firstly the child's own awareness of change within themselves, then the awareness of regular change in the social environment in which they live. Thirdly abrupt changes in their own communities from actions of the people themselves; fourthly abrupt changes in their environment from external factors and finally the changes which seep into their micro-environments from pervasive indirect changes in the surrounding macro world. In each of these categories there is the extent to which the changes directly and indirectly affect children, and each will involve different forms of required and actual pro-social behaviour.

Even if we consider that there is a datum level of behaviour which children may have "inherited" ethologically, genetically or socially, any change which involve children must cover almost all aspects of communal pro-social behaviour. The adults in a community have to change their behaviour to meet or fail to meet new conditions and what they do will be followed consciously or unconsciously by their children; they are pulled along in the slip-stream of adult behavioural patterns. Pro-social behaviour will always be in a constant process of change relating to what is happening around them.

## Children's Awareness of Changes in Themselves

All children are aware that they are growing up and that this affects how adults see them and indeed relate to them. They aspire to reach stages in their lives above the ones they currently occupy which give them personal satisfaction such as working with adults and children as young as three years have been seen hoeing with their mothers in subsistence societies. In such societies all children are contributing to the economic survival of the primary group within which they live; there is some correlation here between what they contribute to their families before they are married off into other families or set up their own semi-independent households. These changes in their status are often recognised by rites of passage and changes in the forms of their language with which they are treated.

Children are not so much aware of changes in the calendar but very much aware of the excitements that go with cyclical rites of passage. For the children of Pangani the Islamic month of fasting and prayer, means staying up late and parties and the Prophet's birthday means new clothes. Similarly weddings, circumcisions and national days in which there is no schooling are all remembered and looked forward to by most children, even funerals means a good meal with meat included.

Children are very much involved in Christmas and in bureaucratically organised societies, birthdays are known and eagerly looked forward to. Children become aware early that their lives are ongoing and marked off by cyclical events. They also become aware that these marked off events are accompanied by changes in how they are expected to behave and indeed in how they perceive themselves.

While puberty means that children experience biological change, this is a slow process for boys in entering adolescence is often marked off by social ceremonies of inclusion which may have no direct biological correlations. With girls this is different.

The menarche in less economically developed societies is likely to occur late in adolescence and to coincide with early marriage and there are often ceremonies to mark the occasion but again these will not coincide with first menstruation as the ceremonies will probably cover a number of girls and in subsistence agricultural communities would be likely to occur in the dry season when there is less necessary work. In economically developed societies particularly among the well-to-do, this is likely to occur earlier and without any public acknowledgement that the menarche has occurred. In Britain in some cases this is now occurring while the girls are in primary school.

Thus there is the ongoing problem that in developed societies biological adulthood does not coincide with social adulthood which is legally put off for several years although the bodies and the minds of adolescents are adult. In subsistence agricultural communities there is not so much of a gap as late adolescents/young adults may live with their parents for the early years of marriage; they are not expected to be independent.

## Changes in the Children's Own Communities

Secondly there are changes which occur demographically in any group however small. Babies arrive and indeed in open door social groups in which there are probably not enough children to allow for the creation of peer groups, this means some measure of responsibility for existing children. Weddings mean someone new comes into the group and deaths mean the loss of someone known. In more developed states the lengthening of life has meant for the child the loss of someone who has not played much of a part in their lives, but when the average age of death is forty years and the infant mortality rate in Pakistan probably ten times the rate in Paris or Beijing, most children will have been close to death among those that they know long before they become adolescents. In subsistence societies the care of the dead and the dying are not subcontracted to outsiders.

Children are also aware of the annual changes in the seasons and the differences between hot and cold as well as between wet and dry season; the differences between times in the agricultural year in which everyone is busy and the times when the adults sit around and the young can eavesdrop on their conversation. They will certainly be aware in subsistence communities that they are likely to be better fed in the months immediately after the harvest and quire poorly in the cultivating season when more work will be required of them.

## Radical Changes Created by the Children's Own Communities

There are times when major changes are organised by the people themselves, when they come to consider that their traditional ways of living and behaving are out of date. Margaret Mead describes (Mead, 1956) the village she studied in the Manus Islands for many years which decided to go modern in one fell swoop; they changed into clothes, moved their houses from the lagoon into a village with orderly lines of houses, even creating orderly time by the ringing of a bell to denote work and leisure.

Everyone, young and old must have been in the same position of creating a new form of social living and there can be speculation as to which age group suffered most and it will probably have been the elderly since their status and the value of their memories must have rested in the lost way of life. What is significant here is that this new form of social life continued so that subsequent children were born into it and while there must have been fringe returning to the old ways in their religious practices and ways of coping with distress, it was an irrevocable move in the direction towards which all Papuan societies were gradually turning anyway; in this change they were to some extent controlling their own destinies. Children would have grown up there in a more positive ambience for accepting change.

Other abrupt community changes have not been so successful since the impetus to change and the change itself either faded away or reverted to something much like the way of life from which they had turned away. In Yucatan a large area of impenetrable thorn scrub and dispersed Mayan populations of subsistence farmers, after a century of intermittent warfare in the War of the Castes, a dominant individual in one community initiated change (Redfield, *Progress*). He moved a dispersed population into building a township with even small bandstand into which the Protestants moved but the Catholics remained in their dispersed family groups. A quarter of century latter, the effort remained not more than a testimony to a religious split and it would have had no new influences on the children's pro-social behaviour which remained differentiated by sub-community; it was a dispiriting run-down sight despite the optimism of the original description of the change. An elder when asked what he wanted for improving his community replied more guns.

The difference between these two sets of changes was that the Manus continued to live under these new conditions as it did not interfere with their survival as subsistence farmers and fishermen. On the other hand the Yucatan changes meant that families would have had to maintain two households, one in the town and one wherever their slash and burn fields were located; social change there clashed with the time and motion economic realities of their lives; children there would have grown up in a social ambience wary of deliberate changes.

A far wider abrupt change occurred in Tanzania where the ruling one-party government decided that dispersed populations could never modernise on their own. It decided that the whole nation should move into villages for which modern institutions of schools, dispensaries and shops would be provided. This happened and communities which had been dispersed for the better use of their environments by methods which had been developed locally over countless generations were destroyed.

These compulsory disguised as voluntary concentrations of population was a failure since it brought them away from their fields into areas which could not support such densities (McCall, 1985: 6302) which became overgrazed and denuded of trees because of the need for firewood. The promised facilities were not provided and people who had led dispersed lives and whose social practices and ideas reflected this, were brought into close contact. The pro-social behaviour required of children in their dispersed hamlets did not apply in these villages which contained people to whom they were not related. Children were no longer controlled by small neighbourly communities in which they had grown up. The new villages meant groups of adults who had little interest in the behaviour of children about whom they knew little and the children experienced a freedom from pro-social control.

On the requirement being relaxed most adults returned to their previous dispersed way of living and after a prolonged period of national food shortages aggravated by drought. These three examples would seem to suggest that rapid social change even with the best of intentions has so many ancillary difficulties that what happens is inevitably going to upset the steady socialisation into the processes of slow change.

### Abrupt Changes from External Forces

Subsistence communities are susceptible to environmental changes over which they have no control. The rindepest epidemic of the 1880s in eastern Africa changed cattle keeping, the diseases brought into south and middle America by the earliest Spanish invaders have continued through the railway lines along which the 1919 influenza epidemic travelled just as new infections are brought in by the contemporary aircraft of Protestant fundamentalist missionaries. AIDS in Africa south of the Sahara has affected the families of many children by making them orphans. In some of these infected societies the surviving children would have grown up in communities without parents and with depleted numbers of adults; the pro-social behaviour of these survivors would have been very different to the social behaviour of the preceding communities. They will almost certainly be aware of the unreliability of nature and many will have experienced drought in Africa and catastrophic floods in Bangladesh and Maputo.

In addition there have been the disasters from floods in Bangladesh and drought in Ethiopia, locusts epidemics which cannot be controlled in areas of civil unrest where the spraying aircraft are shot at, so that very large numbers of children are underfed and in some areas of central Tanzania famine conditions are likely to occur for one year in five. The pro-social behaviour required of children in these conditions would be those worked out by these communities to cope with the possibility of repetitive distress.

Chronic food shortage turning into acute starvation with a sharp increase in mortality causes any afflicted community to go through four stages; austerity, temporary migration, divestment and asset disposal and exhaustion and population dispersal when it is often too late for the old and the very young to survive (Crow,1992). Amongst the Sukuma in times of famine there were two types of marriage "kuhanira" and "kuhaha" (Cory, 1953: 50) which allowed fathers to give immature girls in a form of marriage in return for food or cattle. Each of these stages would correspond to Maslow's Hierarchy of needs and children would conform to immediate needs of selfish survival which would be against the pro-social requirements of communal living. One has only to remember pictures of children picking up grain from broken bags outside famine relief centres to recognise the gross changes in their moral understandings.

In the recent past wars would have affected a narrower range of populations since only a limited number of refugees would have been able to move out of the afflicted areas and be kept alive by the unaffected surrounding population. Even if food was available in such situations including famine, in the absence of wheeled transport, a fit man can only carry so much food as he has to feed himself on the in and out energy consuming journeys for food even if it was provided free. Children would perhaps learn the importance of outsider non-national agencies as in Zimbabwe where a large proportion of the population depend on imported aid for survival since the government without any advance planning took over the productive and commercially viable farms owned by "white" nationals so that the nation ceased to be self-sustaining.

Now large populations fleeing from war are living in large semi-permanent camps where they are maintained by international agencies creating an entirely new form of social living. The refugee camps created by Israeli aggression in 1949 and 1967 are in effect permanent Palestinian towns in which the young are socialised by their living conditions into hating the Israeli outsiders. The Ruanda genocide created in the Ngara area of Tanzania the largest refugee camp in the world which at one time contained a million people of whom a large number were social orphans who had lost parents. Much the same picture has been seen in the areas affected by the civil wars in Ethiopia, Eritrea, Yugoslavia, the Sudan and Lebanon and the destruction of particular cities such as Sarajevo and Beirout apart from the destruction of cities in Germany, Russia, China and Japan in World War Two. It is hard to evaluate the effects on the socialisation of children whose childhoods have been violently destroyed since much would have depended on the stability or instability of their subsequent lives.

## Steady Pervasive Influences on Developing Children

Although attempts are often made to divide the influences of rural from urban areas as well as to discuss changes in terms of pre-industrial and industrial communities, every community is porous to the influence of changes which they have not created themselves. Particularly in Africa where the countryside feeds the town, there is a constant movement of adults and children between relatives living in both localities; every bus station illustrates the extent of this continual process of short-term internal migration. Virtually every community is subject to the pervasive penetrations by internal expatriates; government inspectors from a variety of departments and interests, catechists from various religions and indeed from rival political parties and of course tourists who may come from both eastern and western countries as Bali has found after the terrorist night-club bombing of 2002 which led to a drop in western visitors. Most children would have seen foreigners and would have noted how well-off they were materially and their healthy appearance since they never stayed long enough to be seen to be ever ill.

Despite the constant political pressures by touch and go visiting politicians for communities to become less dependent on outsiders, the whole system of centralised and inefficiently centralising bureaucracies may be creating in children a sense of dependency on outsiders conflicting with their traditional ideology that such dependencies being networks of personally created and regularly maintained reciprocities.

The effect on children must be that of their continual exposure to the erosive uncertainties of difference in which their own quasi-traditional ways of living and behaving are usually seen at a disadvantage. Of course, small collegial groups will always have had their differences but their effects are slowed down by established communal practices which require ongoing personal inter-relationships. Then there are the whims of fashion as in the designs and lettering on women's clothes, so that the making of clothes and cloth from wool, cotton and hides has been almost completely replaced by factory products except for some work which is produced for the tourist trade.

Most communities are now affected by primary schools in which children of mixed sexes are subject to peer group pressures which may not have occurred in their open-door neighbourhood communities. Only Islamic communities previously had a form of school for the learning of the Koran by rote combined with some knowledge of Arabic which for most was not an opening into the modern world. For most the school is an alien, imposed but usually welcomed institution with differential effects on families who may not send all their children there and withdraw them at harvest time when subsistence families need all the help they can get. In conditions of extreme poverty and unemployment girls may be withdrawn from school as they have a better value as domestic servants for others or in their own homes or for prostitution.

These non-urban communities are regularly confronted with people who are visibly different; even nuns are mobile and very visible examples to young girls that it is possible to have valuable livelihoods without men. Most of these outsiders are the subject of envy as with the material prosperity of tourists and the interference of come and go internal expatriates with their record keeping and possibly their out of touchness with the realities of poverty in town and countryside from which they themselves have escaped through education and private influences.

At the same time almost everyone in the Third World are using more and more manufactured artefacts which replacing their own manufacturing abilities which may for a time have worked parallel to these shop goods. In eastern Africa many children are brought up to prefer manufactured or machine ground grain because it is white. Patent medicines replace their own knowledge of herbal medicines and back up the inadequate provision of western scientific medical services; in Usukuma in Tanzania Andrew's Liver Salts was considered beneficial for venereal disease.

So many people in Tanzania now listen to the radio that government time has now entered the lives of subsistence farmers and single party political systems controlling the contents of broadcasts have been influential on the ideas of such communities when they are active in trying to organise change by fiat.

The radio as it uses only one sense is not as influential as films and the television which in some Third World countries is more publicly than privately viewed which uses both sight and sound. A young Tanzanian boy shuffling about with his shoes undone said that he was imitating the walk of a gunfighter in western films. The watching of western television serials is widespread as they are cheaper to hire and show than Third World countries which cannot afford to produce such expensive and lengthy serials.

These continual changes are to some extent not controlled as much as kept in some sort of psychological and social order by the fact that these small collegial communities have always been slowly changing while maintaining in their own minds that they are not changing at all although these changes are easily observed by intermittent outside observers.

**Pivotal Events and the Experience of Crises**

The definition of crisis is a turning point in the progress of anything and a state of affairs in which a decisive change for better or worse is imminent. However crisis and its correlation with stress seems to fit into a pattern of the unexpected and yet there are numbers of critical and stressful events which occur in the lives of children which are common place enough to be part of the expected pattern of their ongoing socialisation, not only to the detriment of pro-social development but also pivotal in its enhancing properties.

On the other hand the lives of children however well they may be theoretically timetabled are necessarily uneven in that numerous events are totally unexpected such as the deaths of pets, others expected such as the delay in the arrival of the school bus, but nevertheless stressful and of course there will always be differences between individual children just as much as with adults in their reactions (Lazarus, 1968).

There are obviously certain crises which are universally accepted such as the death of a relative and that in many subsistence families there will be less food up to the next harvest and for some such as the Gogo of Tanzania one in five years will be famine; this allows the child to see how their society provides for change and the advantages which come from pro-social behaviour. There must always be some knowledge in the understandings of children that some events will occur to them; there are both linear and cyclical rites of passage in which they will be involved as family members and as individuals at the experiential centre of some ceremony such as being circumcised among the Maasai of East Africa, changing forms in a school or being selected or not for a sports team.

However over a much wider area of childhood experience, what is seen as a crisis will always be a very personal affair in which personality and events will vary. Some of these crises in the lives of children are created by the modern institutions in which they are involved; selections for the sports teams and examinations grade children. In some traditional societies this divisiveness is avoided by all children passing through age grade ceremonies and in competitions everyone wins by the provision of several categories of success; overt equality is combined with covert inequality.

Categorisation of events and behaviour always reduces the enormity of events on individuals and it may well be that with children their possible range of reactions and limited social power may make for both the internalisation of stress as much as its external expression. They will look to adults for cues as to coping as well as for behavioural strategies. There cannot be any uniformity in either what is a crisis, and how children will react to particular events; these are personal events reacted to in personal ways.

There are fine analytical distinctions to be made over the experiences of pivotal events in which individuals and groups of children are involved in the understandings of adult insiders, adult outsiders and the children themselves. Further there are even more difficult factors in the individual personality make-up and the cushioning effects of social arrangements which may exist deliberately or accidentally such as the existence of friends, supportive sponsors and compensatory consequences; the pain of circumcision for a Sudanese Muslim girl may be balanced by her subsequent enhancement of status from entering womanhood.

There is reason to believe that the environmental input is vital for the development of pro-social behaviour in children. However "much of this input is usually encountered in the normal environment and not very variable across individuals" (Newcombe, 2002). The surrounding environment for a primary school in an African, Asian or English village differs vastly from that of a child living in an urban slum in East London, Calcutta or Accra, let alone for a child living in contemporary Baghdad or a Palestinian refugee camp. Although this comment relates to cognitive development, the developing child can be expected to encounter within each particular social environment whether urban, rural or nomadic, a broadly similar range of inputs. Feeding patterns, domestic organisation and routine however disorganised this may appear to the organised outsider, impose some consistent influences on what any child may do and think or have done to them. This can only go so far in explaining or at least correlating to unexpected changes from what happens to them as they grow. Normality in a Palestinian refugee camp regularly raided by Israeli tanks would have a different effect to that of a Sukuma child hoping to be regularly fed.

The distinctive differences and ones which may have significant impact on how each child views the social world around them from the moment of their occurrence are crises, pivotal events which either enhance or diminish the normal expectations of living. These events however much they may be part of the inevitable framework of life like death, disease and disappointments are personally experienced and personally evaluated.

These can be broadly divided into experiences that enhance the personal lives of children such as the gaining of status by receiving prizes, promotions and sport successes and negative ones through the loss of pets, property and persons who may have been part of their ordered lives or abstractly loved as pop stars.

There may be little cross-cultural uniformity in these experiences such as the menarche in girls which in developed societies with year round adequate food is beginning to feature in primary schools. This may be a distressing event in parts of the western world where social behaviour may not be so clearly related to biology. On the other hand in Islamic societies this will mean for girls the closure of the relative freedom of childhood. Also in subsistence societies such girls have now reached the status of marriageable women and thus become negotiable assets in the fluctuating social and economic importance of their families.

All societies have stressful social hurdles which children have to pass over as they grow older. Whereas in pre-industrial societies these happen within a social environment which is at least partially known to such children, this is not so in more socially and economically developed ones.

In such societies leaving their homes for participation in institutionalised education is usually a stressful pivotal and almost universal event of recent origin since up to quite recently formal education was only for a minority.

Thus the first crisis shared by millions of children may well be their dumping in schools and their abandonment there by their mothers to be left in strange and uncomfortable surroundings in the enforced company of strange children and under the control of strange adults speaking a different linguistic code to that which they were used to using at home. City living children sent to rural English boarding schools may have the same distressing impact.

There is nothing comparable to this isolation of children in pre-industrial societies. The isolation of adolescents prior to their circumcision is a socially porous isolation among known young people which has none of the arbitrary isolation of schools. In Pangani Tanzania the mothers of children who were nominally isolated prior to a mass circumcision, sneaked in to give them food.

Let us look at some of the pivotal events which children are likely to see as crises and which would cause them stress (Robinsen, 1968). Both stress and crisis are adult words and were created to describe adult experiences for what they consider to have been serious disturbances in their lives; deaths, disease, divorce and so on.

In applying these terms to children it may be that adults are still within this adult framework of thinking and indeed it would be quite correct to see such major disturbances as applying to children. But children are different to mature and socially experienced adults who have been able to diminish in some ways the effects of these crises.

There are many events affecting children which adults might almost laugh about as not being real crises and just childish behaviour and misunderstandings, because they have not yet learned to cope or to understand that this is what is always going to happen. Indeed it is not known whether these micro-events in childhood are more specifically part of western and /or urban-industrial life and thus may not occur so much in pre-industrial and/or subsistence communities.

For some children their position as first or last born and even though this may be denoted by distinctive names and social position, it can be altered by subsequent births and adoptions as may occur in Hindu families in which only girls have been born.

Children build sand-castles or whatever and these are destroyed by the tide or the actions of other children. The children in so-called isolated nuclear families are almost over-dependent on a small group of adults while those in extended families may have their emotions spread over a large number of adults. An English child may only be able to name a dozen relatives while the wife of an Afro-American airman based in Britain stated that she and her children had over a hundred relatives with whom they could stay on leave in the United States.

The loss of property to a child in a subsistence community is going to be more upsetting than to one in an urban industrial setting who may have many toys but in either case ownership will have emotional aspects. Rivalry over friendships may well be intense in urban-industrial societies where many social groupings are short-term and varied.

Children as much as adults do not have any in-born sense of mechanical time and for them it is linked to events; the imposed time of institutionalised schooling and buses create tensions between social and institutionalised needs. There will also be crises when children realise that while they may have some control over their own lives within the home, they are no longer in control at all as to what happens to them outside.

A typology of the pivotal events which may periodically involve most children and which have correlations to crisis and stress would be as follows :

A. Negative and irreversible events

- Deaths of those with whom there are real or imaginary relationships
- Loss of status
- Loss of property to which children are attached
- Broken off social relationships
- Death of pets
- Divorce or abandonment by parents or a parent

B. Negative experience but linked to the positive

- Bodily mutilations; circumcision, scarification
- Menarche

C. Positive and irreversible

- Gaining prizes
- Sport status in teams
- Promotion

D. Ambivalent pivots depending on environmental factors for impact

- Changing house
- Entering school
- Changing school
- Birth of a sibling
- Remarriage of either parent

**Poverty and Pro-social Socialisation**

In any society there are three ways in which poverty can be assessed;

real poverty as assessed by independent researchers and non-governmental organisations, the statutory rulings of governments that anyone with incomes below a certain level is poor and the feelings of the people themselves that they are poor in comparison to what they want and feel entitled to in their society.

The first is what might be classified as "real" poverty but this will also vary with the society in which it occurs; the poor in unproductive farmlands without adequate food, housing or clothes would see the poor in western cities as almost affluent. The rumours of western affluence held by poor Albanians or Chinese is not based on the purchasing power of money, they and their children are influenced by the detached images of the mass media. Statutory rulings on poverty levels make the whole issue into a matter of bureaucratic administration without much relationship to obligations to the state or local authority as providers.

The final form of "relative" poverty is certainly the most widespread and influential in the lives of children. They are deeply affected by not only domestic inequalities such as those between boys and girls as to who gets what and when, but also by the envy introduced into their lives by outsiders and the mass media.

So poverty is a difficult concept to use in relation to pro-social behaviour as what is considered poverty in one society cannot apply in another. The mendicant street livers in Britain are certainly poor by the standards of that society but the statutory poor there who receive supplementary benefits from the state have weekly incomes greater than the annual incomes of many subsistence farmers or daily employed workers in Bangladesh and Zambia. The latter would consider the British poor to be well-to-do.

The first type may have particular concern for the young, the aged and the handicapped and special voluntary organisations as Age Concern and Save the Children Fund attempt to help these disadvantaged, often concentrating on refugee communities in Uganda, the Sudan and Palestine. The assumption usually appears to be that the young brought up under such conditions defined as poverty, are suffering from social and biological deprivation. It is rarely if ever concluded that such children develop appropriate pro-social behaviour for those conditions which helps them to survive and become useful adults in whatever type of society subsequently involves them.

Some governments in economically well-developed states have statutory poverty levels, the minimum cost of living standards and families and individuals falling below this are given weekly payments. Despite these costly provisions, poverty remains widespread despite well-developed and systematically administered welfare programmes.

In practice there is absolute poverty which involves enormous numbers of people in the subsistence economies in parts of India, East Africa and the Sudan as well as among the urban poor in the slums of most if not all less developed countries. In these situations children as young as 5 years old and even younger among the Ik of Uganda fend for themselves and often lead lives independent of adults as the so-called "street children" of Latin America. These children appear to have better health than those who do not have this pattern of living and as "professional" opportunists they are relatively well adjusted to their marginal urban existence.

At best such children and their families lead hand-to-mouth existences on uncertain daily employment as can be seen in the road-side job markets in contemporary Beijing in which people with the tools of their trade in their hands wait for employment. The itinerant sellers of fruit, flowers and vegetables in Mombasa, Kenya are out of work whenever the road and rail links with Nairobi are disrupted by seasonal rain.

In contradistinction to this and just as important for any assessment of the pro-social behaviour of children is relative poverty in which individuals of all ages feel that they lack many of the goods which they see others have around them and which they see on television, in the shops and in advertising. Reasonable aspirations and envy are hard to distinguish and all the forms of poverty fluctuate and overlap to some extent and are subject to personal and objective bias.

While comparative poverty in the economically well developed societies of the Western world certainly has an element of envy to which children conform, it does not have the political significance which exists in Third World countries where the international South can be compared with the ex-colonial and persistently wealthy North. Children in the former grow up within a persistent politicised framework of resentment.

West African thinkers have described this situation as the "disease of the wants" started by the mass media generally and visiting

Westerners, the expensive but work less wanderings of tourists, diplomats, men and particularly women missionaries, aid workers and gap year students who accidentally flaunt their comparative affluence with their clothes and cameras. Children in Ethiopia who acted as guides wanted to be "paid" with a single ball-point pen and the throwaways of departing tourists left in their hotel waste-paper baskets, had to provide room servants with certificates that these useless holed and dirty articles were in fact thrown away. All of this provides both adults and children enduring real poverty with a world of materials to which they must inevitably aspire but have little hope of ever attaining.

Within every country there have always been marked differences in materially linked status but in the developing world, these differences are linked in the popular mind with corruption, political violence and nepotism rather than with hard work. This must also be linked in the minds of growing children with the poverty which is their immediate experience.

However there cannot be children anywhere in the world who are not affected by the existence of relative affluence which is related to a fictional world of well-being. The advertisements on hoardings and in thrown away newspapers and magazines and in the soap-operas on television often hired from Western companies as Third World countries cannot afford to make their own serials.

This leads to envy brought on not just by the subtle gradations in wealth and influence in their own societies which children can see in the differences between houses, the clothes of other children and those who have several step-mothers and in the size of their fields and flocks. Even though money can hidden easily enough, traditional societies do not like too much affluence which is not redistributed to maintain some popularity; lavish hospitality to all in the neighbourhood without invitations at marriages, circumcisions and funerals is a necessity to maintain the inter-relationships necessary for communal living in joint cultivations, carrying the sick and digging graves.

The children see in their visions of the outside world a stark and absolute "us" and "them" which may lead to eliding these outsiders with the tribal enmities of the past and present and make it less immoral to be involved in petty crime and street violence.

Whatever level of affluence or poverty within which children are raised, their pro-social behaviour as in other matters will be a mixture of behaviour dictated by the immediacies of their familial living and external social and economic influences which will always make the former unsatisfying to some degree.

Even for those children who live in families which are quite adequate by local standards, there is probably a feeling of deprivation in relation to standards of greater privilege.

# Chapter-9

# Social and Physical Environmental Variations Affecting the Growing Child

In any society there is an ideological image of ideal behaviour which is implied rather than discussed. A primary illusion which implies homogeneity is possibly a need and a direction of thinking. There is some understanding that there can be variations from this ideal model but not much consideration is given to the possibility that the models could vary.

**Intra-society Variables and Pro-social Behaviour**

One of the illusions of comparing complex and so-called simpler less economically developed societies is the assumption that the latter are inevitably simpler and more homogeneous in their social arrangements. This acceptance of homogeneity is almost certainly incorrect and probably arises from the difficulties of visiting outsiders studying societies of which they can only be a researching part for limited periods. Few researchers have continuous and data collection over several decades as Margaret Mead had with the Manus islanders.

The children of such societies are as much subject to varied influences as in the larger social groupings with perhaps only the differences which come from greater social and geographical distances. Even this may be questionable when we have also to consider the influences which come into the children's understandings in even the most isolated communities from wireless, television and even if they cannot read, the pictures in newspapers which are too valuable to use for personal cleaning. We can only imagine what their minds may pick up in visits to markets, seeing the goods on display and from even watching outsiders in their cars passing on the road.

Just as the characters of members of so-called simpler societies will vary so must their inter-relationships and the ways that these people and their societies influence their children into pro-social behaviour. In Iran the religious settings of the villages and older urban neighbourhoods cater for a variety of religious and social needs of their adult inhabitants (Fischer, 1980: 136) and thus their children learn particular forms of pro-social behaviour alongside their parents, in which social and religious factors mix.

The mosque with its daily routines of prayer for which the children hear the calls to prayer long before they are able to participate, they may sit in on and at least see the giving of sermons which are homiletic entertainment and weekly gatherings for religious discussion and pietistic exercises, they will certainly see as Shiite Muslims the annual passion plays about the martyrdom of Ali and men beating and perhaps cutting themselves out of sympathy; they may go on special pilgrimages with their parents, visiting the tombs and stopping places of saints as well as sacred trees and wells to which picnics may be brought as well as to graveyards to reaffirm ancestral ties and dues.

The boys will be interested in what goes on in the traditional gymnasiums involving the virtues of Islamic chivalry and the younger children will go with their mothers to predominantly ritual feasts for the taking of vows, sociability and homiletics. Only in the bazaars with its language of Islamic morality will they experience the decaying Islamic commercial obligations and the fading taboos circumscribing the activities of non-Muslims. In addition there are the gatherings for marriages and funerals and the night-time excitements of the holy month of Ramadan. These may be less influential as electricity extends the range of television and video entertainment on themes which are both religiously and officially prohibited.

Onto this varied pattern of external influences which are specific to a locality, there will be the individual influences which come of course from their own personalities and those of their relatives but also from their economic position and social status. In that same Iranian village there will be the family of their religious leader, those who are doing quite well by local standards and those who are always on the verge of penury. When the end of Ramadan comes round, and children get new clothes, how well will they be able to show off to the other children with whom they play.

The difference between the so-called simpler societies and the more complex urban-industrial ones may be that the influences in the former are more direct and with less social distance between those that are involved and those that initiate these activities.

In seeking to understand the factors influencing children towards socially acceptable behaviour to the requirements of their families and the surrounding societies, we are faced by two extremes. The bland generalities of numerically illustrated patterns of behaviour taken from studying a large number of children usually provided from those in a school environment.

The alternative extreme to this will be the data provided about the extremes of behaviour from individual children. Much more is known about so-called feral children, child criminals and delinquents and those who are terminally ill (Bluebond-Langner, 1978) than is known about the so-called average child. The vast majority of children in all societies who grow up and pass through schooling into adult life without in any overt way going beyond the boundaries of acceptable behaviour required by their families and the surrounding society.

It is reasonable to suggest that this latter category covers the generality of childhood and that if it was not so such a society either deliberately or involuntarily would change their system in order to make their children better behaved in their families and neighbourhoods either making deviance acceptable by changing the rules or increasing the penalties for deviance and with it creating a further range of reactive deviance.

It is this middle ground lives of children who are not in any particular trouble with anyone which should be the basis of any study of the pro-social behaviour of children. But even if this is correct there are the problems of any assumption of averages in this grey area of normality. Within this average whether assessed from the children in geographically isolated hamlets in Russia or Iceland or in an urban secondary school with a good reputation for educational success and behaviour, no child is average. In schools we have the regular reports on children which show their individuality but of how they behave in their homes we know very little except by intrusive questioning and participant observation of a limited number of families.

In any consideration of the power of culture to mould the behaviour of children, there will always be variations in what is possible to impose or teach. Even in an ostensibly rigidly controlled society of which contemporary Iran may be an example, there are limits to what can be controlled. There is no social system that can provide for all the possible variations in human behaviour and situations. It is not only that human beings are infinitely variable and that parents and children are likely to be mutually variable but that they are all continuing to vary in different ways as they age.

There are two aspects to the pro-social behaviour of children within a society. The actual behaviour of children in particular social settings insofar as it can be observed and recorded without bias and the theories through which social scientists filter what goes on in and around childhood. This theorizing lists a long succession of prestigious names Foucault, Hobbes, Rousseau, Locke, Freud, etc. who have applied their analytical minds to childhood. What has been achieved by this work based on limited numbers or the assumption of averages? We are not much further forward except to establish quite clearly what children are not, in a jumble of theories around the innocent, immanent, naturally developing and unconscious child (A. James et al., 1998: 3-21).

## Intra-society Variables : Motherhood

It is valuable to speculate on whether the image of the mother as the essential human component in the bringing up of all children is a human universal which goes beyond Western ideologies of parenthood and the ideal family. Even in that particular cultural environment it may not be the commonest and lengthiest early relationships which children experience.

In every society there will be large scale demographic variables from what even those societies consider to be both average and best for the bringing up of their children. The statistics if available and accurate will show marital failures and where the children of those marriages now live, social conventions such as the inheritance of widows, early deaths and the numbers of children who share relationships with their mothers as well as children in serial monogamous, polygynous and polyandrous marriages. In these circumstances any conceptions of normality has to remain an ideal for which there may be little statistical backing.

It seems likely that there will always be the unity of alternate generations in which grandparents provide affection without discipline. Even in this there will be variations as in patrilineal societies, children may well be closer to their mother's mother than with their own mothers as these relatives will have greater empathy for children than the more rigorous approach of the patrilineal kin. Conversely among the matrilineal Yao of Malawi and southern Tanzania, the father's mother will be preferred by most children.

While it certainly correct that every child can only have one mother but that is the end of such certainties. The father is usually a peripheral figure in which he can accept biological and legal parenthood, but until science comes on the scene this is a social and negotiated relationship.

Even the simple fact of conception may not coincide with the western understandings that sexual intercourse is necessary for this to take place. There is evidence in the past from some New Guinea societies that the spirits have to agree to a wife becoming pregnant so that a husband may accept as his a children born after he has been absent for two years as a migrant labourer on another island.

Although there may be some physiological resemblance of a child to a particular man, most societies accept that the mother is at least initially responsible for caring for her own child and children. The influence of the male parent whatever the legal position in customary and statute law, is likely to be subject to many variables based on the realities of social and economic life whatever the wishes of either or both parents may be within their circle of family living.

A male parent may not exist with any exactness since the women may have been promiscuous or have just disappeared as soon as he found out that his partner was pregnant which accounts for the predominance of matrifocal families in the slums of the Caribbean and western cities. The sexual and material services which he gets from a childless woman will not be the same return on expenditure if she has children which take up his resources and make her less available to look after him.

The father's attentions may be spread sequentially over several children born to several women in polygynous marriages or two brothers may be responsible for a single woman's children in polyandrous marriages in Tibet.

The commonest form of fathers not taking much part in the bringing up of their children is their gender in which the care of children is distributed by sex between the mother and the father or their respective sides of a single family. Even commoner in urban and industrial societies is the absence of the father because of seasonal or permanent work at sea, in transport or the armed forces in other areas, the daylight working hours of offices or the shift working of factories.

Housewives in such societies who are not in paid employment and who are in monogamous marriages in their own separate houses. They may be isolated from their own relatives will have to perform both male and female roles in caring for their children ín the daily absence of a man for which they have not been socially or culturally trained and for which they may not wish to use their time or have the abilities. Thus the pro-social training of children may not conform to any socially acceptable pattern.

So within any community there may be as many variations in styles of motherhood as there are between cultures variations in the maternal competence of mothers as household administrators. In this there are marked contrasts between subsistence societies in which each household may have little material property and in which the woman as mother has to learn to manage with only a few variables. Even the poorest family housed in government housing in western cities has much more to cope with in property and behavioural alternatives. A wife in a subsistence society either cooks adequately or gets beaten or divorced; the behavioural pattern which the young learn of what is socially acceptable is perhaps rather easier to learn because there are fewer alternatives and no welfare system to appeal to with its statute law and payments underwritten by the state.

Then there is the issue that a mother with one child will have one pattern of behaviour but with three there is inevitably a different pattern apart from the fact that the first and last born in many subsistence societies are treated better than those in between as they have their own special names.

Many women are far from well and it may be that a high proportion of mothers in subsistence societies have debilitating diseases from parasites making for anaemia from hook worm infestations which come from walking in bare feet, apart from the endemic malnutrition to be found in the shanty towns of large cities; it is rare to see a fat Sukuma woman.

Now in Uganda and India there are widows who cannot marry again because of religion or disease leading to a shortage of men because of AIDS or a suspicion that they carry such diseases so they may have to bring up children alone.

Women are certainly responsible for child care in all societies but it is by no means certain that the biological mother will be the one who does this caring for them. Upper class women in all societies have always subcontracted not so much to relatives as to employees as wet-nurses, nannies and governesses. The influence of the latter on the behaviour of the children in their care based on affection and the length of their relationships has often has a depth which has no parallel in that with their own mothers which the novel Brideshead Revisited illustrates so well (Waugh, 1953).

At the lower end of the economic and social scale mothers may live in family groups in which the care of the children of all the mothers in the group is not so much formally shared but informally catered for by whoever happens to be around even in some cases breast feeding the upset child whose mother does not happen to be there at that moment.

In many if not all agricultural subsistence families the last born child is indeed close to the mother but not in ways that involve much personal intimacy with their mothers since they are carried on the back and there is then no eye to eye contact. The babies are there when their mothers are working in the fields moving up and down with their movements as the hoe.

These mothers also have to run households in which little is ready to hand or provided by the husband as part of his marital obligations; each and every day she has to fit in time with the child or children between fetching water which is rarely nearby, getting kindling, preparing each meal from start as there are no means in such households of preserving food as well as cleaning the house and washing the family clothes in cold water away from the homestead. So children are more likely to be left to the care of whoever is at hand particularly older siblings and learning to cope with their own needs at a far earlier age than would be the case in western societies with so much restrictive legislation preventing the participation of children in the wider society surrounding them.

Once families live in towns on low incomes the mother may have even less time for her children as she often has to earn a livelihood from road-side peddling. There are also situations in which two earners in the family are needed to maintain the required standard of living for the family and to pay off the mortgage. This has occurred in contemporary Norway where the majority of women work and children grow up quickly and early enough to take an obligatory share in running the household of which they are a necessary working part as they are in subsistence agricultural families; for these Norwegian children their participation is much more than vague irregular voluntary help of not much economic significance (Solberg, 1997).

So we see that the participation of mothers in the pro-social training of their children is by no means clear cut or the inevitable consequences of motherhood. Both within a community and cross-culturally there are no uniform patterns of what mothers can be expected to do rather than what is thought that they should do.

## Open and Closed Family Lives

When children are thought of in quasi-traditional environments, their social and geographical environments are seen as their villages and the larger distances within which they are progressively able to walk. This is a false methodological assumption as these social boundaries have been and are constantly penetrated by outsiders and mentally by every outsider theme seen on paper or television or heard on tapes and discs.

This theoretical comparison between tradition and modernity cannot be maintained. Roads and wheeled transport have been known and used for centuries apart from rivers and coast lines which in even earlier days provided for the movement of people, property and ideas. Strangers and outside influences have never been unknown, but perhaps it is only in the more recent past that these factors have become a flood of changes.

Perhaps the tendency is to look for and appreciate macro themes in social change and to miss a more basic division between the two types of communities in which children spend their lives in which the family social environment is open or closed. In the open environment a small number of families live together with children growing up under the eyes and ears of a small known number of adults. This is seen today in Bushman encampments with a small number of shelters as housing, the traveller-cum-gypsy caravans in lay-bys on main roads of Britain, the high density old housing of some cities in which generations have lived in the same close neighbourhoods (Wilmot and Young, 1957) for the same industrial reasons where the street was the play area and in small villages or housing clusters of long staying farming residents everywhere in the world where there is a low turn-over of population. The social environment in which children grow-up could be described as collegial whether in China, India or Bavaria and indeed even more specifically in the Mormon communities of Utah and the more narrowly defined contemporary American Amish and Canadian Hutterite communities.

Then there are secretive closed door communities in towns and cities in which family life goes on behind the barriers of defended space. There is a high turn-over of neighbours and the supervision of children is a matter for individual families to carry out or to arrange for others to do so on their behalf as when both mothers and fathers go out to work. This family space is only entered by visiting relatives and friends or penetrated by bureaucratic outsiders with official power to do so.

From the sensed feelings of the children stability of the collegial open door communities is obviously greater than in the closed door ones. In the high density housing in the East End of London there were often families which had lived in the same localities for years with the street outside as a communal play area. It has been shown that in these communities bride and groom prior to their marriage had usually lived within two hundred metres of each other so that daughters and their mothers remained physically close and were at hand to look after their grandchildren (Wilmot & Young, 1957).

In the locked door communities the turn over is high with between 10 per cent in Britain and 20 per cent in the United States moving every year so that there is unlikely to be much association between neighbours. Of course relatives live within a radius of 25 miles and can be communicated with by phone but to actually visit is an expensive and time consuming expedition.

In such locked door communities the child is subject to the same processes of demographic change but uncertainty about neighbours is constant. By the time the parish priest had completed a door to door listing of family details in a Guyana township and gone back to the beginning, 20 per cent had moved. The importance of known faces for the stability of the growing child becomes negligible in such communities.

On top of changes acceptable to their families, the closed door child is subject to polyfacetted changes over which their family has very little control over what they see on television or in the outside world and as to what they read. This is particularly distressing for minority families whether of eastern or western origin who wish to retain as much of their traditional cultures as possible. These difficulties over the raising of children and their pro-social behaviour are particularly stressful in the areas of obedience and the issue of "love" and relationships between the adolescents.

The commonest parental requirement in such minority households would be for obedience and yet the children if they do not actually see, certainly know of what is apparently tolerated disobedience; teachers go on strike, children are let out of school to participate in public demonstrations against the war in Iraq, graffiti on walls provoking opposition. Then in such minorities which want to control the relationships of both their sons and daughters, the public persistence of the theme of personal choice on the grounds of love is a constant source of conflict.

Social change in locked door societies is a much more pervasive influence on children than perhaps their parents and guardians realise. Behind these doors family life is secretive and defensive and indeed the door has great significance in law for its compulsory opening for the enforcement of social change by welfare officials.

Of course "out there" has always been threatening as in the generalised fears of collegial porous groups, but now "out there" is continually threatening because it is no longer something simple which is relatively easy for children to accept and understand without much anxiety.

## The Absence of Child Centred or Centring Families

Although many western based studies concentrate on children in relation to the familial or non-familial social and psychological environments in which they are brought up, this overlooks their basic status. Concern for the child as an individual is overwhelmingly secondary to the concerns of their adults over their own interests; rationally this could not be otherwise. Situations in which the interests of the child overwhelm those of their caring adults is inevitably a western phenomena with handicapped children for whom state support is in the background or when there are financial reasons involving custody as in the bringing up of the very rich and high status children.

It would thus appear to be the degree to which the interests of the child are subordinated to or serve the interests of the adults with legal or customary responsibilities for their upbringing. It is both a moral and social point whether there are indeed situations in which the children can have rights and interests independent of or superior to those of their custodial adults.

Any sentimental approach to this issue in terms of love for the child or the child as an ongoing symbol of the relationships of their parents needs to be treated with some scepticism outside of any biological, genetic or ethological considerations. To paraphrase a sign often seen on the back windows of British cars "a child (dog) is not just for Christmas", children once born last many years beyond the first burst of maternal and less long lasting paternal sentiment.

At the subsistence level children are bred to be economically, socially and indeed often politically useful and their cost in terms of food and clothing is balanced against their utility as part of their parents survival needs until the boys found their own families or in most cases the daughters marry away into other families. This is not to suggest that sentiment may not exist but attachment to children is often thought unwise in creating jealousy within the surrounding community and tempting providence when such a high proportion still die in childhood.

At the other end of the scale in western societies with highly developed systems of social welfare and ideologies of child care, children have been legislated out of any need to contribute to the economics of their families even as regular chores. The economic and social return on the enormous expenditure in time and money in bringing up any child even when publicly rather than privately educated is unlikely to exceed 5 per cent; they are a poor investment.

In the eyes of subsistence farmers this set-up of giving priority to children in terms of some hypothetical moral, national and political interests is an incredibly poor investment. Some indeed are beginning to question the justification for sacrificing the here and now use of children in family farming and herding in order to send them to school in order to be educated which often results in the children's dissatisfaction with their parents way of living and surviving. Something resembling the Amish view that children should be educated for the life that they are likely to lead rather than for an unspecified and in reality unlikely future.

Let us take the family on which politicians, social carers and theologians devote much of their public time in supporting; that it is a "good" by definition without breaking it down into what may actually happen. Is it indeed possible to think of any family in such unitary and long lasting terms when considering how children attain some measure of acceptable pro-social behaviour. It seems unlikely that there has been in any society any customary policy to give priority to the interests of children at the expense of adults.

Let us look at the data which is available from the Netsilik Eskimos before they left their wholesale dependence on a traditional way of living by hunting. Too many female children would threaten the ability of the hunting males to support the group and also they are of no use to their natal group as they marry into other groups, so many are killed (Rasmussen, 1931). Male children are kept alive if possible as they represent future hunters. Thus children in this very simple type of hunter-gatherers are kept alive for their future use to their natal group; they have no value moral or otherwise in themselves as individuals. No doubt the mother may regret the necessity of any child being killed but necessity is more important that what might well be the deadliness of giving way to sentiment by giving the child food which would otherwise contribute keep an adult functionally useful.

A housebound single mother in a council flat in East London is child centred principally because this is enabled by the social welfare system of her society which requires her to be child centred and living in a style which has no connection with costs. In a subsistence community a single mother would remain part of her natal family whose name she holds and her children would be part of the family's daily economics. Her role in caring for her children would be subordinated to the needs of the group; if she wanted to eat she would have to work as part of the producing unit.

In the urban slums of Brazil and East Africa so-called street children may be contributing to the survival of their families however constituted; as often as not such children are not abandoned, but "in and out" members of their families as the children's economic opportunities fluctuate.

Above all the concept of the family is a very elastic one not only in the forms which are theoretically acceptable to and legally accepted by any society, but in the forms that it takes in any society at each age at which the child socially and biologically exists. This can never be a constant when all the members of any family are aging and subject to internal and external factors influencing the behaviour of all involved. Child-centeredness has to be accepted as a largely ideological attitude to which most people and political policies support but which can never be implemented.

So firstly there are the varieties of family in which children may be brought up as for example there are over ten social forms for the Indian joint family (Kolenda, 1960). There is almost certainly as large if not larger number of varieties of nominally monogamous families in the east End of London which can be identified well enough to be group families of extended kin since the forms will involve Bangladeshi, Afro-Caribbean and White families.

The Bengali families in East London would to some extent follow the Indian pattern with several families living in one house or next door in which the economics are joint; it is not known what the extent of polygyny is in such communities or whether there can be such a thing as a single socially separate parent. In such complex households children may be popular but who is responsible for their up-bringing would have to divide between day time, evening with grandparents doing the former and younger doing the evening shift when they come back from work. We know that there is widespread dissatisfaction among Asian and British educated adolescents as to the way that their parents think about children within a traditional framework. Thus in this situation child centeredness is more a question of who is talking.

White English families might have an equally large range of alternatives which children of any age might be subjected to; single parents of either sex for whose children there may be existing involved, not involved or not known partners with biological connections, three generation families with grandparents from either family, siblings with children living together, grand parent and grand children living together, adoptive, short-term caring families paid by the state and children living with unrelated couples. In all of these situations notice is taken of the children but it seems only that in families in which the state pays for care will the children's interests have priority; this is a statistically rare form of parenting.

All these varieties will have little in common with any legally defined marriage based or long-term concubinage as socially acceptable nuclear families which is thought ideologically to be the best environment for bringing up children. It is always the case that the ability for any type of family to bring up children to the standards required by social welfare ideologies and legislation would be constantly changing perhaps even on a day to day basis and certainly on any longer time scale since all those involved are subject to inevitable personal disasters, handicaps and successes.

Much of current social and political thinking, in which there is a social science and social welfare establishment acting within cross-party policies in every country, rests on what society and the parental group should do for children to develop their full potential. There is hardly any focus on what children should be required to do for the maintenance of the large and small groups within which they are living and which are responsible for feeding, clothing and housing them for years.

## Intra-society Variables: Surrounding Families

The analytical image of what any society considers to be a family and the variations which are to be found in any community from this picture produced by the social scientist is always large. The children in any society seeing this variety of relationships is not going to get any practical image of any specific pattern; there will always be a serious gap between social reality and hope. It seems likely that almost universally this gap in almost all contemporary societies has widened under the influence of the mass media and popular entertainment.

The basis of all social relationship groupings which can be classified as families must be the mother-child relationship. In fact this is the only human relationship which is biologically incontestable and socially recognised except for identical twins which do not in fact create single families. All other kin relationships if they are to exist require social confirmation that they are what they claim to be. For a man to state that these are his children is a social creation of a biological relationship for which until recently there can have been no proof available; it may be true but it is social action which makes it into a fact. It is fundamental that if something is believed to be real, it is real in its consequences (Thomas & Thomas, 1928; 571-3).

Thus the family is an abstraction, a mental construct, which even in the terms of any definition would only be recognisable in a few groupings and in each case for a short period of time. It is a social grouping of very variable construction both in its social composition and in its functions. In fact to talk about "the" family is an error when it is actually in the eyes of society and its children "a" particular family.

Mothers and their children while being the most basic form of human association since it is both visible and biologically based are infrequently isolated from their own biological and social relatives and those who have particular significances from culturally supported kinship and social systems; these may be agnatic, matrilineal, polygynous, affinal or whatever system that each culture, society or community recognises.

In almost all cases except in a small number of specialised circumstances women mate exogamously and live in groups away from their natal families. Even in the cousin marriages of Muslims and Amish, there is the setting up of a new household dictated by the man.

Every community will have variations in the degree to which the mothers and their children are entangled in wider family and non-family connections whatever the dominant culture may suggest to be the ideal and correct one. A common variation is the presence of a key relative whose presence in social and economic terms dictates the structure and functioning of a family. This is often a grandparent who insures her own social survival by caring for her grandchildren as their parents are working; this is a common feature in Chinese and Russian urban societies.

The common cross-cultural variations which children are likely to become both part of and aware of in the surrounding neighbourhoods are numerous. The absence of rather than the presence of certain relatives; grandparents, in-laws, uncles and aunts, cousins may exist but out of social reach whether by walking or driving; it seems unlikely that the telephone will keep people in touch when there is no functionally useful need to keep in touch; there is always a time and cost factor in maintaining relationships. A well-off relative in a poor extended family may not want to be importuned by those family members not as well-off as himself and he will do all that he can to avoid them; they want to take from him without providing anything in return.

Then there is also the total absence of certain relatives; they may be dead, disappeared through long distance migration or have never existed in the first place as with biological fathers who were socially unknown to the mother and adoption whether legal or not which may or may not be socially acceptable in a society or family. The mother's brother may be a culturally preferred relative but in a particular family the child's mother may never have had a brother or he had died young.

Some families such as the fictional one described by the play-writer J.M. Barrie as the "dear octopus" in which a family thinks of itself as a corporate one for a wide range of functions such as that of the Marks and Spencer families and a number of Bengali families in East London. In situations of some poverty relatives may hang together and indeed in some cases create the classificatory relationships in order to justify closeness as the creation of fictional mother's brother connection among patrilineal migrants into East African cities.

There are always variations in the degree of acceptance and acceptability of particular relationships involving children. Apart from linguistic, legal and customary definitions. A child may have a mother or father in a series of short-term relationships in which the temporary step-father or mother is referred to as uncle or aunt. In another form this is relatively common for the long-term friends of parents to become classificatory aunts and uncles thus upgrading the relationship to the closer form of friendship.

In this category there are informal and non-legal relationships which may have achieved greater acceptability in the surrounding community than shorter legal arrangements which relatives may have considered unsuitable; longevity of such relationships create their own acceptability.

Finally children and adults always have to recognise that in any family groupings there are patterns of dominance in which power is shared but not loosened. The Chinese family in Penang which met in the patrilineal grand-fathers house every Sunday for tea in which it was alleged that the only matters discussed were family ones; the children of such an extended family would have recognised early in their lives that this was a combination of the Confucian ideal of family submission to its head who also had economic power. The obverse of this is that the child will never treat their relatives equally, there will always be preferences which are entirely personal and ones which are guided by their culture as in patrilineal societies the preference for the matrilineal side of the family and even then one mother's brother may be preferred over another.

It seems likely that a child will usually react to the range of available adults rather than seek out particular ones who should exist; those who were adopted as children may seek out their real parents but this is usually an adult reaction in a minority of adopted ones.

A surrounding society may contain no one to whom the child is related; modern communities have highly mobile members in which between 10 to 20 per cent may move every year. There are enormous numbers of refugees in camps far from their original homes so that there is a likelihood that numbers of contemporary children live in particular social environments for short periods in which their models for familial behaviour are likely to be deficient in the characteristics of a "conventional" family according to local ideas which they might not even know about. In the Kumbh Mela pilgrimage in 2003 to which many millions of people came as in the larger refugee camps, children became lost and remained unclaimed because the parents did not know where to look and were fearful of moving out of their own known space.

Each of the changes in their social environment which the children experience once they are passed the toddler stage, will involve them in relationships outside the immediacies of their primary groups over which they have no control. They venture into neighbourhoods which provide them with very different models of behaviour which will in most cases be different to those of their own primary groups.

Particularly in urban locations neighbours will no longer be known to the children's carers whose wariness about new contacts will be passed onto their children; there are now distinctions over the "right" and "wrong" sorts of families based on rumoured information rather than the certainties of subsistence agricultural communities. Let us examine several types of societies and see what various models there are of family life which children can be expected to encounter and which by the accident of these encounters form models which they may copy by social accident as much as by deliberate design.

Firstly the village near Pangani on the East African coast of Tanzania in which 33 out of the 34 households were related and could be plotted on a single family tree because those living there accepted that there were social relationships based on biological connections. Although all the houses looked much the same, the households were by no means similar except that there was a connection which they ostensibly shared, important enough to live there when there was land available elsewhere.

How might they be divided up in the eyes of children living there. Possibly the first point that their children might notice is that there are not many children there perhaps as a result of marrying cousins in successive generations. Households will be divided up by the presence or absence of children and their ages and whether there was more than one wife living there since this was a Muslim village in which polygyny was religiously and socially acceptable. Certainly there were no single parent households but some families might be three generational because of divorce. These children would notice the age differences between husbands and wives and from the ways in which they have learnt to address them, they would know the relationship and the appropriate behaviour which comes with variable social distances as well as which coconut palms belonged to which household and which fields they cultivated; the patchwork pattern of cultivation which might come from the Islamic pattern of dividing inheritable property according to relationships. In some such villages a child accompanying a parent to help with the weeding of the fields might spend more time walking between fields than working on them.

In a village which had such ostensible unity, all their children would have learnt the subtle gradations of behaviour and its guardedness in relationships outside the home which would enable closely related people to live together without too much overt tensions. Members of families are just as much rivals for status and self aggrandisement as the unrelated and children in such environments would soon learn what can be talked about inside the home but not outside. They would learn the duplicity of behaviour which is a necessary part of living in small communities for long periods which contain few people.

So the children would learn not so much a model of stable familial behaviour but one in which divorce is a constant feature and that probably a kinship network was more socially and economically valuable than something approaching the "isolated" nuclear family of western familial ideology. In a nearby village a prominent member was able to remember what he had given to each family member in the past lunar year and how much he received in return; it almost balanced. In the long run the child may learn that even in the closest of families there is no such thing as a free dinner. So these children would have learnt that a recognised and nearby group of kin is valuable, but that distant kin are less reliable since they are socially invisible. This is probably a way of life that in that locality is very old indeed.

A community of similar size in Ngara, western Tanzania would not be in a village but located over a wide spread of fields which are too valuable to live faraway from; it has an entirely different composition depending on the time of year. For most of the year there will be many women and their children married but functionally single as their husbands are away as agricultural workers in distant areas, often Uganda and Kenya. This unbalanced sex ratio would be duplicated in many areas of low prices for cash crops so far from export markets connected by rail, ship and truck combined with land shortage.

The surplus of women and shortage of men duplicated in many areas in which cash crops fetch low prices, has meant that there is always marital instability since a married woman in this situation spends most of the year in a dual role without relief. Children here will see their mothers moving into whatever social relationships might bring relief from this unilateral oppression which leaves them alone as well as having to fetch water and fuel.

Since this is an area in which almost all are Christians the children will have learnt early the difference between long-term and serial monogamy. They will also realise that the maternal side is likely to be more use to them than the paternal certainly there will be no long standing kinship network in a stratified society divided between land owners and those whose land is less fertile and at a lower altitude.

In both these communities family men who are outsiders and want to live there they have to live outside as clients; "us" and "them" are marked out geographically. The only exception would be women who marry into these communities. Certainly in Pangani the sense of exclusive identity would have been so strong that children would grow up in a social atmosphere of people who think that inlanders are uncivilised. Children would grow up knowing the aphorism that the real natives live on the coast and only uncivilised ones live inland.

Finally a collection of households in East London will probably have an even greater variety of family types than either of the previous communities in which however fluid the relationships within family groups are to some extent acceptable and known within a particular cultural framework; polgynous families certainly but no polyandrous ones, although women with two current relationships are not uncommon. Here we have neighbouring families who have no shared cultural backgrounds and yet are to all intents and purposes forced to live close to each other and use the same facilities under the cloak of shared citizenship.

What is important for children is the immediate awareness that they must physically accept rather than just accept cognitively, that their own family is not and never can be anything like the families of people living next-door and round the corner. The "us" and "them" is not over the horizon but here and now. It is a much more difficult form of reality than one in which there is an element of choice. The difficulty here is that in small "traditionally" inclined contemporary villages anywhere, children grow up with this duplicitous approach to their neighbours; it is neither taught nor challenged. In modern urban neighbourhoods children are taught the moral requirement of equality which clashes with their day to day experience of neighbourly relationships. The schools and local politics teach that such distinctions should not exist and that when they do those involved are in the wrong.

The child is faced with a looking different form of reality which is not just a question of wearing different clothes. The Bangladeshi seemingly overcrowded household comprised of presumed relatives, look different, talk differently, smell different both personally and in their cooking and indeed they are over the edge of a white child's comprehension of acceptable behaviour. In return the Bangladeshi children will think the same thing in reverse combined with some feeling that they are out of place; the divided psychological and social loyalties common to all immigrant community members. An English couple moving into a Welsh community may take years to be accepted even if they learn Welsh.

But in this high density community which does not often have community wide matters of shared interest, other than a varying dislike of the various surrounding bureaucratic authorities and a fear of crime, the children will be aware of the wall of privacy which surrounds each household. The only known factor may be the length of time certain people have lived there and which people are seen together.

The children either have a model of family relationships which they may not wish to follow as in Muslim arranged marriages over which there is a generation gap or one which comes from television and the popular press. The better off families who may live nearby are even more secretive over their family compositions and what gossip there is may be because they are involved in their children's friendship groups and shared school activities. The closed front door is an effective barrier to communal understandings and gossip lines may not involve neighbours.

## Intra-society Variables : Surrounding Community

While it may have been less so historically a proportion of people in every society will have had some knowledge of what goes on outside their neighbourhood and community. Children may have been made aware of this long before they can have been able to walk into outside experiences since they will have been carried to markets on the backs or hips of their mothers. The older walking child will already have had some implanted information memories of an outside world.

It seems likely that historically as far back as trading and curiosity existed, children will also have seen strangers who do not fit into their own communities; the wandering saddhus who so astonished Alexander the Great when he penetrated as far as the Indus, the ships from the east who visited the coast of East Africa with the westerly monsoon. Above all children will always have seen and handled objects which were not made or existed in their own communities; the cowrie shell currency of Uganda, beads from India common enough in the cliffs of east African beaches. Perhaps only people living on some Pacific islands such as Easter Island and New Zealand will have been isolated from such outside cultural and biological stimuli because no people came and none left.

If this was the situation historically in which children will have become aware very early in their lives that the vague categorisation of "us" as different to "them", the contemporary situation is much more varied, pervasive and influential. The modern child grows up within a deluge of objects and ideas which have not been thought up or made within their community; their relationship to this almost entirely passive and they and their families have no part in this creativity; being with-it is at the same time being without it.

Of course there may be some relatively isolated communities in the sense that they are stuck in some environmental niche from which only members can escape by remigration such as the mountain valleys of Gilgit, the isolated Nuba mountains of the Sudan and parts of Irian, western New Guinea. Even these very isolated communities have transistor radios, newspapers and probably the Bible or the Koran.

The majority of children are brought up in neighbourhoods in which a knowledge of alternative forms of pro-social and seemingly anti-social behaviour in terms of individual, familial and communal ideas of right and wrong, is not only inevitable but part of their usual development. They will be faced with the immediacy of variable behaviour as a reality; they have little choice but to be involved in a form of dysfunctional reality.

The individual child is brought up in a circle of closeness, the primary group of their current and individual families and this is surrounded by a larger circle of acceptable, tolerated and known people, families, fields and housing. This is understood by the child as connecting some social and psychological comfort with the concept of home within which there are interpersonal likes and dislikes. Beyond this circle of people who are thought of as "us", there are enormous numbers of social and emotional "foreigners" who are psychologically threatening even if they make no overt hostile actions.

Whereas in subsistence communities "foreigners" start some way away on the geographical horizon, in urban-industrial environments foreigners and foreignness start much nearer to the children's circle of material and emotional safety. It is no longer the limits of sight but a restricted range blocked off by roads, traffic, and houses; free moving space for children is limited by real warnings and their own imaginations.

The important point here is that children in subsistence communities have a pro-social learning process which coincides with that of all or most of the social activities and people which they are likely to meet or be involved in; there is an immediate or at least proximate pay-off. It is related to a general understanding that good behaviour and good food, grazing, etc. are not so much inter-related as dependant on each other.

In subsistence communities the ability of a family to bring up their children satisfactorily not only depends on the use of land but the cooperation of all family members because it is unlikely that a single man will be able to cultivate enough land to feed them all even if there is enough rain, no debilitating illnesses at critical times in the agricultural year and no other natural disasters. So both survival and the good life depends not only on family cooperation but the network of reciprocities which the family has with their neighbours; it is these people who carry the sick girl down the mountains in a hammock in contemporary Madeira. This supportive networking is maintained by a combination of good behaviour and good material returns also occurs in Mexican urban slums (Lomnitz, 1978). The poor there create small networks of reciprocity between neighbouring families which cover protection from outsider crime, child care and the sharing of information about employment opportunities.

There is also the fact that the urban industrial setting is a social environment does not alter with the seasons and it may be seen that it is good or bad for reasons which have little to do with the immediacies of surviving. Surviving may have little to do with personal relationships for which some states assume responsibility in their expensive social welfare systems.

So the first intra-community variable is the nearness of "foreigners", the unknown others who are not like the children looking out on this restricted and restrictive world. Concepts of otherness start at the front door which is locked to get out and to get in. It is not only in law that these outside closed doors have significance.

This realisation of "otherness" has many forms and is often correlated to morally-based pro-social behaviour for which there are no visible returns or no returns at all. The transistor radio, newspaper pictures and increasingly television provide children with enduring images which in their explanatory crudity provide no support for the reciprocal basis of moral behaviour in primary groups. One should never underestimate the possible consequences of mass media images;

the adolescent in the mid-1950s in Tanganyika shuffling along with his shoes undone says that he is imitating the gunfighter in western films and the half-dressed girl in the television play is an example of Western poverty not sexuality.

Children see on television burning mosques and churches in Kossovo, the results of terrorist bomb explosions in Spain and Israel and the funerals of Palestinians killed by Israelis as well as inter-religious killings in India and Pakistan which give them immediate anti-social images for which there are no attached explanations. They all add up to actions against "others" which are not in any way related to pro-social behaviour for which there is no pay-off except psychologically and the apparent fact that those who did these terrible acts are not caught and obviously not prevented.

It is not only in these extreme situations that the modern surrounding community provides other contrasting images of social behaviour which are not knitted into economic and social returns and which are enforced inefficiently by bureaucratic functionaries. A whole system which is outside what the child learns at home, that reasonable behaviour usually pays off. The input from the mass media must surely suggest that at best what might be called non-conformity, pays off. The individual gets away with behaviour which more or less would not be tolerated in any well organised and well functioning family primary group and community; the extravagancies of the pop-star are incitements to anti-communal behaviour. It may not be possible to prove the negative influences of television violence but it seems ridiculous to suggest that several hours watching per day for the average child does not influence thinking and subsequent behaviour.

The children learn of contrasting behaviour which in the context of their primary groups would have had difficulty in surviving and perhaps should be classified as immoral and selfish since they are not based on the human primary groups need for reciprocity to survive.

The school teaches competition largely for individual benefits and at the expense of the majority and its communal aspects are peripheral to the main syllabus. The local shops and more particularly the supermarkets offer what they want but cannot afford and the children in towns are surrounded by visible wealth in cars and clothing. The unit with which this inequality is mediated is money which can be hidden and the reciprocity of which they may have heard is one of corruption and nepotism between the unequal. In such conditions of visible inequality and social relationships which cannot be negotiated quite so clearly as in face to face subsistence communities, pro-social behaviour remains most effective in small groupings of people who experience the realisable and useful materialism in these primary inter-relationships.

Beyond this the children early realise that pro-social requirements in their behaviour outside the primary group relates to a social world of inequality in which the return is keeping out of trouble. Here pro-social behaviour is not self reinforcing and requires special agencies of control; the legalised morality of the civil service in which it is sensible to conform with unconformity.

## Individualism and Communalism

The basic division of themes through which children are socialised into their communities, societies or cultures, is often though to be between individualism and communalism. This is often seen as alternative ways of living typified at one extreme by American ideas and practices and at the other by eastern communalism and that this division is shown in the structure and use of their languages. The frequency of "I" as opposed to "we" language use.

There are always the practicalities to be considered as to how far any communalism is likely to impinge on and control individual needs; at what level is this being considered as overt or covert behaviour? The growing child is likely to see and hear much that is going on around them which would suggest that very little is going to be clear cut in their experiences and much is manipulated and covert.

The difficulty with the Whorfian hypothesis that language both creates and provides the framework for the world view of those speaking it is the instability of the spoken language while it may have a grammatical form, there will be constant variations in how it is used and the meanings attributed to its words. It is ridiculous to suggest that because a language does not have an indefinite future tense, the children or indeed the adults using such Bantu languages, do not recognise that some adults do live a long time or that trees take a long time to grow, while maize and rice grow quickly.

To have a world view is a magnified aspect of understanding which is more philosophical in its comprehensiveness and not a common way of looking at what is going on around them. For most people the use and understandings of their language are socially segmented and situational and are not taught; children learn natal languages they grow but secondary ones are usually taught.

It has been commented (Triandis, 1995: 61-65) that a language which subordinates women to men is situational and social, but may not constitute a world view. In any case men may have authority externally to the home and women control within the home. Where women are in contemporary positions of authority, it seems unlikely that the use of language will continue to show any such patterns of inferiority; there will have been situational circumlocutions to cover the women prime ministers of the Philippines, Pakistan, Sri Lanka and Bangladesh. Whatever the language into which children are socialised it seems likely that they will see its use in the social terms of the environment in which they are living. Their whole experience of language will be in these personal terms rather than in the abstract situations of learning a second language grammatically in the classroom. Anyone learning a language for which there are no texts or text-books will recognise that there does not appear to be any involvements with world-views of those who are speaking it even as teachers.

A major difficulty in such wide ranging grammatical categorizations such as "I", "we", "us" or "them" is the extent to which their use and related behaviour is consistent. It is easy enough to find examples of both individualistic and communalistic behaviour in a group of children in a finite situation but not that this is related to any predisposition necessarily related to language when those children have not been observed in a variety of situations and for much longer periods. Research done in English has to be expressed in English. The Japanese word "amae" to depend on and presume upon another's benevolence has no suitable equivalent in English. It is said that the Japanese never give up their desire to depend upon others and that this is an acceptable way to feel in that culture (Doi, 1962). To make such a semantic point cannot be said to make the individual Japanese communally or individually minded across the whole range of daily behaviour.

It seems likely that children will notice and remember very specifically social occasions in which they were involved with people and daylight events out of the ordinary; a street party for a coronation or jubilee, the end of the fasting month Ramadan in a Muslim community and New Year celebrations in a Chinese one as well the welcome for the success of a local sports team or a presidential visit. An East African child remembers Ramadan as a time for evening parties rather than extra prayers, while adults may see this in reverse.

For children rites of passage for others as well as themselves are likely to be remembered since the celebrations of death, birth, circumcision and marriage are partly a reflection of status and partly of community because everyone comes as a matter of social and geographical nearness and not as result of being invited which is a characteristic of urban-industrial societies and their narrower social relationships.

Then there are aspects of communality in defence of local interests such as village demonstrations against the opening of a local quarry in which children are made prominent by the carrying of placards. The Sukuma child will remember the well attended rain making ceremony at the time of a long drought because it involved people from a range of communities which at other times would have had divergent interests.

Children are also likely to recognise the sheer necessity as much as the utility of communalism even though this may be a matter of social rather than geographical definition. A village is a community by the fact of being surrounded by uninhabited space and it might take an hour to walk from one English or Yao village to another.

In an urban-industrial setting a community might be defined by the occasion as much as the location such as a cul-de-sac, street, tower-block or floor level, even students do not know much about those living in floors above and below them in university accommodation. The Sukuma and Nyamwezi in Tanzania have no villages and might have a sense of community with those who live within their sky-line and it might also vary with the seasons expanding in the dry and retracting in the rains.

In all of these situations the language may suggest preferred social relationships but not their inevitability, or indeed their existence; a child cannot be taught or learn that their mother's brothers are someone specially helpful and sympathetic if in fact there are none. Moreover they learn soon enough that such relationships can be invented for people from whom they want to receive good treatment even though they are no relatives at all as indeed do English children who are taught to call their parents long-term friends as "uncle" and "aunt".

A Sukuma talking about his or her interests out of hearing of his neighbours would be as individualistic as a western town dweller but when they are seated with others round an evening fire or beer pot, they are not likely to talk in such terms because it would be rather like disclosing one's long-term business plans to rivals under the mistaken ideas that because they had known each other since birth they were friends. All children in any culture would become aware early in their lives that their parents behave and talk in different ways to different people of which "on stage" and "off-stage" is one clear division.

Although ethnic and religious divisions account for much very communalism, sometimes a community is divided seemingly on quite trivial differences. The isolated village of Mkwaja on the Tanzanian coast was divided into two by a shallow usually dry ditch over which it was possibly to walk and yet the gossip lines of the people who lived on each side were quite separate.

What children will remember is the sheer utility of communalism cum-neighbourliness; the digging of graves in hard soil when it has to be done quickly. Neighbours are needed to carry the injured and sick to hospital which is as necessary today in the mountains of Madeira as it would be in semi-deserts of northern Kenya.

Children may not appreciate the intricacies of long-term reciprocities, but they will certainly appreciate early on that "we" is a necessary part of life and when it is no longer necessary or does not work because the neighbours have nothing to offer or are always changing, that "I" becomes a more active possibility. In most societies which are subsistence based whether down and outs in London or farmers in Brazil, children are likely to appreciate the importance of a varying communalism to both themselves and their parents.

There are too many variations within these communalistic and individualistic categories to make them into valid separate and wide ranging ones, particularly as to what children become socialized into as they grow up in which family situations may vary if not from day to day but certainly over the seasons.

All must experience their nuclear family or at least the group within which they grow up in collectivist terms; it is a very potent "we" and it is only very gradually as they grow up that they realise the enormity of the outside world. A "them" group which is moreover a mass that is always on the verge of threatening them. No child is brought up to see this outside world as an "us" in which they are freely at home.

Clearly some children such as those brought up as Amish will have the concept of a much wider "us" than their nuclear families in which everyone in this category dresses alike, speaks the same dialect and behaves in similar ways throughout the year. But for these children "them" are even more potentially threatening because they are so obvious so that as they grow up in territorially concentrated communities which are not territorially distinct except in the form of their farming, they are brought up collectively. They are likely to be as covertly individually motivated as any other individuals if only in having to choose whom they wish to marry.

This would be even more so with the Hutterites amongst whom the residentially separate nuclear family does not exist as eating and all domestic functions are carried out collectively, just as it was in the early Jewish kibbutz settlements in Palestine and Israel until many were forced to change to reconstituted family living within their lessening collectivist idealism.

Hutterite children are brought up in geographically distinct communities in which there are no infiltrated spaces filled with non-Hutterites, but in their personal appearance they are not distinguishable. They know that their way of living is different to the outside world and it is as strong an "us" and "them" situation as with the Amish. Both these ways of living are very different if not deviant to what Americans and Canadians would feel to be a normal modern way of living and so catch the eye and imagination of observers. The Doukhebour communalism is even more extreme when the protests of young and old alike at the invasion of their way of life and thinking by the Canadian authorities, is to take off their clothes in public as in the court rooms in which they are being prosecuted.

Indian Hindu society has large numbers of caste and sub-caste communities which have none of the more obvious exclusivities of either the Amish or the Hutterites. Their children are brought up to see themselves as part of social units which are always on the move relative to other such small units negotiating possible changes in caste status by hypergamous marriages and taking into practice some of the rituals of slightly superior sub-castes to improve their own status.

While Hindu society whether in farming or in paid employment in industry, is as individualistic as in any other competitive social environment, it is unusual in that children are brought up to see themselves as slotted in relative to other socio-religious groups either superior or inferior to themselves which are locally expressed. A village may be divided in many different ways along caste lines which will affect where they live and what they do so that children will be socialised into minor communalisms which exclude rather more than they include in terms of their pay-offs. For such children it is a built-in discriminatory situation which has none of the persisting benefits in religious and social equality which comes to those who are living the Amish and Hutterite way of life.

Children are always aware of their own individuality and that this is both constrained and developed through the communal life around them but they become early aware that this is a varying relationship and that when they live in the urban-industrial world communalism is much less strong and does not provide much of a pay-off for pro-social behaviour by those who live there. It is then that the child's individuality may become more apparent without getting any of the reciprocal benefits which were more obvious in subsistence communities.

## Boxed in Nature of Contemporary Child Life

Anything approaching a sedentary walled-in home base may have come very late into human social life and at its earliest it would appear to have been an open-sided cave or lean-tos of branches. Being brought up in a house is comparatively new.

Leaving aside the fact that the ethological background to modern man was that of hunter-gatherers, the majority of contemporary children are brought up under conditions of subsistence farming carried out from permanent housing, not under urban living conditions and this has attracted most of the attention from social scientists. What is the difference between these two patterns of living?

The children of farmers whether in Kansas, Kathiawar or Kwangtung live under open door conditions; they can wander in and out. The surroundings of their homes are known and are not filled with parental warnings other than an overall concern for prudent behaviour. Children may play within a wider circle of more or less tensionless neighbourhood in which people and places are well known. There is no lurking hostility because it is the nature of a small group living to masque inter-personal tensions. It may not be a specifically friendly but it is likely to be pleasantly neutral.

In subsistence agricultural societies the child lives in a social environment which has no fixed boundaries. There are vague social rather than geographical ideas of neighbourhoods, often quite large but probably more so for boys than girls. In an Indian village the boundaries of a neighbourhood may be that of the sub-caste to which the family belongs, while among the village-less Sukuma and Oklahoma farmers it would be as far as the next farm.

Moreover amongst these village-less farmers it is an environment which is not dominated by buildings, roads and railways but one which they themselves have changed for their own survival needs. It is not an environment which is intrinsically hostile to them and their children; it is their land. As particular people they have a particularised personal connection with all that they see.

The child in subsistence agricultural communities once they cease to be tied to their mothers, have considerable freedom of movement, except for the Navaho Indians who swaddle their children and hang the children on their boards on the walls of their hogans. They can crawl where they like within the compound which may contain several households rather than houses, an important distinction within the thinking in to which they are socialised. The compound is often fenced to keep animals in and wild animals and cattle thieves out rather than as a marker distinguishing property and people within an area. There is no particular attention paid to toilet training when the floors are dirt, which most children learn in their own time.

Such restrictions as there are relate to prudence and being under the socially acceptable supervision of a sibling only a little older than themselves whom they will learn to call by the honorifics of their birth order seniority. The main trauma for the child may be related to loosing the mother's breast because of a subsequent pregnancy but breast feeding may continue for as long as two years which is an Islamic requirement and it may coincidently related to the spacing of births since lactation delays the resumption of menstruation (Feyisetan, 1990).

In contrast to this the urban child is boxed in and the front door is locked. There may be known neighbours but they are not necessarily friendly and the turn over in occupants is high varying between 10 and 20 per cent annually in Britain and the United States. Even if most moves are within the same postal district, it is always a change in the composition of the immediate neighbourhood and for the children a change of school involving a newset of adults and school related peers.

In most if not all neighbourhoods the proportion of known to unknown people is low whatever the proportions may be, tensions in the neighbourhood of which the growing child is made aware very early in life, make them learn that they live in an unfriendly world in which the primary family group residence may be the only place in which safety can usually be assumed. This would particularly apply to children of minorities with their own languages.

In the contemporary urban-industrial setting particularly in Western societies, the contrast with the subsistence farming pattern of upbringing is very marked. There is no sleeping in the same bed as the mother and little breast or bottle feeding on demand as too much of the mother's time is spent outside the house where this behaviour is either not acceptable since the breast is primarily a sexual object or inconvenient as the mother is working.

The child grows up separated from the mother in a separate room and in the confines of a cage and the mother only becomes aware of the child's distress after prolonged crying. So very early in their lives children are rigorously segregated and penned in from which they cannot escape. When not in a fenced cot, they are often put in play pens and when not in that they are strapped into push chairs, prams or car seats or controlled by harnesses like horses. There is little to distinguish their physical treatment from that of privileged pets as indeed does the form of language with which both are addressed. Great expense and effort is put into very early toilet training for reasons that are social and economic and again rather similar to that used for the training of puppies; it is for the convenience of their parents/owners. It would seem that the Western child experiences not so much a patchwork of restrictions as a comprehensive prevention of any freedom of movement and an almost total inhibition of any natural tendency to explore.

Outside the home the child is surrounded by buildings with which they have no relationship at all to which access is prohibited by a combination of fear, alien faces and closed doors. Once the child goes beyond the home into school, they are similarly boxed in by the requirements of educational administration; they can only enter certain rooms at specified times and have to sit in required places; a world of territorially marked out spaces related to rules (Jenks, 1998).

It is not that the modern urban world can be changed because of its effect on the growing child but to stress that the form of the social and psychological life within which they develop is so very distinct from that into which humans have developed their social institutions.

## Chapter-10

# Parental Care and the Scarcity of Uniformities

If we can assume that there are styles of parenting that are part of the ideologies of particular cultures, then we are faced with two methodological contradictions. Firstly the individuality factors of both the parents, alloparents and children. How in fact can these be identified and studied except by intensive and intrusive studying of families which will alter the social environment of any group being observed.

The second problem is the difficulty over what are supposed to be the cultural patterns for parenting. Those who are prepared to come forward with statements about cultural parenting are a specialised group with viewpoints which may not be elaborations of their own experiences. These opinions could not include within their generalities the varieties which are an inevitable feature of any community regardless of size, traditions and stages of economic and social developments. There can be and are no communities or societies which can be homogeneous to such an extent.

From this we certainly have in existence cultural ideas of what is the correct way for parents to bring up their children and for children to behave while this process is continuing. In the economically developed world child care is subject to fashion and in every society parental care will be inevitably subject to immediate necessities occasioned by deaths, new births, disease and economic and environmental misfortune.

In addition to this we are likely to find patterns of generational differences in what is considered to be appropriate behaviour and in particular disconnections between popular instructional books, professional advice, political expectations and the existential realities of everyday life. The cultural ideas may be crystal clear but quite indistinct when subject to closer inspection.

Cross-culturally the realities of child care and what is considered to be the pro-social behaviour of all involved into which children are deliberately or by accident socialised is along the divide between family situations in which the children are seen from the earliest ages are seen as and are required to act as economic assets necessary for the family to function more or less successfully. The opposite side of this divide is which children from the same ages are recognised as economic liabilities and as continual restrictions on the lives of the adults responsible in law and custom for their socialisation.

In the former situation emotional attachment to children certainly exists but it usually runs parallel to high juvenile mortality rates and the economic usefulness of the survivors; they as it were pay their way in the families in which they are living. Emotional commitment would not be considered to have any priority, while in the latter it would be considered the only valid reason for having children in the first place as they are just not assets. The idea of family continuity is no longer dominant overall.

This division is not a simple one between subsistence cultures and more economically developed ones, but between the "haves" and the "have-nots" in any society. In Western societies with well-developed social welfare systems the differences are partially disguised so that for most families with children there are only economic and social handicaps. Elsewhere the children of the poor can have economic uses despite legislation forbidding such uses.

It seems unlikely that there can be large scale blocks of homogeneous behaviour in which it is safe to conclude that children are brought up in a certain way except in small exclusive communities such as the Amish. Current social analyses may divide societies into rural and urban patterns in which there are broad uniformities. London a large and rambling city contains socially distinct pockets of Orthodox Jewish, Chinese, Afro-Caribbean and Bangladeshi families which have been established there over several generations or which contain several generations within individual families. These families will certainly have some uniform cultural and social features, but uniformities will also occur in the families of diplomats and military personnel as well as in a range of professional occupations in which marriage is often socially endogamous. Such patterning is probably just as common in Delhi, Djakarta and Detroit.

Beyond this there may well be common denominators within which families operate but it is difficult to compare the uniformities in the socialisation practices of Amish communities with their all-round social and economic effectiveness with those of Iranian villagers in whose communities there are clear-cut economic and social divisions.

It would seem likely that there are some cross-cultural themes which involve children and how they may or may not behave. Schooling might be classifiable as a prolonged social and economic disruption of family cohesiveness. Certainly television watching is going to take up an increasing amount of solitary time which might otherwise be taken up with developing inter-relationship skills; the child developing an interior world in which reality has little assessable access.

Secondly whenever and wherever children are no longer potentially economic assets, the family size diminishes whether this is the result of prudence and self-interest of cohabiting adults or under the national compulsions for one-child families in the Peoples Republic of China. One child or no child families are likely to become commoner so that the "Little Emperor" syndrome is likely to become much more than a particular Chinese characteristic.

So it would seem that where children do exist, they will grow up with pro-social requirements which are no longer part of family networks of reciprocities. They will have to learn to create their own networks for which there will no longer be any familiar or family bases. In such situations children are likely to grow up in families in which grandparents not only increasingly survive and contribute to younger generations but for whose terminal care will no longer be shared with siblings but bear directly on only children or devolved onto the State.

Difficult though it may be to study systematically social behaviour at all, it is much easier to study children in situations where their behaviour is restricted by adults responsible for their care than it is to study adults into which most children eventually develop or to study the long processes involved in turning children into adults. Correlations of all sorts have the awkward quality of being unable to decide whether the chicken or the egg came first so that a commitment to a viewpoint contributes to the correlations which may be chosen.

So we have the problem that these enclaves of particular forms of pro-social behaviour may have their origins in the social backgrounds of those involved whether those observed or observing. There is also the added complication of individuality and whether they alone or as a group are subject to what influences from the surrounding society which may have ideologically different concepts of pro-social behaviour and how it should be instilled into children and adolescents.

## Nature *versus* Nurture

When we are faced with the enormous variety of the cultural forms into which children are socialised into pro-social behaviour patterns combined as it must always be with individual personality differences, nurture must be the predominating influence on how children may behave, but it will always be a matter of degree.

It is often taken that nature and nurture are two poles of explanation for human behaviour and indeed for the development of children, and that they have to be expressed as opposition as if one excluded the other in some sort of zero-sum play-off. Both nature and nurture are lump together headings for multiple genetic and socialising factors which come together in specific and highly variable physical and social environments.

This is particularly so in the dilemmas of feminism over sexuality for which social science objectivism twists and turns over physiological sexual differences, ethological and primordial foundations for human social behaviour and the individualism disclosed by psychology (Rosaldo, 1987).

We see it more that nature and nurture are at the most intertwined co-equals in which any form of sectional conclusions must obliterate opposing inevitabilities. It is not a dichotomous situation since there are now numerous examples of the higher anthropoids learning new patterns of behaviour such as the baboons round Lake Naivasha in Kenya learning to chase and kill flamingos and Nigerian monkeys using the leaves of particular shrubs as insecticides. Indeed if it is seen as such it must be because the variations in both dimensions have been abbreviated into unitary concepts. Scientific advancement commonly consists in a progressive complication of what once seemed a beautifully simple set of notions but now seems an unbearably simplistic one (Geertz, 1973 : 33).

The search for origins as a way towards understanding contemporary human behaviour is inevitably fruitless because of the absence of comprehensive enough data and the absence of any datum line from which projections can be made. Certainly nature has its ascertainable dimensions as in DNA identifications, bipedal locomotion, sexual bimorphism and the position of the eyes and thumbs in humans. But this is a gross simplification not only of the number of factors in any consideration of nature but in their dependent variations and the permutations and combinations with which they have reacted to factors outside their control and which even in Parallel Distributive Processing has defeated computerisation except for the simplest of human movements although it has rightly been described as a lure towards finding ways of using multiple data outside a sequential system of analysis (McClelland, 1986).

We can conclude that we are what we are naturally and whatever that is, is too varied for any exactnesses despite this acceptance of nature as a necessary foundation, but if there had been any rigidity in this then nurture would have played a very limited part indeed, and probably as a consequence humans as a species might have died out.

We accept that there has been evolutionary change through processes of constant adaptations which affect the development of children but that these changes need not have been adaptive; they may well have been short-term dead-ends which might have benefited others while leading to the extinction of their own genetic peculiarities as dead-end mutations. It is obvious that new-born higher non-human primates have a social and physiological competence which is only reached by the human child after several years of protected growth; taken out of its social context the human system of immaturity could be classed as maladaptive. Evolution is one way and not necessarily forwards so the direction of what occurs may be obscure and not enabling adaptation to varying environments.

In the sense of child development leading to a biologically and socially adaptive existence as a adults, it seems obvious enough that many biological facets of existence are maladaptive so that a particular biological pattern will die out; it does not reproduce itself as in Turner's (girls born with vestigial ovaries) and Klinefelter's (boys born with vestigial testes and the usual absence of spermatogenesis) syndromes (McKusick, 1969). These are biological dead-ends for any child born with them but not necessarily preventing them from conforming social lives which may influence others since these factors are not visible imperfections since nurture covers them up.

While these abnormalities would not affect gender attributions, their sexual status means that their chromosome abnormalities are not going to be passed on and that if any social behaviour is passed on to a subsequent generation because of their bearers institutional or personal charisma will not have much to do with their biological status.

Now social ability to reproduce or not may not be considered the most obvious of biological characteristics in the sense that individuals can or cannot produce descendents. But when this is tied to visible abnormalities such as cartilage hair hypoplasia a form of dwarfism of which the number among the Old Order Amish (McKusick. *et al.*, 1965) equal the known number in the rest of the world, then clearly nature and nurture coincide in attempting to block off the reproduction of this abnormality without of course nurture knowing about the carrying forward of recessive genes in otherwise normal people.

Other biological characteristics which are visually accepted as abnormal are all negative ones against reproduction but the positive ones which presumably have a similar genetic origin have yet to be identified so exactly. The Amish who in-breed for socio-religious reasons have so far provided 12 previously unknown genetic disorders in their communities and a further 18 which occur amongst them as well as in the wider population could certainly be described as a quite unusual accumulation of biological disadvantages in any breeding population; yet the Amish way of life is successful enough to have continued communally for several centuries while being surrounded by quasi-hostile social environments.

Amongst the Amish nurture has responded to overcome these multiple problems in the sense that their defectives are never institutionalised unless their behaviour proves dangerous to their community. But despite endogamy which they certainly see as the best way to perpetuate their religious and social ideals and to bring up their children in righteousness, the relative absence of birth control or rather the restraint on sexual intercourse by only the older multipara, has meant large numbers of children offsetting the loses from continued inbreeding. This would seem to be a clear example of at least partially planned nurture overcoming the handicaps of nature.

Nature would certainly seem to provide the genetic programming for continued breeding without much regard for specific biological characteristics of breeding pairs or indeed the extent to which man as a species may be over-breeding. So we cannot state that even this characteristic is adaptive.

An example of the possible direct intertwining of nature and nurture may be the Papuan degenerative disease of the central nervous system which was first thought to be hereditary through the female line since only women were affected. Then it was found that the women were eating parts of the bodies of dead non-relatives (Glasse, 1967) which was taught to young children as part of their socialisation. When this was discouraged and replaced by other meat in their funeral ceremonies, the disease died away so it was no longer thought to be genetically carried (Gajdusek, 1973). It has now appeared again suggesting either that it was genetic or alternatively that some women have returned to this practice as its abolition had been correlated in their minds to a variety of misfortunes associated with modernity. In either situation but to an unknown extent children are being socialised to some unusual moral understandings according to Western thought which is similarly a product of nurture.

Thus it would seem that nurture socialises humans to a preferred degree of inbreeding which is likely to lead to the carrying forward of disadvantageous genes which nurture again manages to circumvent unless the carriers are not seen as socially acceptable for breeding purposes. To a noticeable extent nurture develops ways of coping with what would otherwise be the restrictions of nature.

It is perhaps easiest to see how the foundations laid by nature in providing most individuals with one or the other forms of sexuality which dominate their social behaviour but nurture has turned this into an enormous variety of different social forms into which children are socialised apart from related fantasies. The predetermination of biological sex and its failure to account for its social and psychological forms argues "the case of the cognitive self-construct in the minds of the individual over his or her organic programme in the determination of action" (Reynolds, 1976: 125).

Nature certainly provides some restrictions and enablement which humans receive at birth but the varieties of societies, sub-societies and groupings which humans have development makes nurture a much more important factor in considering the moral development of children in what are now all polyvalent social environments.

Even if we accept as we must the mathematical inevitabilities of inherited DNA with its multiplicity of unduplicatable individual alternatives, there is another aspect which points to the dominance of nurture over nature in the moral developments of the contemporary growing child.

It has been pointed out that some fifty thousand information "chunks", units of meaning, are needed to play a sophisticated game of chess and to speak a language reasonably proficiently a typical adult probably knows between several hundred thousand and several million "chunks" (D'Andrade,1981:180). These are the "chunks" which almost all children who are not mentally handicapped, learn quite early in their lives.

If knowledge is so distributed in society that everybody does not have all the same "chunks" as indeed it must be with regard to age, sex and experience, its total information pool may be a hundred to ten thousand times larger than the knowledge of any one individual. It would this contain something between a few million and ten billion "chunks" of information. There is a greater complexity to this if culture is seen as a collective rather than an individually based structure of meaning. Some cultures as indeed would be those in which the average modern child is developing, would have larger inventories of differentiated meaning (Hannerz, 1992: 7-8). These children accumulate the "chunks" which in smaller societies and in family groupings are largely obtained from consociates with whom they are in face to face relationships. However through the media they have a much wider range of contemporaries who may and indeed will influence children although they never have and never will meet them (Schutz, 1967).

In our analysis of the cross-cultural moral development of the growing child it would seem that nurture is overwhelmingly the most important factor while in no way diminishing the foundational importance of nature.

## Early Influences towards Pro-social Behaviour

It is perhaps unwise to conclude that the earliest influences on a child whether for good or bad, can be correlated to their behaviour latter in life since these are always going to be overlaid by subsequent serious and influential experiences in any social environment.

Traumatic events are just as likely to mark a child's consciousness and determine behaviour at whatever age they occur and in fact there can be no child, adolescent or adult whose lives are not regularly marked off by what they experience as crises which will have radically altered their ways of living and presumably their accompanying patterns of thinking.

It is more likely to be the other way round that individuals normally have lives which consciously and unconsciously move from one crisis to another in their own eyes, if not also in the eyes of outsiders; this is the dialectical ability which makes individuals and the human species as a whole able to survive in so many radically different environments.

We tend to concentrate on what cultural patterns suggest and indeed lay down this as normality. This is not the normality within which children are reared; an amorphous indefinable state with its pervasive minor variations but how they are socialised to cope with the invasive changes with which each individual at whatever age or in whatever community are faced.

The ways in which macro outside changes affect the upbringing of children is rarely a singular one despite the case with which it can be attributed for example to the Chinese and Russian revolutions. Humans have always affected their environments which can be destructive as in some of the Indian irrigation societies of the south-western United States leading to their extinction or emigration or constructively as with the Mormon dominance of quasi-deserts in the same general area in the 19th century. There must have been differences in the adult attitudes of those involved passed on to their children which will have been reflected in their abilities to survive. The need to achieve in the Mormon case will have enhanced the pro-social demands on children in such areas.

The point may be that much social and environmental changes affecting Chinese and Russian farmers when agriculture was centralised into communal farms much too rapidly for the chain of influence in child–training practices to have affected infant personalities and then to have gone on into adult behaviour (McClelland, 1981: 84).

In such situations the adults may have reacted in one way as their previous ways of livelihood were drastically modified while their children may have reacted differently in the need to achieve in situations which were communal rather than familial. The adults change perhaps because they have to or their ideas may have changed through ideological conversion to religion, communism or whatever which is passed on in a different form to their children. This may have more obvious affects in adulthood than centuries of culture bound child rearing practices.

Patterns of behaviour learnt in childhood and which continue into adulthood are bound to reflect the particular conditions of the families in which they are reared as well as the surrounding geographical and social environment. An adolescent Arab boy in a well-to-do Gulf family with over fifty indoor servants is not growing up in an environment likely to stimulate either initiative or effort. On the other hand the higher achievement motivations of the Nigerian Ibo as a whole and their relative success in business, combined with an open status mobility social system seems to have encouraged personal efforts and the public recognition of success (LeVine, 1973).

More ascetic Protestant Christianity has on occasions caused small endogamous sects to be materially successful. The Seventh day Adventists became dominant in the early years of the Sukuma cotton cooperatives in Tanzania as they did not drink or dance which kept them apart from mainstream Sukuma society. Apart from this their Saturday worship kept them socially isolated which led to their business mindedness becoming appreciated by the cotton growers who voted them into executive positions. This seems also to have occurred in two neighbouring Mexican villages in which one converted as a whole into a form of fundamentalist Christianity so that their children showed signs of higher achievement motivations than those in the traditional village (McClelland, 1961). In both the cases children will have grown up in communities in which religious commitment gave them local advantages. Had this religious sectionalism been socially and economically dominant over a wider area, this stimulus might not have been so common or visible. In the Sukuma case the Seventh day Adventists came to prominence over a five year period in which the cooperatives were formed and this can have had no obvious correlations with child training.

## Official Concern for Parental Failures

A distinguishing feature of the urban industrial world as well as those societies which aspire to this status is their concern over children whose parents have failed to care for them or who have failed to become socialised to pro-social patterns of behaviour and in many cases have become actively anti-social. Most of the legislation has been patterned on laws passed in western democratic states which have long histories of involvement in welfare of deprived children and their employment at early ages which together with women was certainly to the advantage of working adult men.

In economically developed societies parental control of children occurs all the time within the privacies of their homes and proportionately behind closed doors out of sight and hearing of neighbours. What happens there is not particularly enabled or restrained by what the law allows them to do or prohibits them from doing. Violence against children in family settings which seems to have generational correlations, may be more related to the sense of what is right to do in particular circumstances than by the background restraints which exist in the officials of Social Security departments and public charities for the protection of children.

There is certainly ample literature about the activities of governments and charities attempting to counter parental failure to socialise children pro-socially and the activities of juvenile courts. By starting out to have as its objectives the socialisation of children to the pro-social requirements of the larger surrounding society, it is inevitable that should always be children who will fail to behave according to these minimal standards.

Contemporary urban-industrial societies are much concerned with these disruptive failures and so have developed social welfare industries to cope with parental and juvenile failures to conform. The potential to be delinquent is coped with by the social structures and behavioural systems of traditional societies which thus appear to avoid having any such classification as juvenile delinquent just as bad parenting appears to have been coped with by internal social politics of each extended family. This seems to be the contemporary case with exclusive communities such as the Amish, Hutterites and in Israeli kibbutz.

However today the majority of young either live in quasi-traditional communities of subsistence farmers or herdsmen or in urban slums which are outside the range and capabilities of centrally organised city development; the septic fringes of Cairo, Lima, Calcutta and Capetown.

Parental care and the pro-social behaviour of children varies with the types of communities in which they occur and it is only in small scale exclusive communities that this now occurs with any degree of social success.

## Pro-social Behaviour in Exclusive Communities

Exclusive communities such as the Amish have had much adverse publicity under a range of contexts; they are considered to be over-restrictive of individuality and forcefully preventing their members from modernising; by outside standards the Amish environment is limited and restrictive so that their children are deprived of their American rights of opportunity to personal development.

The children are brought up in on-going communities in which they benefit from an early age as being responsibly active in farming and are taught all that is necessary to fulfil this role and its religious justifications in a non-competitive environment by teachers who are part of their own believing community. Since the Amish are so visibly different by their pattern of living and appearance they have been well researched for biological (Reynolds and Tanner, 1995) as well as social characteristics.

Amish babies are rarely alone and are held during most of their waking hours and are rarely fed on a strict time schedule. As children they are taught to respect authority by obedience as in less developed societies. Work is seen as helping others and fulfilling their responsibilities to them for which they are rarely thanked. The switch is used freely but not harshly and tears are discouraged as a response to physical pain or in self-pity. Physical but not intellectual initiative is encouraged and asking questions is severely channelled. As in other cultures children learn by observing and imitating rather than by asking.

The Amish believe that children have inherited a sinful nature but are considered to be teachable in the proper environment of this community so that in adulthood they would be responsible to God and man for their actions. Parents are responsible for training their children rather than their schools (Hostetler and Huntington, 1971).

This form of upbringing and its success in comparison to the more frequent failures in the wider outsider society has to be seen in the social environment which these Amish communities provide; a high standard of living, community self-help and successful farming. In many ways the Amish way of ensuring the pro-social behaviour of their children is a modernised version of traditional subsistence communities which may have once existed in Asia and Africa.

## Pro-social Behaviour in Subsistence Communities

If one examines the role of children in subsistence families it would be more realistic to describe them as production units for insuring the annual survival of a small group of adults; it is hard to see children as having any immediate roles other than contributing to production.

Of course they are links to the social, economic and political futures of particular men and in a few cases women but their primary purpose is to provide an additional source of farming labour in proportion to their abilities. They do not have separate roles as children who should be protected as far as possible from the difficulties experienced by their parents and alloparents.

As soon as they are able they start to be integrated into the needs of their guardians so that they do not have separate social lives nor special periods when they are at play. The use of children as workers is necessary and constant. It may even be that children who have such supportive roles feel that they are useful and indeed important in their own ways; they take the cattle to water and grazing and they sit on platforms above fields of ripening grain throwing stones and balls of mud to keep off birds and monkeys. They lead useful lives from which education takes them away so disturbing the balance of work in their families who get little if anything in return from the absence of these extra pairs of hands.

## Pro-social Behaviour in Inclusive Communities

There are certainly societies which have an overall theme some which relate to political dominances such as Communist Russia and China until their recent relaxation of ideology. Others have much more persistent and long lasting religious dominances such as Hindus in India and Muslims and their diasporas.

Hinduism as it is without definitions and sacred dogmatic literature, has many variations around the overall dominance of caste which are visible in all villages and towns as well as in their overseas communities in Trinidad, Fiji, Britain and Malaysia. The orthodox religious subordination of women to father, husband and son is clear enough is likely to be highly varied in practice as a result of education, poverty, employment and the political opportunities provided by the democratic vote and the absence of husbands working away from their home environments. There are so many variations of family composition that it would be hard to find any overall patterns which are not subdivided by social circumstances.

What Hindu children learn from their homes is likely to relate to the permutations of caste in village communities and their relative freedom from this in towns. Rather more than the pro-social requirements of domesticity, they will learn the importance of caste solidarity in the new political environment of democratic India. In the families of the diaspora Hindu values will have been increasingly subordinated to the social requirements of their new economic environments. Children will be made aware of Hindu values in the celebration of rites of passage and popular communal festivals almost as an antidote to the anonymity of these new environments.

Islam with its divinely inspired legalism has a more pervasive influence over the pro-social learning of children when the national law is Islamic and there is no provision for reinterpretation concerning personal and local situational factors. The very rigidity of Islamic laws over marriage, rights of men, women and children and the distribution of inheritance would suggest that there is always going to be locally accepted variations. Other than the acceptance of the Five Pillars of Faith which are obligatory on all Muslims there are likely to be substantial variations in their domestic arrangements between Kabul, Cairo and villages in Morocco, the Sudan and Iran within the framework of marital instability and the prevalence of domestic alloparenting.

The Latter Day Saints of Utah would appear to have had a substantial influence over the pro-social behaviour of their children with much lower rates for most forms of social upsets than in other states which do not have such an overall particular institutionalised political and social influence.

## Pro-social Behaviour of Children in Septic Fringe Communities

A striking feature of contemporary life must be the growth of cities without adequate provision for the immigrants moving in from the countryside to have a reasonable standard of living. The slums of Rio de Janiero, Addis Ababa, Caíro, Lagos and Calcutta are perhaps beyond the capabilities of any government to remedy, however willing and competent so it is not surprising that there has developed a culture of poverty. Its characteristic feature is the predominance of matrifocal families in which any male presence is irregular and transitory.

Where there are no welfare systems to support such family groups, they are subsistence communities with far shorter periods for which foresight is possible. Employment is short-term and irregular and children are expected to help where they can so much so that often the street children of Latin America may be major contributors to their families. Girls can get domestic employment and their paid jobs in match and carpet factories despite being forbidden by legislation as well as juvenile prostitution are the only barriers against destitution. What children learn in such environments is not the cohesiveness of a family based on shared work but almost certainly a strong trend towards selfishness.

**Pro-social Behaviour in Bureaucratically Controlled Communities**

In most societies there has been a growth of the involvement of children and indeed adults in communities and organisation in which standards of required behaviour are laid down by authority and usually in written form. Expatriate communities in Islamic countries, military cantonments, boarding schools, factories and so on are all controlled by written regulations. Even in housing blocks in city settings there are tenancy regulations. Even the time-table with behaviour controlled by the clock is an imposition on natural behaviour which is not created for the convenience or on the wishes of children and adolescents.

The arbitrary nature of these institutions ruled by regulations leads almost inevitably to the creation by children and adolescents of alternative behaviour patterns which run counter to such official requirements. The children learn to live in a two tiered system in which much behaviour is pre-defined as both illegal and often as deviance.

**The Cultural Frameworks of Thinking**

In this context there are two issues affecting pro-social socialisation. Firstly situations in which the children grow within a single culture and do not have any personal contacts with outsider adults and their experience of other cultures is essentially peripheral to their focal experience of being brought up within a single cultural neighbourhood.

Secondly there are children whose domestic family experiences are within one culture and in a language connected to that culture, whose experiences outside the home in education and economics are within other cultures and in other languages. This would include Turkish children living in Hamburg, Bangladeshi ones in London and Punjabis living in Delhi and any number of quasi-tribal children living in Shillong, Kampala, Onitsha and Las Vegas.

While it is easy to point out the differences in patterns of thought between small distinct cultures such as that of the Dinka of the Southern Sudan or the Yanomamo Indians of Brazil, this may be largely due to their isolation in anthropological studies. They are not literate or indeed numerous enough to make them distinctive in comparison to the broader and more comprehensive Eastern-Western patterns of cultural thinking and behaving and the influence of subsistence imperatives on all such cultures as factors in the socialisation of children.

The Dinka (Lienhardt, 1961: 149, 155-6) think that memories are acting extensively on them and are the sources from which they are derived rather than things retained in the mind. So Dinka children would have been socialised to see their personal past as a living present parallel to what they are experiencing now. But the study on which these conclusions were made took place in a relatively peaceful time except for their constant skirmishes with the Nuer to their south. It is not known to what extent such distinctive patterns of thought have survived prolonged civil war and famine. Children would now have been brought up within the needs of continuing gun carrying uncertainties in which cultural distinctions may have been blurred and new ones created.

The distinction of such micro-patterns of quite distinctive metaphysical understandings perhaps rely too much on the findings of individual anthropologists and cultural biased missionaries and the difficulties of translation into macro-languages long committed to literacy. It is always an important practical issue as to whether metaphysical matters can indeed be translated at all over the boundaries of language groups.

The macro-cultural divides between the East and the West and the overriding concern for survival over the next hand-to-mouth period of time, must be the matrix which will dominate the socialisation of children. Firstly the macro-cultural divide between the East and the West in which the former has existed in a literate and influential form far longer than the more recent West which has tended to dominate social science thinking and practice.

This distinction came to the fore in the prolonged discussions between Jesuit missionaries in China and their Chinese Confucian counterparts, who found themselves in a different cultural system and its supportive ways of thinking (Gernet, 1985: 146, 203). The Jesuits found that the whole range of classical Western dichotomies did not exist; mind and body, self and world, spiritual; and material, rational and sensible. As the philosopher Huang Zhou wrote "the mode of action of Heaven and Earth can be summed up in a single word, it is not double" (Gernet, 1985: 205).

A high proportion of social science evaluations of pro-social behaviour of children have been done within the schemas devised by thinkers in Western patterns. Whether or not this is the right one is not the issue since there are other systems of thought which have social consequences and to which children are exposed domestically which may be quite distinct from what they encounter under the literate regimentation of formal schooling.

There are and have been many "immigrant" communities in Europe, Asia and Africa in which adults have the fluent use of one language outside the home for business, administration and politics, but use a "home" language domestically and in talking with friends. It is not possible to walk near to young people in Britain who are visibly alien to the dominant culture without hearing that they are talking Yoruba, Arabic, Spanish or Mandarin, even when they have just emerged from the doorways of language schools teaching them English.

In the case of Eastern thought it has been able to continue independently of any Western scientific and linguistic influences; these cultures involve so many millions of people that their understandings are self-sustaining. Nevertheless there are some small cultures which retain their identity in thought such as the Ojibwa Indians of Canada as a means of psychological survival despite being meshed into a social system dominated by "whites". Amongst the Canadian Cree Indians to live like a white is close to being stupid and crazy (Berry & Bennett, 1992).

Thus to the Chinese thinker such divisions as "us" and "them" should be expressed as "we" and it seems likely that in Bantu language use "we" is more frequently used than "I". The personal prayers of Swahili girls were predominantly couched in terms of "we" rather than "I". Max Weber (Weber, 1951: 156) wrote of the Chinese central concept of propriety in which the individual always aims at being harmoniously attuned to all social situations with watchful self-control, self-observation and reserve. Similarly the Japanese are apt to view themselves as objects in the eyes of others rather than as being the subject (Heine et al., 1999).

Western cultures emphasize self-experience as an autonomous independent entity. In the tight interdependent East Asian contexts the self is fundamentally interconnected in relationships with important others. They construct a spontaneous social reality from a less ego-centred but more overall vantage point than Westerners do (Cohen and Gunz, 2002). The overseas educated Malaysian Chinese adolescent went round every Sunday to his grandfather's house along with other relatives in order to talk about family affairs and nothing else.

The macro-context in which Eastern children are raised and maintained through the medium of their domestic environments and languages to which are subtended their religious-cum-magical understandings, have a stronger control over them than Western style education because it extends beyond the micro-environments in which they are raised.

The family's involvement in Hinduism which is likely to be the substratum of their domestic life is immediately reinforced by their children's experience of life outside; it is too general to be relegated to a more circumscribed religious slot of behaviour. The child in a Western Christian family unless they are members of Amish and Hutterite communities, leaves anything remotely Christian as soon as they step outside; there is no correlating reinforcement.

In Buddhism, Hinduism and Shinto there are fundamental questions such as the identity of the self, the relationship of the body to the mind, the place of nature in the constitution of human individuals and of society and the nature of logic and science are there addressed in a way that allows the formulation of an alternative cosmology. These factors are so fundamental to human understandings of the environment in which they live that they are bound to affect the socialisation of children within such cultures whether or not these ways of thinking have been committed to writing.

## Inter-society Variables: The Question of Values

It is obvious enough that there are immense and to all intents and purposes unbridgeable methodological gaps in studying cultures as divergent as communities in Greenland, the society of the capital of Iceland and that of the Norwegian capital Oslo, even though they are more or less in the same cultural strata. When the comparisons are extended to the Toureg living on the edge of the Sahara, refugee camps in Palestine and Thailand and those living in Brazilian urban shanty towns, then the hopes of having scientifically acceptable comparisons available evaporates.

We are left with the comparisons of customs which are more or less parallel to the volumes of Frazer's Golden Bough in which behaviour is grouped under themes which may or may not have any underlying similarities (Frazer, 1922/1963). What is being linked in such an enormous compendium of disparate behaviour, is the cultural understandings of the author as when he links religion and magic in the subtitle.

When social scientists trained in the western traditions of a culturally based science, reach comparative conclusions about the childhood of people living in the flood plains of the Yangtse, Ganges and Euphrates. Then using the same terms and their understandings and apply them to the slum dwellers in Moscow, Karachi, Ibadan and Lima, the futility of comparison becomes self-evident.

It is not that the behavioural patterns of children, parents and everyone else involved with children are different since they have to be fed, housed, clothed and disciplined, but the standards within each culture by which acceptable and unacceptable ways of bringing up children are not shared across cultures and probably not even between the different social sections of a particular society.

Western standards of child care and development are focused on particular children as individuals being cared for within long and predictable periods by legally obligated parents. This is very evident in the assessment of the needs of children which are assumed even in the pronouncements of the United Nations. 'The child, for the full and harmonious development of his personality, needs love and understanding. He shall wherever possible, grow up in the care and under the responsibility of his parents, and in any case in an atmosphere of affection and moral and material security; a child of tender years shall not, save in exceptional circumstances, be separated from his mother (United Nations, 1989). This is a statement from within Western cultural understandings in support of monotropism. Thus there can be substantial criticism of any politically motivated and well intentioned documents which talk about the universal value of a particular pattern of bringing up children (Woodhead, 1997).

This viewpoint nevertheless is one which is globally stressed by many social welfare agencies as the standard which is best for children and which should be supported internationally. Variations to the theme of monotropism do not have much say in the creation of these standards so that they continue under the implied slur of deviance since there may be little or no evidence that the children of such societies suffer from what Western values define as unsatisfactory care.

Many societies have the care-taking of children by several individuals and in almost all subsistence societies siblings dominate as the carers of younger children (Weisner and Gallimore, 1977), just as there are societies such as the Ghanian Gonja (Goody, E, 1970) in which a high proportion of children are fostered out to relatives and friends. In fact there are numbers of societies in which the biological father may have little to do with his children since authority over them is vested in the mother's brother as among the matrilineal Yao of Tanzania and functionally dissipated in polygynous families in which the father maintains several separate households for fecund wives. There is little compelling evidence that monotropism is the only way in which children can be successfully reared although it can be shown in particular societies and social conditions that its absence can have unfortunate results. In western societies it has been shown that children who have been institutionalised for long periods are likely to have behavioural problems in adolescence (Hodges & Tizzard, 1989), but this accurate but culture bound data cannot be used for assessing the behaviour of children in other cultures who may have little to do with their biological parents and who have relationships diffused over several adults. We have already referred to the Zigua child in Tanzania who in the first five years of his life, spent only eighteen months with his parents; no one in that village thought that this was unusual or indeed the subject of comment.

The inheritance of widows by brothers of the deceased when it has often been the case that men marry younger women, is a reasonable provision for their care and that of their children. The British attempt to abolish this custom in parts of Tanganyika had virtually no effect on what families actually did to care for widows.

The monotropic thought of Western societies has made the step-mother the personification of misery for the children involved, just as the co-wife in polygynous societies is made to perform the same role of having a wide range of malpractices attributed to them. However in many societies in which long lasting marriages are unusual and the normal pattern whether caused by early deaths or interpersonal tensions, the step relationships may be the commonest type of parenthood experienced by children.

Of course in some types of societies there are points in common so that a mother-in-law English joke translates easily enough into a Swahili speaking patrilineal audience, but this same joke would be unintelligible in a matrilineal society in which a man's struggles would be with his sister's husband's family trying to get control of the children which are not his responsibility.

The behaviour of monkeys has been found to be far from uniform. Some are gregarious and share the care of infants while others live in closely knit family units and are exclusive in their patterns of child care (Schaffer, 1977). While direct parallels to human child care cannot be made but it would seem significant that it can be assumed that if the children of one species were brought up in another type of community, there would be some very socially disturbed young monkeys. This would suggest that there can be no uniformities in how children should be brought up to the best advantage of both themselves and the communities in which they are living.

It is by no means clear that there can be a "best" or even a "worst" system of bringing up children or indeed that there should be any model at all of what should be aimed at once they have been fed, clothed and protected from violence and mass diseases. It could also be argued that the monotropism of Western societies has been less than successful in bringing up children adequately with its high levels of juvenile delinquency and the inability of these children in adulthood to maintain permanent relationships.

We have to conclude that cross-cultural comparisons have their best value in stimulating thoughts about the dead-end of cultural biases and that once children have their basic needs met for health, the question of the pursuit of happiness in the context of what is required of children pro-socially, has to be studied and the conclusions retained for each society in partial and fragmentary isolation from its neighbours.

## Parent-child Typologies

It is difficult to find any research on the pro-social behaviour of children that does not have as their key data based on their relationships with their parents and their families as a whole, but these families however defined are always part of some wider society which dictates the parameters within which they function; these parameters are similarly always a mixture of the ideals at which societies and individuals aim and the realities of each separate individual social existence.

Any typology of parent-child relationships is bound to provide problems, firstly because existing ones are likely to be based mainly on the knowledge gained from social science research on small samples of western European and north American families usually tied more to laboratory and experimental work rather than on long-term field work observations.

Secondly because such typologies are based to a large extent on ideal concepts of stability; that family forms are either stable or should be so for pro-social behaviour to be developed. To describe a social relationship as stable enough to be part of any such typology must impose a consistency over-time which cannot exist in human relationships particularly parent-child ones. We can presuppose that in any such relationship the children are proportionately changing more rapidly in behaviour, understanding and overall biological and psycho-social capacity than their parents. If stability has to be given as the principal characteristic of any social relationship it might perhaps be applied to an elderly couple who have lived together in the same community in reasonable good health and economic stability for ten years or so. It cannot be applied to any parent-child relationship.

Also every family however constituted is being continually and irregularly changed by crises which effect what its members do and are able to do; there is always ill-health, quarrels with neighbours and relatives, short-falls between what its members want to do and what they can afford; the relationships are in a constant state of flux due to factors which are usually outside their control and which they can only ameliorate or come to terms with.

Thirdly there are substantial cultural differences in parent-child relationships both within a society and between societies and cultures. It is necessary to take into consideration contemporary American Indian, Chinese, Japanese, Indian, sub-Saharan African and Arab cultures. The many and varied ways in which the families in these cultures vary from the ideal isolated nuclear family of western urban-industrial societies; isolated moreover only in comparison to societies in which families are more closely integrated into their immediate social environments. These modern urban-industrial families are integrated into other and more distant social environments but never isolated except in rare cases of extreme deviance from all acceptable social norms of their societies. This is without going into the parent-child relationships in small "exotic" groups which vary from the more average ones in their millions within any large culture. There is no particular value in bringing into consideration such family systems as can be seen in United States Mormon polygynous families relying on social security for their survival and the various types of urban and rural communal living.

Finally there are the difficulties in considering the parent-child relationship in theoretical isolation when in fact no inter-relationship can be isolated except by artificial categorisation. This theoretical triad of father-mother-child always involves many more people for various periods; other relatives and in-laws, friends, neighbours, employers, employees, fellow workers, together with the demands of earning their living or survival in subsistence or competitive societies which may mean that a parent or parents are often absent and the child in effect becomes a worker, apart from the separations involved in formal education. These situations may change not only on a daily basis but within the day so that in any analysis the child may be moving from one category of analysis to another. This chess-board situation means that the pro-social behaviour required of, learnt by and taught to children involve many more factors than the assumed stability of any formal or quasi-formal parental relationship.

Thus we start by looking at parent-child relationships in what are assumed to be relatively enduring relationships because they are easiest to study and because they have special significance for the individuals concerned as they provide strong, frequent and diverse causal interconnections (Kelly et al., 1983). Further where there are interruptions in these inter-relationships which have created mutual expectations then there are likely to be emotional upsets affecting both parents and children (Bercheid, 1986). These are of course culturally loaded expectations which may or may not involve any one form of stability or indeed emotion and may in fact exist nowhere except in the emotions of those involved. While we know of the emotionalised romanticism in popular cheap novels in literate societies, there is no reason to suppose that non-literates and oral cultures generally do not have some equivalent hopes and dreams interior to themselves of equal force.

There is a constant process of adaptation of all those involved which has pro-social importance and which may circumvent the development of emotional and social problems. Even when the child is a pre-conscious infant there are linkages in which the former adapts to the caretaker(s) and the latter adapt to the infant; there is a continuous process of adaptation (Maccoby, 1999: 157-175).

It is the cross-cultural variations which need to be examined as to which are more efficient in producing pro-socially motivated children and what are the parameters for the pro-social behaviour required of children; what are the requirements in cultures or sub-cultures in which the father is deliberately and acceptably absent and those in which he is just absent as in the majority of West Indian parent-child relationships; the presence or absence of scheduled relationships between parents and children in which the children are looked after by non-relatives as in boarding schools for professional class children in Britain and the widespread fostering out of children in Ghana

(Goody, E, 1970) who were assessed as not being handicapped latter in either marriage or careers; the situation in polyandrous families in which there are several fathers married to then one mother and polygynous families in which the children functionally may have several mothers; finally the differences for the pro-social requirements for children in patrilineal and matrilineal societies and between patrilocal, matrilocal and neolocal families.

It is also possible that within a single family there may be a variety of acceptable parent-child relationships; a coercive one over school and family work; an hierarchical one in when it comes to arranging the marriage of a child, the network of benevolence within a family for which the playwrite J.M. Barie coined the phrase "dear octopus" as well as the segregation of sex roles as to who does what during a normal day's inter-relationships.

## The Factor of Coercion

Few if any families are run on democratic principles in which the children's votes have equal value to those of their parents although in some families in economically developed societies there may be a range of discussions of what the family should do as to holidays. In most families in urban-industrial societies, the children are an economic and emotional drain on their parents who get little return on their parenthood. In subsistence societies the children are expected to work as early in their lives as possible and to the extent of their abilities; this is not voluntary and usually receives no thanks; they are expected to help their own families to survive in a straight forward material way and there can be no argument as to whether they should or should not do such work.

In patrilineal societies the boys may see their family as something from which they will eventually get a material return, but not so clearly if there is a segmentary social system in which the first born inherits and the other sons hive-off. The Islamic inheritance system which limits the amount that can be left in wills to individuals or outside institutions such as religious trusts, gives all children, relatives and wives a fixed proportion of any inheritance so that children are brought up with these expectations and no doubt find out early in their lives that these assessments and divisions divide families and are sources of dispute, just as they do in families in which there is testamentary inheritance.

In societies in which there are arranged marriages and the payment of dowries as well as payments to brides and grooms, these sums are economically important to both families. The bride-wealth in some African societies is paid for daughters may be thought of as contributions to the getting of a wife for a son. Overall the giving of a daughter in marriage is one in which their families remain vitally concerned for a variety of reasons of which the daughters are usually not brought up to expect their views to have much weight except possibly to make difficulties by refusing the choice made by their parents as to whom they should marry.

In many societies families through parents control the lives of their children as rigorously as they can and in many contemporary societies the children avoid these controls by running away with partners of their own choice which is often easy when there are no financial reasons for keeping within the disciplinary requirements of their families; the wealthy land-owner is able to keep control over his children more easily than a subsistence farmer with rented farm land. Freehold farmers and financiers are able to control their children much more effectively because the latter come to realise early in their lives that it is to their advantage not to press their individualism too far.

Where there is adequate land to feed the family, the male and female children earn their keep in such a way that the costs of bringing them up and the work they do, balance out by the time that the boys set up their own families or the girls are married away into other families from whom compensation may be obtained. In Bangladesh and Egypt the Islamic system of inheritance by divisions of the property has always meant that successive generations get smaller and smaller parcels of land so that there is a greater incentive for pushing the children out, than pulling them in to obey their parents for future gain.

In some parts of Latin America where there is rural indebtedness there may be considerable pressure on children to work towards reducing the debt burden of their parents, a heavy burden of obligation which the children may try and avoid; these attempts are punished with beatings and abuse because of the precarious nature of their daily existence with the children seeing the step-mother as being the responsible parent (Bernand and Gruzinski, 1996). Overall we can expect considerable direct or indirect coercion on what children should or should not do wherever they are part of the economic and status needs of their families. The absence of coercion may well be part of the individualisation of societies where parents do not have the means or the need to enforce discipline on their children as they are not necessary parts of the lives of the care-taking adults.

It has to be accepted that in all societies existing social practices are to some extent coercive; they provide an outline to what children and adolescents are required to do if they are to behave pro-socially. To the individualistic child and indeed to perhaps all children this is experienced as coercion and similarly to some extent all children avoid this coercion which if successful and paying off in their own thinking would lead to changes in the required behaviour for succeeding generations.

## Sex Role Training and Pro-social Behaviour

It seems obvious enough that males and females are biologically different and are easily identified as different whether they are naked or clothed. Census enumerators in Tanzanía in their preliminary training found this dichotomy too exact and almost their first question was to ask how they should classify people who were neither one sex nor the other. It would seem therefore that there is widespread recognition even in subsistence societies even if it is not semantically marked out that this distinction involves women who have manly characteristics of form and character and men who have the obverse.

So children enter a social world with sexual differences having a biological base, but that through nurture this does not appear to be as constricting as it seems to be in other species. Nurture as involving these sex differences regards them as parameters in which there are immense social and psychological variations.

It is a mistake to concentrate on the possibilities of uniformities when there are bound to be an obvious predominance of exceptions if not differences based on personality, social and geographical environments apart from emergencies, apart from the larger cultural framework and methodological shortcomings.

Sukuma children and adolescents will have noticed that there are young women diviners and that high ranks in the Buchwezi cult are held by older ones just as on the Tanzanian coast at a political meeting the Swahili men attending were told to stand up to greet a woman political leader when she arrived apart from their knowledge of homosexual behaviour and cross-dressing.

Even if it is accepted that the higher aggressiveness in males probably has a biophysical basis from experiments with non-human animals which cannot be carried out on humans, aggressive behaviour has many different social forms and need not be related to human inter-relationships.

In any case aggression has to be an occasional form of behaviour; no one can be aggressive all the time. Even in age-grade socials systems in which young men become junior warriors as a matter of course, their aggressiveness is socialised towards surrounding communities and cattle theft. Many Sudanese Nuer young men had special cattle which they decorate, compose poems about them and dance before them, which cannot interpreted as aggressive.

Amongst the Ssonjo the young men who have formal roles as defenders of their fenced in villages and cattle, are taught to control their aggressiveness since they are not allowed to come armed to communal religious celebrations in which they might become possessed and uncontrollable.

In economically developed societies there are families in which the children are expected to become soldiers, butchers and demolition workers and in many societies the ambition of adolescents is to become footballers which requires a high degree of professional but controlled aggressiveness.

We have to conclude that aggressiveness as a male characteristic in early childhood is always periodic and takes various social forms according to the culture into which the children are socialised. Children absorb a variety of images and many will have seen that the bodyguards of Colonel Gadaffi, the Muslim leader of Libya are unveiled women.

There are a number of all-encompassing factors in considering sex roles and their relationships to social behaviour in particular circumstances. Firstly there are the requirements of the culture which are usually based on what has happened historically and not so much related to what is happening in the here and now. It is what people think they do or consider that they should do which predominates in conversation rather than what they actually do and this applies to the socialisation of children.

Secondly humans show an immense variety in the environments in which they function. The social requirements for the behaviour of boys and girls in a Brazilian urban slum or in New York where there are now girl gangs quite as violent as those of the boys, are not going to be the same as those for adolescents of the same ages in a middle class suburb of Paris or amongst the pastoralists of the Sudan during the current prolonged civil war.

If there are parallels it would seem likely that the key words used in the interpretation of behaviour may have different meanings for nurturance and aggression. A Japanese child growing up in the use of a language which has numerous ways of avoiding actually saying "no" will have very different ideas about aggressiveness to an English child of the same age.

Thirdly in all cultures and environmental circumstances there will be inevitable situations in which culturally required sex role behaviour is impossible. Children grow up in parts of Tanzania where a high proportion of fathers are away as migrant workers leaving their wives to do the work of both sexes. The effect on children who see and experience this functional equality which they equally see as dysfunctional, will be the same as in Chicago, Johannesburg and Birmingham where such women are classified as single mothers who similarly carry out the roles of both sexes.

A study of the Kenyan Luo focused on boys doing female jobs when there was no older sister at home and often when the father was absent and who were thus required without choice to be involved in child care, housework, fetching water and firewood and milling flour. The conclusions were that they showed less overall egoism, less egoistic aggressiveness and more pro-social behaviour when compared with boys who did little "feminine" work (Ember, 1973). But it was not a clear division as boys who did outside feminine work seemed to have enhanced overall egoism possibly because they had to be more aggressively defensive in their relationships with other boys. Inside feminine work made such boys social behavioural profiles more "feminine".

## Hierarchical Exchange Relationships

All societies have hierarchies into which families and their members fit. The age-set systems of Nilotic and other tribes make each male have a position in which they are always above and below men who were initiated before or after them; they cannot jump a grade just because they are successful. This usually means that husbands are much older than their wives and the status of children will reflect that of the age-grade position of their legal rather than biological parentage.

In urban-industrial societies the fathers social status influences the position of children from which they may benefit so that their pro-social behaviour or its absence outside the family may be a reflection of this. The violence within a family in physical, abusive or sexual forms may be reflected in violence outside and in the latter parental and social lives of such children.

In general the emotional lives of children in most societies prior to the individualisation of modern urban-industrial ones, were subordinated to the requirements of their families in which children are expected to marry cross-cousins or to marry someone from a particular community in a marriage circle. Hindus are expected to marry at least within their own sub-caste and if it can be arranged hypergamously through a cash transaction so that the girls' children take on the caste status of her husband and her family then inches up in relative sub-caste position. It is perhaps a mistake to see children in any society as making individualised choices as to what they do and with whom; there is a process of channelling not so much of aspirations but of limitation which applies as much to Bavarian as to Bengali and Basuto children.

In Latin America god-parenthood was important and usually among kin so that it reinforces existing horizontal bonds in what were then relatively homogeneous societies. It became more important from the 19th century onwards as kinship alone was no longer effective in ensuring a family's economic and social survival. So god-parents for children became asymmetrical and as far as possible advantageous to the current family as well as to the future of the child. The well-off and higher status individuals would accumulate numbers of godchildren to whose expenses they were expected to contribute (Mintz & Wolf, 1950). This also involved with population growth parents might try to put a daughter into domestic service with a godparent as a way out of the cost of bringing them up.

In Sukuma conversion to Christianity and the prohibition of polygyny, was to some extent circumvented by a high status person taking on godchildren whom he would help and more importantly they would help him as if they were his real children. In both these cases children would grow up into realising that these fictional relationships were socially useful in ways that were more directly advantageous than classificatory kinship.

## Communality

Whether a society and the families and individuals within it are predominantly collectivist or individualistic, there is always elements of communality in how they function. There are large families in the sense of recognising membership at both ends of the social scale; both the poor and the rich have selfish interests in keeping together which children recognise and appreciate as they grow into socialised individuals.

Andean children often sleep in the same beds as their parents against the cold and the loneliness of sleeping alone. In these quasi-Roman Catholic communities in which marriage in church as a rite of passage is considered important, the marriage between cross and parallel cousins has increased despite the cost of obtaining Church dispensations to allow marriage within officially prohibited degrees, since it is an effective strategy against the partition of land. Children there who participate in farming tasks from an early age will be well aware of the economic advantages of such closeness.

Migration into cities in many societies often involves gross overcrowding with families sharing accommodation such as in contemporary China where it may be rare for a couple even with children to have more than a single room and children grow up sharing water points and lavatories with strangers forming a "culture of poverty" (Lewis, 1966: xiv).

Children brought up in urban-industrial environments do not experience the narrow communalism of subsistence farmers as their communalism is distributed over a number of interests; their experience of sectional communalism may involve the membership of a religious group, sport and other specialised interests and that of house-housing block communality. Even if this communality may not have any positive values it may have the negative functions of distinguishing children from other children who are defined communally as outsiders.

The individualism of urban-industrial societies is only an important analytical point; few if any children do not have their individualistic tendencies even in the smallest and most isolated subsistence groups, subordinated to both intermittent and regular sub-cultural obligations outside for both conformity and avoidance.

## Domain Specifics in Parent Child Relationships

While much work has been done in trying to allocate different parent-child relationships into overriding styles (Bugental and Goodnow, 1997), it seems likely that it may only work by extracting specific details into provided categories (Baumrind, 1971). It now seems more likely that while there may be broad categories, in fact each parents-child triad has its own specific characteristics of which most if not all are transitory apart from the difficulty of tracing long lasting effects with anything like the requirements of scientific causation.

The domains of communality, hierarchical exchange and coercion are present to some extent in all families and are part of the pragmatics of social living anywhere. The parent-child relationship is a multi-purpose socializing arrangement (Maccoby, 1999) providing training for role requirements which are constantly fluctuating. If in fact any relationship was within one type, the child would become at least partially unable to function outside this parameter. It may be that societies provide schemas with ill-defined but negotiable boundaries which influence to varying degrees the behaviour of all those involved.

## Authoritative Parental Behaviour

While the family is often described as an important institution for society and for the adequate raising of children in a pattern of pro-social behaviour, its characteristics and influences have always been hard to define except in ideal and static terms. Except in some aspects of written legal systems, it does not and indeed cannot conform to the formalities of institutions related to Weber's definition of a bureaucracy.

The obligations of family members to each other are not closely defined or definable but are both variable and negotiable often on a day to day basis according to the circumstances confronting them. This is apart from the fact that the cultural forms of the family are extremely varied and its demographic composition is always different.

It is hard to conceptualise a family primarily because its members are always ageing. The parents and the older generation members of a family are ageing slowly and the children much more rapidly; a process of catching up. It can never have static social inter-relationships except as a useful concept by which to locate and study variations from what a society at any time might consider to be ideological normality. Thus in any social grouping there is never sufficient firmness in its day to day practices to be able to assert that its members have persisting characteristics except by taking particular aspects out of context by some abstracted categorisations.

There will always be social ideals of behaviour which will suggest in general terms that family members are required to behave in certain ways without this being correlated to some adjustable scales to allow for demographic and social factors. As to whether this idealised conception of the family is conformed to must depend on the day to day needs of family members and the pressures of the surrounding society to make some conformity realised. This is a very loose framework indeed within which to tie down a particular pattern of behaviour.

Family members talking about their particular way of behaving will usually differentiate between the ideal to which they might aspire and what actually happens for which they will usually be able to explain away quite adequately for their own satisfactions that the circumstances were against the fulfilment of these ideal patterns; the father had taken to drink, the mother was often sick and the children had got under the influence of bad companions. The reasons for exceptions are as many as the social scientists wish to bring into consideration.

A father may in theory and practice indeed be authoritative but there can never be an across the board static or similar pattern of behaviour. Within the family there are always dyadic relationships in which one half of the dyad is just not there by accident or deliberation. An authoritative parent is not there all the time and when he is, wives and children soon find ways to circumvent his authority. There are always allies to offset what some family members may experience as oppressive such as affines, aunts and uncles as well as grand-parents from the non-authoritarian side of the family. The Nobel prize winner Naguib Mahfouz has shown in detail the intricacies of Egyptian family life under a would-be authoritarian family head (Mahfouz, 1994).

There are also likely to be variations in the situations which dissipate authoritarianism involving co-wives collectively and individually and step-mothers in sequential monogamy with various sets of children and affines. Families are not united by their demographic classifications since each member will have different interests to pursue which cannot be shared with others.

Finally there are the realities of familial inter-relationships in variations in favouritism and tensions, the secret threads of family hatreds and loves which remain with relatives over the years and which make for the most serious of all long lasting quarrels.

For instance in Saudi Arabia there is an Islamic system of family law in which the authority of the man is superior to that of the woman whose power in the giving of evidence is adjudged to be half the value of a male witness. However in a variety of on and off stage behaviour it would appear that many family decisions are made by powerful senior women and that the titular power-holding men merely endorse what their women have already decided on for instance the matter of arranged marriages of sons and daughters.

This may not be a particularly Islamic characteristic. In public the man of the household will answer the questions of the visiting social scientist with confidence while his women will reply in terms which suggest that they are not all that intelligent. However if one is sitting latter against a grass fence behind which the women are working apart from the public areas of the household, these same women will be dissecting what had happened previously with clinical efficiency and understanding. "On stage" and "off stage" behaviour is of overriding importance in human behaviour; the strong voice of an English women coming from the open window of a hotel demanding that the man "get on the bed" might well be an example of this.

When it comes to identifying a particular pattern beyond the aspects already described, there are other intermittent factors to consider in any inter-relationship. If the family was an institution, there would always be ways in which it reacted to and adapted to various intrusive factors or it would collapse.

An authoritarian parent cannot impose too much or the reactions of family members would lead to the family dissolving unless there are other factors overriding this such as property hopes, status considerations and the possibility that the ancestors must react with hostility to family disunity by creating ill-health, infertility, cattle disease and low harvests as rain falls just round the corner but not on their fields.

If parents give an order to a child then they have to see that the order is carried out which can be done if it is something which has to be completed at once. But if there is no immediacy then the parents have to follow up these instructions; they have to remember to do so and to be there to do so. It would seem that authoritarianism can be self-defeating particularly when there is physical punishment.

On the other side of the coin children soon learn to manipulate the authority of their parents and indeed this may be one of the most valuable lessons which they learn for themselves and are likely to be taught by their siblings. This is just as easy to do as in the much more formal circumstances of the school where supervision is more formally intermittent and clock related.

We thus probably have a bipolar reality in which there is an ideal system which lays down often with considerable force what families are supposed to do. On the one hand there is the emotional parameters of the Western family based on the immaterialism of love and that of the subsistence family in which behaviour on a larger social screen of reciprocal inter-relationships in which emotion may have low priority; food may have a constant priority over fun.

There are still other dimensions. A parent can be authoritative because in public to be seen to do otherwise would be to lose status so to overplay this would be socially risky. In private authoritative behaviour might well have a higher personal pay-off in an hierarchical situation.

The extent of physical violence by parents will vary between the accepted and tolerated and what is regarded as reprehensible and inappropriate but it is always an alternative in authoritarian environments. We have seen in Bernstein's theory of behaviour correlated to linguistic codes that those with an elaborated form of English are better able to control their children. On the other hand those with a restricted knowledge of English do not have the resources to control their children verbally and thus tend to be more violent with them (Bernstein, 1975).

This might well apply in non-English or Romance language environments. Linguists almost inevitably find that the languages of non-literate peoples are complicated and indeed sophisticated. However they probably get their understandings from the more sophisticated members of these societies. The Sukuma have been found to have a language which is not only tonal but has twenty-one tenses but how many of those speaking Sukuma use these tenses at all or in the ways that linguists have defined their use grammatically.

It seems doubtful whether parents in contemporary quasi-traditional societies see the corporal punishment of their children as authoritarian; it is just the way that disobedient children should be dealt with and that it does not require long explanations to make the children understand why they should behave in a particular way. The reasoning behind behaviour is not a common way in which people explain why they have behaved in general and in relation to the upbringing of children; this is the way that we in this part of the world have always behaved.

Thus it would seem likely that this is a universal division in the use of all languages between those who use and do not use the complexities of their own languages and that this is reflected in how authority is exercised towards children. One would expect that those who try and control their children through a second not natally learnt language would have similar problems. So that someone moving out of the semantic range of his own language might lead to authoritarian behaviour as in the Tanzanian headmaster who was seen to be beating all his primary school pupils.

### The Pro-social Development of the Single Child

The single child is in an unusual social position for the learning of pro-social behaviour which may have been developed for larger social groupings. Apart from the fact that such a child has no siblings, it can be presupposed that such a child has a greater share of the attention of parents and relatives than a family which has several children.

The growth of the numbers of single children in Western societies is either a matter of parental choice or of fecund women leaving conception to the latter years of their biological lives. The economic cost of having children has risen steadily and women now have control over their own fertility, have acquired marketable skills and have become aware that marriage may not be a stable relationship so that they may be left to care for any children born to them as single mothers. Even in situations of some relative affluence, such a child has difficulties in learning the pro-social behaviour required for reasonable family living. The matrifocal families of the poor are less likely to involve single children and those families tend to be less isolated than the mother with a single child after divorce or separation from a partner.

In this Western social environment while there may be a general pattern of thinking that supports small families, there is certainly no political policy for birth-control and certainly not one which advocates single child-parent families. The government of Singapore has taken the official view that the failure of educated rather than poor women to have children is not in the national interest regardless of the fact that there is no inevitable hereditary connection between the education of parents and the abilities of their children; child bearing is subsidised but the effect has been mainly on the poorer rather than the educated women.

The People's Republic of China has an enforced national policy that women should have only one child regardless of its sex. Early in Communist rule birth control was regarded as a way of destroying

China's future strength, the doubling of their population since 1949 has made the restraining if not the abolition of population growth a political and economic necessity. China now has a large number of single child families in which the behaviour of and treatment of such children has come for them to be called "little emperors". Both the Constitution and the 1981 Marriage Law impose family planning on all Chinese citizens and each community has a birth control planning and enforcement team which can require multi-para women to have abortions.

The long-term problems resulting from the increasing predominance of the one-child family are now recognised by both the Chinese government and social scientists. Young Chinese see the issue in terms of dead-end families with a greater need for personal self-reliance and individualism when the one child is a daughter moving out when marrying and the difficulties for young men in getting married at all (Rice, 1992: 221-238).

However these legal and enforced requirements are still subject to the cultural ideas of the Chinese that boys are necessary for carrying on the family name and to care for their parents in old age whereas girls marry out of their families and thus do not have the means or the incentive to contribute anything to their natal families. Whereas in most societies there is a surplus of women as they live longer, the 1982 Chinese National Census disclosed a sex ratio of 106.3 men to a hundred women which suggested to the authorities that there had been millions of female infanticides which would allow their mothers to try again in the hope of conceiving a boy. So the pro-social model for these single children is not only that they are in a preferential position in which they can enforce their wishes but that the culture is still telling them that to be male gives preferential status, even in their chances of surviving childhood.

Most children grow-up in one of a variety of socially acceptable or at least understandable kin networks; there are known relatives with whom they have accepted and expected reciprocal relationships. But there has to be relatives with whom such relationships can be carried on; children cannot be socialised into feeling that their mother's brothers are good and well motivated towards them when such a relative does not exist and indeed never has in their particular families. A single child will soon come to realise at least by the time of their adolescence that they may well have and certainly will have in their adulthood very few relatives on whom they can depend.

It seems likely that most moral and indeed conventional pro-social practices are developed within a circle of kin which for all children will antedate any experiences of the wider world involving peers and strangers in schools, streets and shops. Of course the pay-off for this learning of pro-social behaviour through the socialisation by kinsmen and kinswomen is that the consequences are essentially benign, the child benefits. It can also be a neutral background which just in general terms keeps children out of obvious trouble. It is a situation in which certain behaviours are tied to certain people in named relationship roles; x is a paternal grandfather and y is a maternal aunt. Behaviour and unavoidable relationships go together and this is likely to teach the advantages of conformity to social requirements whether they are classified as moral or conventional.

However in a society which is largely composed of single children in infancy, adolescence and adulthood, a whole new range of contingencies is facing them; an absence of moral learning correlated to a range of personally known, linguistically titled relationships. So it would seem that the individualism which is thought to be largely the consequence of industrialisation and urbanisation, can be correlated to the consequences of an enforced national birth-control policy or wide ranging personal choices. Certain terms which denominate relationships such as paternal or maternal aunts and uncles and their children may disappear as applied to known legal and biological relationships. In Western societies the contemporary size of unavoidable kin networks is much smaller than in previous generations.

The growth of classificatory kinship is which relationship titles are applied to people with whom satisfactory social relationships have been established or in hope that they will be. The young Iranian woman begging for support for a charity there, would refer to the British man she has approached as "uncle". In this process pro-social behaviour might well loose its "natural" and traditional foundations and become more obviously utilitarian. In contemporary China the channel though which employment and advancement has to be sought is one of created kinship linkages in which classificatory terms are used on the most tenuous links to create a sense of obligation in the person to whom the application is made.

The concentration of attention by grand-parents on the single grandchild and indeed the usefulness of such relationships when both parents of the child are working. This brings about competition between agnates and affines as each side may well have only one grandchild. This situation will certainly increase the bargaining powers of the child and in adolescence may well make them more self-reliant and selfish.

It seems likely that the numbers of single children is likely to grow in many societies and that there will a steady move towards new forms of pro-social understanding from the only child as a symbol of parental selfishness to one in which it is seen as beneficial for such children as they become more the centre of parental attention and economic benefits.

## The Pro-social Importance of Play for Children

There may well be a distinction between play or at least the concept of play among subsistence societies which do not have their children segregated into formal, obligatory educational roles in which reciprocities are not a major factor and other societies in which children from an ever earlier age are segregated in order to be both socialised and educated.

Play as a children's activity must primarily be with neighbourhood peers or in the cohorts in which they are being educated and which is usually an activity integrated into the social requirements of the adults who care for them.

The phrases "go and play" or "play periods" would not appear be part of the semantics of subsistence societies; there would be ways in which children behave when they are not required to support their controlling adults in the day to day business of living.

In these circumstances it is a peer group activity in which there is a wide range in their ages according to those who are available in the locality or hamlet. It is thus likely to be dominated by older children and thus would appear to be an early introduction into the hierarchical nature of subsistence and indeed all societies. Zigua children in Tanzania play a form of the English Game of "I am king of the castle get down you dirty rascal".

However in urban-industrial communities, time is likely to be cut into segments and not just as behaviour of children left over from adult requirements. Secondly the range of peers into which children are regimented by the structure of formal education is likely to cover a narrower range of ages; there will be social pressures to avoid contacts with those above and below their own peer group either for age or to coincide with the institution's structure.

It may be that play will always be with peer groups and not usually except in urban industrial societies, something that children do alone since much of their lives are in compounds with open doors; an including rather than an excluding way of behaving.

It would not seem reasonable to see play however defined as an unimportant activity. It may well be seen as such by adults who see it as wasted time from the efforts needed to keep the family alive biologically and socially. Even a minimal observation of children shows their intense pre-occupation with play even though their span of attention may not be very long. The fact that children's play may appear to be aimless cannot be to suggest that it is without organisation within their minds and its main purpose may be to get away from adult supervision and involvements.

In all this there is often the simplistic view of subsistence communities are of necessity holistic and developed more opportunities for the individualism of each child to develop. There are of course no holistic societies in the sense of an absence of individualism and in each and every society there are the means and the opportunities for each person to work out and develop their specific talents. The children in economically simpler societies have ample opportunities to experience the diversities in adult and peer behaviour and their play will depend on how it is imaginatively viewed and developed. Afghan children make models of AK 47 rifles out of plywood just as Ugandan children make models of cars and aeroplanes out of clay. Zigua children in the approach to the menarche and circumcision will have been shown two hundred or more clay models which they could have made themselves in play to each of which is attached some catch phrase menmonic of some aspect of approved and necessary social behaviour. Play just as much as growing up is not a simple and mechanical process in any subsistence society (Fortes, 1938: 44).

To what extent can children's games be seen as independent of the surrounding societies. For most of the world children do not have commercially created toys and games and purchased for them by adults; they have to be made with the materials available to them locally; twine for cat's cradles, wood for spinning tops, clay, wood and bamboo. In these activities the children are creative in the sense of manipulating materials but individual creativity is not likely to occur (Ashton, 1952: 35) except for exceptional children in subsistence societies of which little is known but who can be presumed to exist.

Many subsistence societies have adult "games" but they are not easily paralleled to the segregated sports of economically developed societies in which teams of players compete which have little external social connection with their promoters. In subsistence societies there may be intra-communal competitions such as the Sukuma form of rule-less hockey and the rivalry of the Bugika and Bugaru groups of young men. But such activities are so closely integrated into their social lives as to be outside any definition of play and their competitiveness is not in the sense of some winning at the expense of others who do not.

It seems likely that only in economically developed societies is play something which can be identified as separated from other activities, but in all societies children and adolescents will engage in activities which they have not themselves created but which have an external focus.

In subsistence societies the focus will be connected to the immediacies of their surrounding social lives and what children absorb of adult preoccupations which they have seen or overheard, and this is not particularly imaginative; the copying in miniature of warrior and domestic roles. The Palestinian rather more than the Karamajong and Maasai youth grows up in a society dichotomised by immediate hatred, just as the Afghan, Iranian and Iraqi ones grow up into which outsiders are classed as infidels.

The environment provides the background for play involving social and physical skills which are negotiable rather than innate so that it was not so much imitation as a valuable preparation for that particular form of anticipated adult life (Kenyatta, 1939: 101).

What seems to be characteristic of the ethnographic understandings of play is to see it as not being a valuable sector for the learning of particular forms of pro-social behaviour even if this involves the killing of Israelis or stealing cattle from the adjacent communities. It is often portrayed as desultory, passive, aimless and totally lacking in imagination (Schwartzman and Barbera, 1976: 11).

The fact is that this imitation of adult activities is the only way available for the children in subsistence societies to contribute to their own socialisation. On the other hand much of the play of children in economically developed societies does not contribute much to their socialisation for the future in which they are likely to participate whether they like it or not.

## Chapter-11

# EDUCATION

The assessment of formal education in contemporary thinking is that for most of its known history it was always specialised training for particular predetermined jobs and usually involved only a very small proportion of any population; it was intended to be elitist and remained so until very recently.

Thus universal primary education in even the most economically developed societies is no more than a century old and is by no means a universal feature of all states other than as a political aim. Above this level of primary education, whatever the provision, may be, it remains elitist because in most states it cannot afford to provide secondary and higher education for those who do not show an above average ability. Since there may be few opportunities for higher level employment, any national investment in advanced education may contribute to a brain drain.

The other important feature of contemporary education is its socially disruptive structure in which children and adolescents are taught for many years by strangers for short discontinuous sessions. Moreover they are taught subjects which have little relationship to much of anticipated employment and are largely dictated by the needs of the surrounding macro-society and that formal education whether it is functional or not for the anticipated needs of the children and adolescents is a "good" thing in itself.

Parents in developing societies may send their children to school in the hope that they will achieve some measure of upward mobility out of the existing status of their families and away from the comparative penury of subsistence agriculture. This can only be achieved in expanding economies and without the society being dominated by the on-going necessities connected to high birth rates and lowered infant mortalities.

In this process the definition of success is competitive assessments of excellence which appears to have little to do with the practicalities resulting from such a system which leave many children with an abiding feeling of inferiority; it disguises elitism under an ideological veneer of equal opportunity which is impossible to achieve within the economic realities of human and environmental variability.

This somewhat extreme evaluation gains its strength from a comparison to subsistence societies. These societies which must have been in existence in one form or another for many millennia before any historical data is available, have followed on to some extent the varied patterns of child care exhibited by the higher non-human primates.

These societies have no teaching roles which separate children from parents and alloparents and in its imitative functions prepare them as adequately as possible for the lives which they are almost certainly going to follow. It would not have made sense in these pragmatic societies to develop roles dependent on communal time and motion support for which the community has no use.

In such communities the children are taught agricultural and animal husbandry methods which have been adequate for their survival for many millennia. By all means teach the children of such communities the nature of plants and scientific causation but their classification and uses will conform to patterns of thought which are already culturally predetermined and probably maintained by the structures of the languages within which children are socialised; they will have no abstract components beyond this. The rationality of the Amish in teaching their children locally no more than is necessary for the maintenance of their own communities in which their children are most likely to remain, is an approach which deserves wider recognition.

In these hypotheses can we be certain that there are typical children and adolescents in typical environments. Such typicalities are usually rather concrete and generalisable and thus often far from the lives of particular children. An educational system provides text books for syllabi, but there can be no uniformities in how these are actually used and how those taught see such knowledge. Knowledge of French can be used to read Proust and pornographic literature and arithmetic is a useful asset for betting and petty market trading and not for the building of their houses which they will learn by rule of thumb. Paper in many societies is costly in societies where cigarettes are bought individually. Almost every term which we use in classifying human behaviour are definable in self-restricting ways and exclude variations in their functions. A minority function may still loom very large in the understandings of particular children who in their thinking and behaviour are non-conformists. Perhaps we can suggest that all children are in practice non-conformists.

So when we suggest that the education of children in subsistence societies is to make them useful and conforming to adult needs, this is an abstract concept which will not correlate to the realities of the lives of individual children. Anymore than it does for children in any school in any country, except for the uniformities of national syllabi. Indeed perhaps the only constant feature of all educational systems anywhere is the presence of a time-table on a notice board in the dominant language according to scientific and not social time.

Initially this apprehension of uniformity comes from the absence of knowledge about many social systems and in particular details in the use and holdings of property and power. Since there is little variation in housing in which children may be raised except in terms of their maintenance or in their material culture except for wear and tare. This is an illusory uniformity but becoming less so with the spread of consumer goods to less economically developed societies.

How children are taught in subsistence societies will show large variations in even the most seemingly uniform community. The personalities of parents and alloparents will vary as they see themselves and their children. First individual children might or might not receive extra attention when their younger parents have the energy after a day's work or when there is less work to do during the dry season.

In fact it may be the case that the education of the young may rest largely with the mother or range of alloparents involved in parenting, then shared between parents and older siblings and finally split between parents on a sex basis. But much may depend on whether these role bearers exist; mothers may change, fathers may be non-existent or absent and rather than siblings it may be the children in the neighbourhood who teach them almost by accident.

Much of what they need to know to get by in these societies which in terms of actual functions are likely to be small in range no matter what variations exist in the large encapsulating society. The adequacy of the education available for children in such subsistence societies for even the most limited of contemporary lives must be questionable however ideal it may be conceptualised.

What does this subsistence educational system and that of developed and developing societies have in common. The environmental, social and material limitations are replaced by a range of legal and educational restrictions filtered through the personalities of the teachers. It would seem at first sight that the latter system despite an ideological aim of equal opportunity is much more deliberately restrictive than the individualised unsystematic educational processes of the former.

Similarly the latter is subject to very slow rates of adaptive change since this has to be conducted through the tentacles of bureaucratic structures. The former is immediately adaptive to the needs of families, adults and children because it fits into their current situations within the widely accepted cultural requirements in which they all live. We should look at schools in their peculiar institutional forms for the influence they may have on children and adolescents.

## The School as an Incarcerating Institution

If we compare the school environments in economically well developed societies with those in which development has in general been less successful, there are clear differences which may affect the development of pro-social behaviour.

In the former situation the children going to school are moving from one part of their society to another which they can recognise as being more or less similar parts; run by the clock, expensive material property, electric light and lavatories with running water. There is no great cultural leap for these children going to school.

This is not so in subsistence societies where the educational experience in almost all respects is different. Such societies have no regimentation and now their children in school are required to sit still in groups under timed restrictions to be taught by strangers. In Eastern Africa the Swahili word for teacher "mwalimu" may still have a Muslim flavour to it. Often there is a long walk to school but as the eating schedules of most subsistence societies is for the main meal to come after the day's work is done, the children are not fed before their day's work and walk begins and may well arrive tired.

While the children in developed societies may expect to go to school as an aspect of normality, this may not be so elsewhere where they may be sent to school at the expense of their parents in the payment of fees, school uniforms and lost labour in the home and farm. Overall it would seem that for most children, education is a form of incarceration.

In the context of learning pro-social behaviour it has to be remembered that what goes on in institutionalised education is a relatively new form of specialised social behaviour which for centuries has only been experienced by relatively few for special purposes. In terms of universal primary education is even newer within the policy that education is a "good" regardless of what it may lead to in the lives of the children who are passed through this process.

Christianity and Islam have led in this respect for religious reasons but the content and form of contemporary education is now largely secular. In its current forms it is a system which has spread from Western economically developed societies which can afford to have educational systems which are not geared to economic needs and possibilities to societies at all stages of economic and social development which may well not be able to afford general education as a "good" thing in itself.

Certain types of organisations are distinguishable by the fact that they incarcerate those involved (Giddens, 1991: 293-4). The clearest examples are prisons in which prisoners are locked in and to a certain extent their custodians are locked in with them. Hospitals are another example in which patients and staff while not being locked in, are isolated from the surrounding society and develop distinctive cultures because of this occupational specialisation. Both these types of organisation have styles of behaviour linguistic codes, exclusive costumes and ways of interrelating which are quite distinctive.

A third type of imprisoning organisation is the school of which the clearest example is the boarding school with its uniform, geographical boundaries, limited contacts with the outside world and interrelationships which are not only distinctive as educational institutions but develop into specialised patterns distinctive to each school.

The day school similarly as prison characteristics. It has fenced boundaries into which pupils come and are retained inside until they are released at the end of the school day. There is often a school uniform by which they are easily identified in much the same way and for more or less the same purposes as farmers mark their live-stock.

The inter-relationships between members of staff, staff and pupils and between pupils is a combination of the official educational structure of the institution and what the children themselves develop within this structure for their own purposes and often in reaction to it.

It is not just a question as to whether schools promote pro-social behaviour because it is clearly in their own interests to do so. The type of behaviour which is built up is itself moulded by the structure of the school because what the school creates almost by accident is a style which is totally different to that of the domestic primary group from which the children come. That even the children realise this can be seen in the pleasure which they show on leaving school after classes, often visible expressions of relief.

The school architecture makes for certain types of behaviour, classrooms designed for particular purposes, closed off by corridors and these rooms have hierarchical significance with a raised front. The physical proximity of certain children to each other in these rooms on a regular basis creates distinctive non-kin primary groups with built-in hostility to other such room or house based groups which are thought to be inferior on some official or unofficial system of classification.

Since the numbers of children in a school is too large to form a primary group, a sense of corporate identity can be created by implied or real hostility to outside groups usually in other schools or outside juvenile gangs. More than anything else this behaviour is created by a combination of geography and architecture. A school, in which the boarding houses are on different roads, will not have their pupils seeing as their equals. The inequalities of a society are pushed into the understandings of children by their experiences in school which even those societies with age set systems have nothing approaching this, and which they will not have heard about much less experienced.

The blocked off nature of forms may not occur where there are streams for different subjects so that a child may not have a single educational status; she may be good at arithmetic and he may be poor at geography. Children who come together more frequently in shared streams are likely to form primary groups or at least have these groups the basis from which they choose their friends.

Then schools are run by time-tables and sectioned off by the ringing of bells and the filling up of corridors which will be a totally new experience for most children except for Muslims whose children will have had an early understanding of the times for prayer which is often linked to loudspeakers calling the faithful to prayer and the presence of large clocks in mosques. But this is religious time-keeping and children will not have experienced anything like its regularity in their homes or if their parents work in markets in their businesses. Similarly the complicated cyclical calendrical system of the Maya was religious and involved year keeping rituals rather than domestic time-keeping (Farriss, 1995). Time is forced on children in schools for the first time.

To make children conform to time and to see time as related to blocks of behaviour with specific requirements might well be interpreted as learning a form of behaviour dictated by institutional requirements rather than as a contribution to pro-social needs. The time-table efficiently distributes the bodies of children around the organisation (Foucault, 1979: 228); is it surprising that prison resembles factories, schools, barracks, hospitals which all resemble prisons.

Domestically only a few households are run by the clock so that for most of the world life is regulated by the sun with times varying with the amount of cloud cover. In rare cases time is regulated by the stars as in the Ssonjo of Tanzania night time distribution of limited water supplies to their small plots (Gray, 1962). Children walking to school will take longer going up hill than down. Time is overall very much quicker in the cultivating season than in the dry season in which men rather than women spend more time just sitting around and talking (Evans-Pritchard, 1939). Time for most children is social rather than a detached and impersonal controller of behaviour so that schools teach the implacability of abstract time.

Of course it is reasonable to argue that organised life is a necessity for large scale living but the large cities of the past seem to have carried on efficiently enough without clocks and even gongs or guns announcing the closing of the gates or the end of the day light fasting in Ramadan could well have been guessed without any such marking off by sounds.

So this form of grouping created by a combination of architecture, conformity to clock rather than biological time and the narrow hierarchical nature of all schools, teaches the children the need if not the necessity of small exclusive groups for immediate social purposes. These groups as far as primary school children and to as lesser extent in secondary schools do not last long.

These physically isolated forms of social groupings in forms, departments, housing and schools creates quite specific "us" and "them" which are far more rigid than the more porous concept of a neighbourhood and classificatory kinship and the "ins" and "outs" of family and local social activities at various levels and on various occasions. Most children status rank forms, subjects, residential accommodation and schools and these subordinating hostilities are only to a limited extent channelled into competitive team sport.

Then children by architecture are subjected to a new form of surveillance which is quite distinct from the forms which go along with family living in which interdependence and necessity control a range of behaviour on all those involved not just the subordinated children. The children are tied into rules about noise, running and prohibited areas which are laid down, considered to be self-evident.

The school class-room has children sitting in rows which are all under the visual supervision of the teacher on a raised dais. They are supposed to look alert and pay attention more or less continuously to show that they are absorbed in their work; there are no ethological parallels to this which might suggest that this is natural.

These required rigidities of behaviour over long periods of time which does not occur in the home, provokes a new type of behaviour which is common to all imprisoning organisations, the anxieties over conformity. It also leads to the children developing and maintaining arange of behaviour which to a varying extent is in opposition to what the school system and the teachers are requiring. Children do not like this permanent overseeing so that all schools have parallel social systems requiring conformity.

The pro-social requirement of having to sit still is an organisational necessity in the institutions of developing countries whether in schools, factories and indeed public transport, but it is a created and imposed requirement. The children's will find all sorts of ways to create free space and free-time for themselves out of sight of authority. In terms of the children ideas and needs this is their own pro-social behaviour but it undercuts the pro-social requirements of the school with its wider terms of reference.

These parallel social sub-systems exist in all closed organisations whether hospitals, prisons, ships and armies. In all cases this pro-social behaviour which is learned and practised is quite distinct from the aims and for the perceived benefits of those not directly involved in the school. Every school has 'back areas' where the children carry out activities independent of the staff and in opposition to their aims.

The children not only learn that they are being continuously over-looked but they are now subject to written records which go to their parents and which are kept on record by each school. Their current status and future prospects are being dictated by numbers recorded in books accompanied by the comments of teachers. At least in economically developed societies and in more well-endowed schools these results are increasingly computerised and not necessarily confidential.

Some of these records are indeed posted on notice-boards so that there are social consequences for children who are put publicly in order of success and failure which has nothing to do with their more familial relationships. This is a noticeable contrast with the customs of traditional societies which indeed do have competitive aspects but who nevertheless usually manage to have each situation so organised that no one is left outside in a demeaning situation of lost status; everyone passes the grade and everyone comes to local and indeed familial celebrations without having to be invited.

School replicates the factory in many ways since it is basically a conveyor belt system to which the individual child must comply or be penalised in a largely competitive world. It has set administrative divisions and an organised bureaucratic promotional system dictated by bells, days, weeks, terms and years. However pro-social behaviour is defined, the school would not appear to be a system designed for its development despite the efforts of teachers to develop individual children.

It may be that some parents send their children to school to be educated but the majority see education as the way to do better in life than their parents and in subsistence societies as the only way in which they can get out of the drudgery of farming, School education with its methods of teaching which have no parallels in either traditional societies or in domestic life in the eyes and understandings of children, is involved in processing them through learning of information that they will rarely use in their subsequent lives. The fact that they see it in economic terms as to what they will get out of it, means that pro-social behaviour is experienced and understood in those terms rather than in what the wider society imposes on them in its own political interests.

## The School and Pro-social Behaviour

The aspects of school education which involve pro-social behaviour are not clear cut except perhaps that most societies expect schools to do more for their children than they collectively and individually accomplish. The factors to consider that prevent schools from successfully doing this are numerous.

The teachers are not responsible to their customers except in the case of individual tuition paid for by parents in addition to the normal schooling. Their contracts as workers are with individual school governors or the local education authority. Only in extreme cases does the local community have any solid corrective say in how their children are taught.

Teaching is founded on curricula not usually designed with particular communities or individual needs in mind except for the handicapped and those who have reached the higher levels of educational achievement. With the structure of terms even the teaching of agriculture cannot be correlated to the farming year.

The intake of pupils to a school is only loosely correlated to any community except in the case of schools which exist in actual villages. For children who do not live in villages but in widely dispersed family hamlets or in highly populated towns, the neighbourhood correlation is low; schools with good reputation get pupils from wider social watersheds and of course boarding schools have no correlation at all with neighbourhoods except for day pupils. Whether for good or not children are usually forced into mixed social and ethnic groupings which would correspond to their adult lives.

Schools which have pupils daily have these students under their official supervision for only a few hours each day and then only in high pupil teacher ratios which make close supervision unlikely. There is no supervision in holidays, weekends nor for any time spent outside the schools grounds.

Boarding schools exercise official supervision for longer periods and the pupil teacher ratio is likely to be both lower and closer. For both the teacher and the pupil there is likely to be a professional and emotional pay-off from the development of such closer relationships; in some cases this would parallel that of classificatory relatives and particular teachers are remembered for their influences and eccentricities into the old age of their onetime pupils.

Each school has an official narrowly defined institution static in time and space functions round social generations of pupils which is usually five years by which time there has been a complete turnover of students. Thus for some schools there is an ethos which has grown up independent of both staff and pupils paralleling the cultural memories of self-identified non-literate social groupings such as clans and lineages. This accounts for the strong solidarity of the student bodies of some schools and their hostility to other bodies which do not have this largely un-codified ethos.

Any school has three levels of social behaviour, viz. (1) The official level dealing with teaching and the codified requirements for behaviour within the school grounds, (2) An official level which the pupils themselves have created and administer in opposition to the official requirements; the undercover ways in which the pupils develop their own personalities and group requirements; the rites of passage for entering and leaving forms and the ways of getting round regulations and (3) then finally there is the system which inter-relates these two systems; the staff know when and where rules are broken but do not see that it is their interests or that of the school to interfere too closely kin what the pupils do within mutually accepted limits.

The school is geographically separated from the surrounding social and geographical area; it is a disjunctive relationship however much those involved may try to establish closer inter-relationships. Both sides of this institutional barrier have different reasons for peering over this functional separation.

Children have to fit into the requirements these educational institutions marked off in space and time in which they learn that its functions are broadly similar to all other bureaucratically based ones, which are organised for social, political and economic purposes. It is similar to the ways in which blocks of offices, and factories are run as well as probably markets in which the product of differential learning is bought and sold; top forms, top teachers and top subjects and their obverse are always being socially negotiated.

Children and adolescents associate largely with those of the same age, a grading system more closely articulated than the age-grade systems of Nilotic peoples in the Sudan and northern East Africa. The educational lives of most pupils is largely cohort related.

As we have already stated the overall effect of formal education is competitive in which a minority succeed and the majority are formally graded as less successful. The passing out ceremony for a Croatian urban primary school had the pupils graded in different coloured imitation academic gowns; some of the very young pupils behaved accordingly. The Norrington annual table of the success rates of the various Oxford Colleges is certainly of active interest to admissions tutors; successful entrants equal successful exits.

It would seem that in practical terms children have to learn to keep within the confines of the different systems of social control and influence. There are the pro-social requirements of the social environments from which children come and in which they spend most of the calendar year and which may well represent a consistency which is absent from the school environment with its turnover of staff and pupils as well as its abstract nature and unrelatedness to the pupils anticipated futures.

The school regime and educational system responding to formal regulations and their interpretation by those in authority, involve set pieces of learning which are clearly different to that of their home environments. Of course there are exceptions as in Guyana where East Indian children tended to do well in arithmetic as so many of their parents were petty traders in shops in which their children helped from time to time whereas the Afro-Caribbean children had no such experience. Refugee communities of Vietnamese hill tribes identified so closely with the aspirations of American society that their children did well in school.

Finally there are the pro-social requirements of the cohort to which they belong by choice or by the fact that they are graded in this way by their school system. Any school contains larger numbers of informal and formal groupings other than those provided by the school system which the children and adolescents have created for their own needs. An English secondary school was found to have over a hundred recognisable groupings.

Although these different styles of pro-social behaviour involve each child and adolescent as an individual, there is little deliberate correlation between them except when the aspirations of professional parents as well as Indian immigrant families in Britain, fit into the aims of particular schools and their systems. Except for such exceptions it is unlikely that the pro-social behaviour required by the school will replicate that of the home environment in which timings are not imposed and the code of behaviour entirely different. It seems likely that the peer relationships of children and adolescents have important and long lasting consequences.

## The Peer Relationships of Children

It has often been suggested that there is a voluntary element in the inter-relationships of children and adolescents as opposed to those with parents and alloparents in which there is a built in element of compulsion. The children have to comply with the requirements of these domestic power-holders.

But what are the relationships of the young outside these fixed parental relationships and those based on kinship generally. Firstly the young are never faced with a wide selection of others with whom they can choose or not to inter-relate. In a subsistence community the possibilities for choice of relationships is going to be small just siblings and neighbourhood; there is an element of compulsion to avoid overt rejection of a relationship over which there are not really any alternatives. Even in a Mexican urban slum in which family and all other social groupings were based on an almost day to day survival needs, there were local groupings of families aiming to provide mutual support and child care in which there was not much choice in who each child had to maintain reasonable relationships (Comnitz, 1978) as there were small clusters of three to four nuclear families.

Children as they grow up are faced with two sets of inter-relationships. Firstly there are those from which there is no escape. They are tied into obligatory relationships by the bilateral "blood" and marital relationships recognised by law and custom from which there is no escape without psychological and social hardship with relatives of varying social closeness; parents, siblings and classificatory kin.

Whatever form the relationship takes at the end the other person is still there in person or in memory; they cannot be abolished. After a serious quarrel the other relative is still there lurking in the periphery of personal consciousness; they cannot be taken out of reckoning. There is no voluntariness in these relationships and conflict shows itself from the second year onwards between siblings; these are conflicts over the direct control of possessions and indirectly over access to emotional resources (Vandell & Bailey, 1992), they "learn ways of opposing, disagreeing, compromising and conciliating within the safety of one of their most durable social relationships".

Because they cannot be abolished, their existence teaches children that there are involuntary relationships, emotional walls of arbitrary containment. As Dawkins notes everyone has particular ancestors (Dawkins, 1995), they existed long enough to start each individual into life and in that they were an influential success. It is no surprise that in many societies, ancestors have an important part to play in the lives of their descendants and have to be propitiated.

It is equally important to recognise that many of these relationships in their social effectiveness are time restricted; they are active in containing the child for only a few years. At the end of this period the balance of power shifts away from actively controlling the children but remains in their minds in the idea that they ought to keep in contact if only for material reasons. The inheritance of property and power is a powerful incentive to the keeping of social contacts which would be recognised early by developing children. It was the writer J.M. Barrie who referred to the family as the "dear octopus" rightly combining in that phrase power and pleasure.

Secondly there are relationships which are matters of choice or of being chosen in the fluid and ephemeral system of peer relationships. In most cases these inter-relationships are restricted to those with whom contacts can be made; the "real" relationships with school friends and work associates and ones which are less physical in pen friends, fan clubs and chatting on the internet without the supervision of parents.

In peer relationships children, adolescents and adults have to use the same methods to gain admission to such groups and to maintain indeed to earn membership in the first place. The basic need for reciprocity; both sides have to gain and loose something which gives them a shared interest. Everyone pays a subscription for membership on which there is a return. Even the girl who kisses the picture of Michael Jackson night and morning feels that there is a personal return.

Almost as soon as toddlers cease to be dependent on their mothers, they are more and more in the social world of negotiated and obligatory relationships. The extent to which the former dominates the developing understandings of these children will depend on how much they are involved in the social world outside their primary kinship group.

Whereas within the primary family these negotiations are small scale and linguistically sophisticated, outside it is a cruder world; in school, in the "hustling" of the street children or as employees as a child, adolescent or adult worker or as an exogamous sexual partner, inter-relationships have to be worked for.

It is the pro-social behaviour required to gain and maintain peer relationships which dominates much of the activities of developing children within the boundaries of the culture in which they are growing up.

In the sense of particular children's popularity with their peers, there is bound to be a difference between the earlier open-door peer group situations in which the opportunity to discriminate is limited; it is a set group of peers in which the inter-relationships are dominated by birth order.

In communities in which the door marks the boundary between a degree of free association and imposed limitations through either the school or territorially base gangs or indeed a mixture of the two, freedom of choice is similarly limited. The gang group in school or outside has membership depending on a mixture of popularity and usefulness to the group; it is anxious situation for children.

In the school with its much larger number of available peers issued to the incoming children on admission, individual children can to some extent choose their specialisation and thus be issued with a set of automatic peers from amongst whom closer inter-relationships will be chosen. But the larger the school, the larger is the number of alternative on the spot official and unofficial groupings which provide choices for individuals and their particular abilities and with these more immediate satisfactions. These cover the specialisations of music, chess, debating and a variety of team and competitive sports.

Although the school may contain hundreds of pupils there are social limitations on association as there will always be a preference for the near and thus more convenient relationships. In some schools children seated in alphabetical order and those that sit around a child may be the same for some years. It may be socially and psychologically risky to venture out of the known into the unknown social world. So the child probably has a choice from the numbers in a class. Theoretically once a child is in a school, the range of choices for inter-relationships is wide but only wider in comparison to the domestic neighbourhood; it is certainly not unlimited. A child may live in Bombay but the chances of meeting children from Banaras and Bhopal are virtually nil.

So it may be that the choice of with whom they will associate is in terms of those who are available and least unsuitable rather than the most suitable. They will cut out from possibilities those whom they actively dislike in the same way that the ability to stop a relationship is handicapped.

Even in these peer groupings of choice there are dangers for the children who are too incompetent to retain effective membership and the alternative one that being too successful will diminish peer group involvement; variations on the theme of "hogging the ball"; popularity is multi-facetted.

So in each type of freer choice peer-grouping there may be different standards of popularity according to gender, age and various forms of social competence. But there is always the factor of individualism which may not correlate well with popularity. Success in school work with its publicly displayed competitive marking in which every child is above or below some of their peers, may well be a handicap as well as enabling certain peer relationships.

There are two constraining aspects of this as it is only in economically well developed societies that such a range of choices are institutionally available and economically supported and secondly in their absence the presence of free forming gangs will be an attractive alternative.

## The Lack of Moral Teaching in Western State Schools

What do we know of moral teaching as it involves children and adolescents in pre-industrial societies. As far as we know such societies did not have any category of behaviour which was classified as religion and that their moral behaviour would have been the requirements of maintaining a balance of behaviour within each social groupings; a dislike of obvious disruptions but not the covert manipulations which might circumvent overt behavioural requirements.

It has to be recognised that there can be few if any such societies which did not have and do not have now at least some peripheral contacts if not continuous ones with specific religions created and maintained from outside their social and political boundaries. Wandering Buddhist monks, Muslim traders, Christian missionaries and colonizers with Christian preferences were commonplace everywhere.

In all such societies the assumption of homogeneity must be an illusion as without literacy there cannot be anything which approaches uniformity and much behaviour would be based on individual personalities and social circumstances. Scepticism is built into the more private thinking of most such subsistence cultivators and herdsmen about the locals diviners and a Sukuma man on being asked his religion took the questioner to look at his cattle.

In such societies there is no word for religion which would keep it has a separate category of behaviour anymore than there is for economics or society. A Sukuma man on being asked his religion replied that he was a Sukuma although he knew full well what was the purpose of the question; he was not saying that he was not a Muslim, Christian or Hindu of which faiths they have had definite almost neighbourly knowledge for over century.

So such people would see moral behaviour as something that integrates children and adolescents into being useful members of their own micro-societies even if that behaviour is at the expense of other neighbouring groups whose interests are at variance with theirs. This pro-social behaviour is not only integrated into all their inter-relationships correlated to social distance factors but is also integrated into the spirit world.

The ancestors expect their descendents to act in further of their interests as a descent group and will act hostilely against those whose behaviour disrupts this by inflicting misfortunes on them. But again the ancestors are only interested in the one organisation and clearly the success of one group in a populated area will almost always be at the expense of other families. There is no moral system in any such society which furthers the idea of universal peace or that individuals should not steal from people with whom they have no social relationships other than antagonism into which they have been socialised. At all levels the pragmatics of survival of small family groups and moral-cum-religious ideas are integrated; the spirit world is either on your side or on that of people with whom you have reason to suspect have hostility towards your success.

Thus moral training or rather the socialisation of children is into the prevailing necessities of getting on with those people with whom they have necessary relationships. Even without looking into the ethological basis of these necessities and associated feelings, it is a series of micro systems without any abstract and generalisable basis. It cannot have been designed or developed if indeed these are appropriate word, for any wider view of moral obligations beyond their existing social horizons. Moral behaviour if it has any basis in such societies it is the maintenance of satisfactory primary relationships in the interests of each individual having them.

In some societies certain religions and their supporting establishments have become dominant so that specific practices are taught in Christian, Jewish and Muslim schools which certainly had the abstract God given abstract aim of being of necessity applicable to everyone in those societies. In practice these rules would have been applied in various ways according to the ability of bureaucracies to apply them. This is a process which is very difficult to apply in urban industrial societies which have immensely varied requirements for which the originators of these religious regulations did not have in mind. The requirements for training children and adolescents to fill roles in such societies are not necessarily met by the school syllabus in Saudi Arabia which contains seven compulsory religious subjects out of twelve (Wright, 2004: 53). There are parallels here to the compulsory teaching of theoretical Communism in all Soviet educational institutions.

These religious rules put their primary group necessities within the frameworks of moral understandings which link all manner of men and women in all manner of situations. Those in those contemporary societies which at the moment are only Islamic states or sub-states know that it is beneficial for their children to be socialised into a religious framework to be used by them as adults.

So believers in the "religions of the book" including small exclusive groups such as Jewish and Christian fundamentalists feel that their children should be schooled in institutions which have their particular moral requirements as providing for a life-time way of thinking.

Of course, this results in the perpetuation of intolerance as in Ulster, Cyprus and Yugoslavia and in Saudi Arabia where even the possession of a Bible would be considered objectionable and no Christian rituals can be publicly performed. However this can be combined with the practical need for tolerance in any society in which there are networks of inter-religious relationships which have continued for centuries as in the presence of substantial numbers of Muslims and their mosques in Banaras, the most sacred city for Hindus.

However western democratic states despite a nominal recognition of the supremacy of God are secular in form and understandings, so that there is in state funded education an absence of moral teaching. In the United States the Supreme Court has ruled that morning prayers mentioning God contravenes the secular provisions of the Constitution that the state should have no religious connections despite the fact that God is mentioned in their foundation documents and that the Congress has a chaplain. Hence the need from the wishes of parents for the provision of denominational schools or at least ones which are privately funded in which their children are taught morality based on religious foundations.

This wide-ranging politically supported secularism which is carried through into public education may have its origins in the ways of thinking initiated by the western Enlightenment which thought and may perhaps still think that religious ideas and practices would disappear with the general increase in the standards of general education and the use of scientific understandings in public life; this does not appear to have happened. It may also be that the majority of contemporary teachers in state schools are not prepared to teach any religious doctrine as a moral necessity or as a guide for the behaviour of children and adolescents.

It may also be the consequences of a liberal political need for tolerance to all religions in heterogeneous societies so that they are taught in outline a series of religious alternatives which more or less all have similar aims. This appears to lead to children and adolescents not receiving moral guidance from those in authority.

## The Teachers view of Pro-social Behaviour

Teaching is a profession held in high regard in most societies and accepted as part of the political, social and religious purposes of a society and secondly as part of its economic future. While teaching is aimed at making the most of the potential in any student with which teachers are confronted, the realities of teaching often have limited coincidence with their professional aims.

The ability to make the best of the intellectual potential of the children in a day school depends upon a number of factors which are likely to detract from any such possibility. These relate to the pupils, the institutional circumstances in which the teaching takes place and the teachers involved. All these factors come together in affecting pro-social, anti-social and neutral behaviour of the children during the formal processes of education and the informal social system of the pupils which may function parallel to the official system and largely independent of it.

The children will come to school out of social relationships which may have little ability or willingness to support and encourage them to make the best of these educational opportunities. It would often seem that children are educatable and largely conformist until the beginning of adolescence when they may or may not see the competitive educational system as related to their real or imaginary futures.

In the contexts of London and the United States children from Asian families are noticeably ahead of those from other ethnic groups because there is substantial family support for making their children as successful as possible from their education. This would also be the case with the children of professional families where there is already a social ambience for educational success correlated to economic well-being. These children are not in general likely to be non-conformist.

Girls in most schools are likely to be conformist which may have originated in some sexual patterning but now possibly due to their recognition that life-long marriage has become uncertain as well as the fact that in the political environment of opposition to sexism, employment opportunities are there should they qualify. Boys in societies with high unemployment are less likely to conform; they see obstacles to their ambitions which involve ethological and social conditioning for male dominance.

There may be other factors which contribute to the pro-social behaviour of children. In African schools such as in Uganda, the children may have high levels of hook-work infestations reaching 40 per cent in some schools where there is much standing water and shoes are not worn all the time. This makes them anaemic and listless; a form of pro-social behaviour which easily and combines with the walk to school and no breakfast. A Baptist secondary school in Mombasa found that by providing the pupils with bread and tea on arrival, their alertness markedly improved.

Then there are the institutional circumstances of each school. Some are well set up with adequate equipment but schools are expensive to run and there may be a shortage of books and materials. Ethiopean and Peruvian children acting as amateur guides for tourists preferred to be paid in ball-point pens than money.

When the schools are in poor states of repair and ill-equipped the children may be more inclined to avoid the required pro-social behaviour and develop their own undercover standards. This is particularly so in urban schools which have a poor reputation and are even seen by the pupils themselves as dumping grounds for the less successful.

Lastly teachers. If their success in developing the talents of the children in their care other than by production line methods, then there have to be stimulating personal relationships. Only in such schools such as those of the Amish are they likely to be taught by a few locally known teachers and even there the numbers of pupils in a class are likely to be large and much will be devolved onto older ones teaching the younger ones. In many schools in developing nations the pressure on schools is such that teachers work double shifts with different pupils in morning and afternoon; an exhausting process for all involved.

For any pro-social influence to be effective then class numbers would have to be small but in most schools these are likely to be more than ten with different teachers teaching different subjects so that an individual child may be under the possible influence of may be as many as a dozen adults. What then is the reality of teaching as an influence to pro-social behaviour?

Teachers are committed to conforming to a syllabus and to complete it in time for periodic competitive examinations. Their means for doing this is the regular provision of information, periodic availability for questions depending on the size of the class, conformity to time tabling bells and the correction of written work. Thus it would seem likely that teachers might be overworked during term time and when it is combined with extra-curricula activities, they will have little time for more than peripheral influence on individual children and adolescents.

It would seem likely that teachers will have expectations of and preference for the type of pro-social behaviour expected in the professional class from which they have come or to which they now belong by professional training; that is an ostensible conformist quietness regardless of what might or might not be happening off stage.

Disruptive behaviour of any type would prevent would prevent keeping to the time-tabling of the curriculum and handicap not only the progress of the other pupils in the class but the critical evaluation of teachers own professional status. It would seem therefore to be the teachers' view the pro-social behaviour of pupils should be conformity to the requirements of institutional life with such variations as might stimulate well-motivated ones.

## Pro-social Behaviour and Personal Ambition

Children attending school and in developed societies this is for a very long period indeed extending to well over ten years and over the menarche which divides biological children from biological adults. If the children aim for professional status such as medicine, this may involve twenty or more years of economic and social dependency on their parents or the state; functionally they are adults in the roles of children. This of course does not happen in subsistence societies where no parents can afford the luxury of useless dependency.

Children from an early age will have ambitions which may indeed be unrealistic, but whatever they may be, education and earning capacity are closely connected in their minds. At the end of this long process for which most of the acquired learning would appear to have little relationship to potential jobs; what will be their chances in the outside world if they conform.

Here there is a fundamental split between budget conscience elected politicians and educationalists. The latter group states almost as a dogma that education is good in itself and should be available indeed compulsory for all children in terms of equal opportunity.

It seems likely that children and adolescents and their parents as well pass over such an idea as well and good but see education as a means to getting and retaining a job. But there is a crude equation here that the more people who qualify educationally, the status of a particular qualification will decline unless the overall economy expands at more or less the same rate to provide more jobs. In Tanganyika in 1948 the long serving chief clerk in the district office had three years primary education but by 1958 the same post was held in Pangani by someone who had passed out of his secondary school with credits in half a dozen subjects.

In Britain today there are more qualified students than jobs for which they may feel themselves entitled. The gossip lines among students in any school will be aware of these facts. Education may not be appreciated as a "good thing" unless it provides jobs and those may come from the qualifications which are hardest to earn.

This educational oversupply is perhaps more obvious in developing countries where jobs in government departments are in short supply and not well paid so that moonlighting becomes a necessity or at least keeping their family farms going. In countries becoming independent there was a lurch into high level employment from the departure of expatriates and then to fill posts from the optimism of development plans.

In Zambia where there is widespread unemployment and underemployment parents are questioning whether the costs of education for them in lost family labour when their children cannot get jobs out of the penury and uncertainties of subsistence farming. Indeed the movement now is away from the unending uncertainties of urban-industrial living into the better known and to some extent socially controllable uncertainties of farming their own land. Beyond the obvious advantages of primary education, there are less obvious value in struggle for secondary education and beyond.

## Chapter-12

# ANTI-SOCIAL BEHAVIOUR

The analysis of anti-social behaviour whether by children, adolescents or adults is handicapped by two major considerations. Firstly at one end of the scale of understanding it is entangled in moral values that certain types of behaviour are wrong regardless of the circumstances. Secondly the very general social reluctance to accept that whether acts are pro-social or anti-social depends on the circumstances over which individuals may have little control; that a particular type of behaviour may be right or wrong in a variety of situations which are never similar.

In this there appears to be some systematic differences between the non-literate thinking of people in subsistence societies and the literate thinking and codifications of more economically developed societies. In general subsistence societies rarely if ever see behaviour in abstract terms but rather in relation to the social circumstances in which they occur dividing anti-social behaviour between delicts which are of private concern to those involved and those that upset the communities in which they occur. Thus murder may be seen as a matter to be settled between the families concerned while urinating in drinking water sources while drunk is more serious as it affects all the users of that spring.

The solution as to anti-social behaviour will not be seen in the clear cut categories of guilty or not guilty of western criminal justice but in terms of contributory minimising or maximising factors and penalties are devised towards restoring social balancing relationships between those involved and the community as a whole; social relationships which are valuable should be kept a intact as possible. To find someone guilty does not solve what is in effect a social problem for those who see each other regularly in the course of their social lives.

Learned elders who help to construct manuals of customary law may have some general background ideas of what is right and wrong in discussions which are detached from the realities of communal life; the practicalities of coping with an upset are always situational since they know the background to what has happened before they have to arbitrate. It is not the bad behaviour of a particular child or adolescent but whose which is important.

## Issues in the Moral Development of Children

The pro-social behaviour and socialisation of children to this end in the contemporary world tends to be seen and evaluated in terms of moral imperatives which in their abstract definitions tend to be detached from the social and economic realities in which most if not all children are raised. Indeed the phrase itself is not one which most parents would recognise in their natal languages if it existed there at all. Anti-social behaviour is also seen in moral terms of being "bad".

It seems unlikely that children as a matter of course go through stages of moral development as detailed by Piaget because basically this implies if not requires a stable social environment not only for the individual child but for their surrounding society. Such a possibility of children passing through such stages would not apply to the street children of Brazil who are stuck in the necessities of daily survival or for Amish children who become aware of wide ranging moral obligations almost as soon as they leave infancy.

It seems unlikely that children as a matter of course go through stages of moral development except in the ideal and somewhat abstract social conditions in middle class nuclear Western families rather than communities in which every one is living in very variable conditions.

In social reality there are different types of moral systems into which children are socialised typified by religious and social differences involving polygyny, bilateral inheritance, communal feeding and single parenthood to name just a few and while they can be called stages under certain possibly rare social conditions, there is little reason to suppose that they are necessary stages. J.G. Ballard's novel about an English child in Japanese occupied Shanghai showed the extreme ranges of behaviour which that child required in order to survive which in Piagetian terms would have been a reversion from previously held higher stages under the force of circumstances; with the disappearance of his parents there is the moving depiction of the boy begging in school uniform (Bauaro, 1983).

If we take the position that there are stages (Eckensberger, 1994: 71-78), it is quite illusory to see that children brought up in the harsh conditions of subsistence farming in India or in the equally restrictive but pleasanter ones of a Hutterite commune in Canada are going to go through similar stages or that they will have much in common with those brought up and continue to live in the urban slums of Lima, Accra, New York or Johannesburg.

Let is look at these stages. Stage One in which the child connects obedience with punishment which is described as the universal primitive view of morality; one questions why this should be considered 'primitive' when it is a common enough contemporary view. Stage Two in which the child follows rules only if it is to their advantage to do so; what is right is an equal exchange, a good deal which is described as both individualistic but primitive; this appears to ignore the calculating nature of most adult inter-relationships; a subsistence farming Sukuma keeps it very clear in his head what he is owed and what he is owing in a combination of social and economic values. Stage Three in which the child does what he or she is expected to do by the in-group and their role in it, described as a primitive collectivist position; again one wonders why this is described again as "primitive" when this is no more than the child conforming to requirements of family living . Stage Four in which the child does her or his duty and what is required of them by law, described as a more sophisticated collectivist position which is more likely to be the case when children feel that they are under supervision. Stage Five has an emphasis on social contract and individual rights; the growing children may hold a variety of opinions and although most values are relative to the group to which one belongs, they should usually be upheld. Finally Stage Six in which there is a focus on universal ethical principles and particular laws and rules are valid if they are consistent with such principles. Principles such as justice, equality of human rights and respect for the dignity of human beings as individuals are not negotiable.

Apart from the fact that circumstances may dictate that individual children and their parents may be forced by circumstances or choice to move up and down on such stages, there is also the fact that the Amish way of living with its absence of punishment and the dominance of example would seem to mean that their children are in Stage Six from the earliest ages at which they have social identities.

It seems certain that these are not stages although they may correlate with age-related awareness, but once a child becomes aware of rightness and awareness, then these are no longer stages but alternatives. They become matters of choice within the options provided by their personalities as genetically endowed and the social and physical environment within which they are constrained by social distance factors. A child may be taught universalistic principles by people with whom they are socially distant but it seems unlikely that they ever coincide with the realities of social distance and this is the most important issue to consider in pro-social socialisation.

## The Dominance of Social Distance in the Socialisation of Children

It is in the nature of social science to look for similarities of behaviour in children and their development from infancy into adulthood and yet we must always accept that there are no such overall similarities. There is in the individuality of the child both genetic and environmental factors, the basic units of difference but these are always modified to some extent by the obligations of living in common which is often treated as communalism.

Living in common whether in the semi-isolated nuclear or extended families must involve a constantly adjusting balance between individual needs and those of the primary people with whom they are living on and off for a range of calendrical periods and correlated to age. Communalism as expressed in secondary and tertiary relationships has none of this quasi-permanency and correlates to situational pressures.

The extent to which the individual is integrated into common living submerging his or her individuality is controlled by social distance factors. The nearer other people are in space, kinship or affinity, the stronger their influence on and socio-psychological control of the individual.

As social distance lengthens, the individual is more and more surrounded by people with whom there is no or limited inter-relationship, so that the possibility of individuality increases as communality diminishes. So for all practical purposes the child grows into forms of pro-social behaviour dictated by the immediacies of primary relationships to which are attached in diminishing circles obligations to the state and the abstract ideologies of religion and social justice. Anti-social behaviour thus may become more frequent as the controls of the primary group become less and less relevant.

So while it is theoretically possible (Triandis, 1995) to assess whether the individual child, adolescent or adult has individualistic or collectivist motivations, this would appear to be more the assessments as to what at any given time they believe to be the correct behaviour.

If situational questions are asked, the answers would be similarly abstract. Real life reactions to stress would fluctuate in and out of individualism and collectivism in ways that might vary from day to day. The child's feeling of happiness or unhappiness or whatever would affect their reactions; they are not going to cry in the same way for the same reasons in successive incidents.

It would not be possible to find any social activities which are either individualistic or collectivist. For the subsistence farmer to go and drink beer at a neighbour's rite of passage or for a skilled worker to buy a new tool combine both aspects of social living, increasing their socials options and personal satisfactions. Few recognise the extent to which children are socialised into the practice of deceit with their neighbours with whom their parents are rivals but have to be in public tolerance. They will see the expressions on their parents' faces and note the tone and content of what they say which will change as soon as those people are out of hearing and sight.

Children may be brought up to think that certain dimensions of behaviour are correct but they are not taught that these requirements change with social distance from tight obligations to vague guidelines which adults rarely feel much need to follow because of time and material expenses. Children realise that caring for a sick sibling and a sick neighbour are not the same but that both in their own ways are social and psychological investments; there are individual, familial and communal pay-back factors. There is nothing to gain or maintain in helping a stranger away from the primary environment.

Children grow up into and are faced early in their lives with relational realities; nearness is a reality and combined biological and social subordination is the first factor of importance in their lives. Hindu children in a village learn very early that everyone in the village outside their own sub-caste is either superior or inferior to them and that the only partial relief from this may lie in the anonymity of the nearby town. Those who are seen less often are less necessary and less influential. Social distance may be a factor in extended families and children may feel more emotionally close to matrilateral than patrilateral relatives and of course there are always the personal preferences of the children which may override socially rational considerations. They learn soon enough to evaluate the proportional differences between the emotional and material aspects of relationships.

It is necessary to see communalism in this light as only existing more or less consistently in the family within the reality of everyday living. What is involved in living in a community is always a periodic dilution of this and the necessary as much as voluntary participation of their adults in this which will be noticed by the child. The Soviet child in school will have been constantly exhorted to show practical consideration for others in the school, but however persistent and efficient this may have been, it will always have been less important as an influence on these children than their home environments in which there is a pay-off for conformity which covers more social space and time than the school environment.

There is not much in communal activities which relates to the importance of everyday activities; cleaning the local dam, repairing roads or the local shrine, festivals for harvests, national days, local rites of passage and the need to pray for rain or the reduction in epidemic diseases. Horizontal communality of the neighbourhood or village depends on the matters in issue and something has to be very important indeed for the child to recognise that the primacy of their own family which leads to social distance disengagements from their neighbourhoods has to be overridden for the common good. Whole communities may turn out to build or repair a local earth dam but not for shrines in which the spirits may have connection with families not communities.

Pro-social behaviour is directly linked to what both children and adults know to be the realities of social distance. Any sense of communalism becomes increasing attenuated with social distance. Individualism while being a constant feature in any social situation becomes easier to express as the enforceable obligations to others become less efficient and more ideological.

In attempting to find any cross-cultural themes in the social behaviour of children, it may be that different cultures are not deeply different but that the information provided by different researchers who have different ideas and forms of their professionalism. The fact that one study does not mention sibling rivalry may mean that there is a shortage of siblings or high rates of long distance migration, just as the absence of affectionate relationships between alternate generations may relate to the high mortality rates of middle aged adults. The abstract categorisations of researchers may be correct but how children and adults see their lives will be in the immediacies of their particular social environments.

## Anti-social Behaviour in Subsistence Communities

In such communities the children are so closely integrated into the round the clock lives of the people who care for them, that anti-social behaviour may be an inappropriate phrase to use. Within the family children will be required to obey their parents since from the earliest ages they are participating part-time adults; any reluctance to do so would usually result in beating and it is unlikely to be a please and thank you situation. Both boys and girls are expected to be obedient but girls are expected to be more deferential and mothers often allow their sons to get away with minor infractions of behaviour when out of sight of their fathers.

Since there is no form of diminutive scaled down language which is used to children, they are brought up to hear and understand its use in an adult environment. In Okinawa conversation is not changed in the hearing of children as they are not thought to understand but of course they do (Maretzki, T.W. & H., 1963). The complications of the use of language in its social environment as it relates to sex, age, status and caste would be easily absorbed and with it conformity to a network of relationships with whom their carers are concerned. Children will not be praised for conformity but will be penalised for behaving in word or gesture ways which bring shame to their adults. Children who behave so badly that their surrounding community reacts not against them but against their parents will anger their carers.

There is also a religious factor in controlling the behaviour of both children and adults in families which are not adulterated by migration; good cohesive behaviour may not be specifically noticed by the ancestors, but behaviour certainly will be and shown in the misfortunes which occur to adults. Adults are not going to tolerate behaviour by children which are so disturbing as to displease both the living and the dead. In Mexico Mixtec children are brought up to be wary of the spirits and in particular of the evil eye of jealous neighbours and those who may be witches (Romney, K & R., 1963).

In Hindu families such as the Rajputs the child is seen as an incarnation and they are breast fed for long periods because of the fear of food pollution which combines with a suspicion of outsiders and the influences of the evil eye. As a refraction of this the children learn early about the inferiority of women and the rudeness of a boy to his mother or to lower-caste servants would not be penalised (Minturn & Hitchcock, 1963). In all such communities the school going of children will be seen as disruptive and not much allowance made for home work.

If children misbehave in a subsistence community at any age, the community has immediate social and economic sanctions which it can impose when a family's child becomes a public rather than private nuisance. Letting livestock stock break into another family's fields, excreting in an area not reserved by custom for their sex, taking maize cobs to eat from a field owned by persons to whom they are not related and behaving disrespectfully to unrelated elders.

For private delicts within the family the mother is likely to be more lenient but beating is likely to be the reaction of most fathers to disobedience. The options open to the child are to keep quiet or to runaway to a nearby relative until matters cool down. For the child to runaway to a town is probably self-defeating because relatives there are not likely to welcome an additional mouth to feed with food which has to be bought unless they are prepared to act as servants.

Subsistence communities are not similar in their moral and behavioural codes despite the fact that they are usually only concerned as individuals and families with their own short-term needs. Hunters and gatherers, farmers and herders will have different perspectives of appropriate behaviour which are not itemised written codes, since in their day to day functioning these are non-literate systems.

The behaviour required of children will relate to the cultural and economic needs of their guardians within broad cultural understandings of what is considered sensible in the circumstances probably largely based on what has been seen to work in the past. These are not child centred family systems.

In societies with low accumulations of food resources usually covering the family and individual needs from one harvest to the next, adults tend to be individualistic, assertive and venturesome, many short-term quick decisions would have to be made over the time of planting and harvesting. On the other hand in societies with high accumulations of food resources, cattle, coconut and oil palms, adults tend to be cautious, complaint and conservative because their thinking would be more long-term. So child training and behavioural expectations would be linked to the type of behaviour useful for the adult economy (Barry et al., 1959).

So it would seem that these two types of subsistence societies would expect their children to behave accordingly. In the former to be quick off the mark and in the latter more considerate of the implications of what they do. Consequently anti-social behaviour in the former might well relate to not taking advantage of opportunities, what might in a modern society be called street market trader awareness and in the latter acting too quickly over matters which might have long-term consequences.

## Anti-social Behaviour in Exclusive Communities

Exclusive communities are just that; groups of people living largely defined lives within defined social and geographical environments. Of course individuals can belong to exclusive communities in their minds for which there may well be only infrequent inter-relationships which give these exclusivities corporate form and without this these can have little influence on child behaviour.

Exclusive communities which have continued over generations have sets of rules which their members feel is in their own interests to obey or to negotiate changes. Without such sets of rules which are largely independent of charismatic individuals, exclusive communities which may be high on ideals but low on the practicalities of communal living, do not last long.

Exclusive communities which do last and thus involve the bringing up of children, tend to have rules which make their exclusivity obvious to children as much as to adults in what they wear, eat, behave and their manner of providing for the continuation of the community; successful farming, ample good food as well as the excitements and drudgeries of communal life are as obvious to children as they are to adults.

An exclusive community is one in which its membership includes people of all ages and both sexes and as far as possible is responsible for its own social and economic life; it is an independent enclave in the surrounding society. A boarding school has only a limited range of functions and it is not an integrated demographic unit. An exclusive community has a designed purpose in which everyone as far as possible is integrated into a common way of life round the clock and throughout the year.

The Amish are surrounded by people who are visibly dissimilar as they are to them. For these people it is not so much a question of avoiding the outside world as a preferred way of life as a community which provides for a high standard of living without the distractions of materialism. Their children are indeed brought up to conform to that productive wholeness which is communally sustained rather than to anticipate individualised non-communal futures.

Obedience and helping others is not so much an abstract ideal as part of the practicalities of living in small communities in which a high proportion of daily living is spent in primary relationships. Those with outsiders are often found to be unfavourable in their latent hostility and the fact that they have not been as successful as themselves in providing for a continuing reasonable standard of living frees them from many of the deviances which seem to bedevil the outside world.

Outsiders tend to see these exclusive communities such as the Hutterites in terms of their deviant characteristics from what the macro-society generally does; it is foolish at best to wear special clothes and it cannot be humane or sensible to eat and live communally so that a married couple only have a single room and have few individualised parental duties. So it seems that these critics concentrate on the isolating nature of what they define as deviance into which their children are socialised without accepting the advantages of such away of life from which there are few drop-outs.

The lives of these exclusive communities provide a range of material and psychological advantages into which their children are socialised and through which the individual is subordinated to the functionally successful communal good. In fact their children may well grow up into an understanding of what they gain from this subordination of individualism which can be seen as destructive elsewhere.

While the Amish appear to outsiders as living restricted lives, for their children there would be a known range of social behaviour enforced at its edges by the use of the cane and in adolescents by a certain amount of tolerance which their adults accept as part of their growing sexuality and their need to taste something of the outside world before commitment to their way of life through adult baptism.

After all the Amish child is surrounded not only by a caring community which looks after its own handicapped members but a successful one with a high standard of living; the amount and variety of food taken on a picnic shows this well enough. The communal concern for the welfare of all is shown in communal barn raising and their material support for young couples to start up their own farms.

The children see uniformity but they also do not see disturbing and ostentatious differences in standard of living and behaviour. For most there is quite enough individuality to satisfy their average needs in the ways that they decorate their horse-drawn buggies and indulge in inter-personal intrigues. The behaviour of children in their schools shows that the uniformity of much of their lives does not suppress their individuality. From a child's point of view their early involvement in the farming activities of their parents must be exciting. Their participation at far earlier ages than would be allowed by employment laws, gives them actual responsibilities; driving horse wagons, ploughing and haymaking.

Their experience of one room multi-grade schooling would be less stressful and useful training for their subsequent communal lives than participation in State schools with their structure of inter- and intra-grade competition, stress on sports and subject segregation. They are educated for the lives which they are likely to lead not for one which is unlikely to follow.

Not only do these schools remain community ones in which the children are always being educated among children and adults whom they know from their home lives, but one in which the older children do much of the teaching of the younger ones which is also a successful part of Russian primary schooling. The school social environment may mean that all involved are treated in some ways as classificatory relatives.

Of course there are disadvantages of such narrow forms of socialisation in a multi-facetted world but it may be that this is not deprivation from which such children as the Amish suffer. A comparative study of such children to non-Amish ones showed them to be more submissive but emotionally well adjusted (Engle, 1943). The hostility of the outside world to their passivism and the intermittent and continuing objections of government educational authorities to what they see as the "primitive" nature of Amish schools is unlikely to alter the positive socialisation which their children receive from their inclusive way of life.

Parents are considered responsible for bringing up their children into God fearing and useful lives as farmers and discipline is enforced with a switch but not harshly. The children in effect are controlled into an all embracing pattern of behaviour in which continuing anti-social behaviour would tend to lead to leaving the community in late adolescence rather than remaining as an erosive element within communities.

It would seem that for children in Amish and Orthodox Jewish communities there are sets of rules pragmatically enforced and that as they grow up they sense that through this socialisation there are boundaries beyond which they cannot go without inconveniencing themselves and leaving the community; this is a high price to pay for being persistently deviant.

Thus anti-social behaviour is basically limited by the inevitability of exclusion from a known and very particular way of life which is much more than the commonplace leaving home of adolescents in outside western society. The alternative of secretive anti-social behaviour is again self-limiting by its secretive nature and that if it became known, there is not so much the problem of breaking the law, but of self-expulsion from a wide ranging particularised way of living.

## Anti-social Behaviour in Inclusive Communities

In many societies communities are defined by their minority or majority status whether by religious, ethnic or by the development of inter-communal tension, those involved and their children grow up in an understanding of opposition; they are Muslim, Catholic, Shia, Pakistani or whatever.

This sense of inclusiveness is not enough to provide the round the clock largely beneficial social and economic exclusiveness which is seen among the Amish and Orthodox Jewish communities. Thus their inclusiveness is always a matter of degree as this is always watered down by the fact that they live in societies dominated by different principles and to whose practices they conform by unavoidably or as a matter of convenience; schools, transport, banking, shopping, housing, electronic entertainment and health services. Their eyes and ears are always confronted by the "others" against whom they have been socialised more by ideology than social necessity from their parents, their places of worship and often the special schools which they are allowed to run on denominational principles. A Roman Catholic in Ulster remembers that in his youth that "to go into a Protestant church was to commit a mortal sin. They hadn't the true faith like us Catholics; God alone knew what horrible things they got up to inside the church and when they died they would all go to hell" (Hoban, 1994). In its extreme forms many children in Muslim countries grow up into similar views of unbelievers. In such situations children can be anti-social in the views of the surrounding society while being conformist within them.

The children of immigrants are often socialised into two language communalism used inside and outside their homes. The home languages will carry their own special inclusive meanings tied to the practices and ideas of their parents. The out of the home languages of the dominant society will carry with it a similar range of practices and ideas continually reinforced by the surrounding culture. Similarly children can be behaving socially or anti-socially behaving in the same way but in different localities; the front door is a passage barrier between two moral systems.

This form of socialisation is more frequent at the lower end of the social and economic scale where the sense of inclusiveness provides a partial domestic and communal antidote to the functional handicaps which they experience in the surrounding society. A confusing world for children wanting or perhaps needing clearer guidance on how they should behave.

## Anti-social Children in Fringe Communities

Much depends on the key words used to describe behaviour as to whether adults and children are considered to be behaving pro-socially. In well-organised economically rich societies the behaviour and social environments of children are looked at with predefined terms in mind such as home, family protection, responsible adult and regular supportive relationships. These are seen in totally different terms by fringe communities which have their own ideas of normality which is certainly the case with so-called street children of Asia and Latin America. If the word "children" is linked with the word "street", there is a semi-automatic build-up of concern as in Western eyes and assessments of welfare which are based on Western standards, the street is almost by definition a dangerous place in which no one would want to spend their lives or indeed should be forced to do so. Thus the phrase "street children" has a stigmatising effect associating such children with delinquency rather than with the views of the children themselves and whether or not they are spending their lives on the street (Invernizzi, 2001: 79).

In all societies there are groups of people who are defined in popular thinking as a social such as the gypsies in Britain despite the fact that in welfare terms they are described as travellers. In India prior to independence there were groups legally defined as criminal sub-castes because they were thought to get their livelihoods as professional thieves. Now they are still defined as scheduled and thus the objects of special official treatment and popular bias. Thus the pro-social behaviour as part of their communal lives becomes anti-social only in terms of the surrounding macro-society.

In countries such as Britain and Germany with comprehensive social welfare systems there are still groups containing children which successfully evade this system because they do not wish to have their way of life modified by officialdom or because they have practices which could make them liable to prosecution; in either case they see the implementation of the ideology of the majority about how children should be socialised in terms of interference or persecution.

The families of the extremely poor or the improvident and addicts with children who will always live on the fringes of short-term deprivation. There are also those that live in short-lived communes or squats or use their children as a means of regular support or have ways of treating their children of which their neighbours disapprove, will always be liable to have their children removed by court order and put into care. These children are likely to be brought up to see what is required of them by this outer world as best avoided and certainly not copied.

Within these social welfare systems there may be two parallel worlds into which the children of such families and communes are socialised. That of conformity to the demands of their immediate social environments into which they are socialised of which obedience and helping in the day to day survival of their families would predominate, combined with the parallel set of behavioural avoidances related to the wider society in which they live.

There is also the distinction between the children and their problems when they are brought up in what their surrounding societies would call deviant conditions which their official views of correct socialisation is rightly or wrongly constantly invading their privacies; pockets of inadequacy over which the majority may feel an amalgam of guilt and hostility.

However outside these societies with their comprehensive welfare systems, there are societies in which the majority of citizens live under conditions of intermittent or indeed permanent deprivation in comparison to the standards of Western societies. In these societies welfare agencies often provided by non-governmental or international agencies can only deal with the extremes edges of child misery in which their pro-social behaviour is geared to their own survival.

The pro-social behaviour of children tangled into such situations as in other social environments has to be evaluated more analytically than by abstract standards. Do the children see themselves as acting pro-socially in ways acceptable to the conditions under which they live with their peers, then to their families as actually existing, the immediate surrounding society and lastly to the administrative structure of the state; these are likely to vary and have very little effect on what the children can do and the possibilities of variation.

When children are employed in identifiable enterprises such as Indian match factories or the carpet weaving of Pakistan and Egypt, then the state welfare concern can find a focus and indeed a rationalisation for their employment as contributors to the subsistence of their own families as a better solution than ever wider destitution.

But with the street children there is an absence of any consistency; some are full time on the street, others weave in and out of children's homes, others are seasonal and some harvest opportunities on the streets from some sort of family home. There are several factors which suggest that the social conditions under which they self-govern themselves are more favourable than the alternatives. They rely on networks of peer solidarity and even though there may be shortfalls in what they are able to earn, this may be higher than if they were formally employed and working from home (Scanlon et al., 1998).

It may well be that these so-called street children are admirably resilient and display creative coping strategies for growing up pro-socially in difficult social and economic environments (Veale et al., 2000). Furthermore it may be the case that some of these children are caring for incapacitated adults rather than the reverse as the primary income earners in their households; they are performing pro-socially in more effective ways than would be the case if they were dependent on official or non-governmental agencies for help.

On the other hand slum children who live in shanty towns or in sidewalk bivouacs, may have little contact with the adults which they acknowledge to be their families as they are often away looking after their own livelihoods and many indeed report that they have never known their fathers. This has meant that their dominating peer group contacts may start very early in their lives (Singh & Pothen, 1982).

These slum children will have had an early and long experience of themselves and their families both from other slum dwellers and from the authorities who periodically try and clear away slums with bulldozers (Mtshali, 1982). In the case of Brazil the police are suspected of having death squads killing troublesome juveniles grouped in gangs.

Slum children certainly have a wide range of income generating activities. The young girls are more useful than boys as they can work as low grade domestics by neighbours and classificatory kin. School even if it is available is likely to be an intermittent experience with no positive holding force on them either at the time or in its subsequent influence on their thinking and behaviour. Children of both sexes offer a wide range of informal services such as sexual services through being offered food, money and clothes as well as semi-formal employment as beggars, pickpockets and bag snatchers (Swart-Kruger & Donald, 1994).

There is also the wider issue that if children have rights, then they have the right of choice when the more officially satisfying alternatives are just not available (Panter-Brick, 2002). There is an important pro-social aspect as the notion of freedom is consistently reported by street children with their autonomy and self-directed choices rather than being held in institutions. This is even though the relationship with their peers is by nature erratic and temporary it is nevertheless the source of shared information about economic prospects and safety.

In societies which are theoretically stable in the sense that parenthood and childhood are connected in a high percentage of social situations, systems of pro-social socialisation can be found, analysed and nudged into improvement away from the fringes of what is seen as social delinquency. Leaving aside the distress which follows disaster and civil disturbances, this does not allow for the social disorder following specialised epidemics.

The AIDS epidemic in sub-Saharan Africa which has heterosexual epidemiological characteristics, is creating very large numbers of orphans for whom pro-social socialisation by their parents is neither an ideal nor a possibility. Of course this has often been the case in which fathers have married younger women and the average expectation of life is still around the mid-40s. But such orphans have always been cared for by their extended families which have also been decimated and have never had the characteristics of such enormity as to become a major social issue.

Currently according to UNICEF there are around 11 million children in sub-Saharan Africa who have lost at least one parent from AIDS which is eleven times the estimated number for 1990. By 2010 there could be as many as 20 million orphans in this area. UNICEF estimates that orphaning rates above 5 per cent exceed the capacities of local communities to care for parentless children and in contemporary Zambia a high proportion of orphans are AIDS related.

Under normal circumstances orphans are cared for by extended families but these are already much less cohesive than they may have been traditionally with the migratory pattern of young male employment, the instability of marriage leading to matrifocal families in both rural and urban localities and high death rates in the middle age range of relatives who might otherwise have cared for orphans.

The result is often that orphans end up being cared for inadequately by grandparents or a single grandparent at the end of their productive and supportive lives who instead of being cared for by their own surviving children, are now expected to care for extra dependents.

In every biological and social sense these orphans are at great risk with fewer opportunities to acquire a range of pro-social behaviour patterns; they are at high risk of carrying HIV themselves, apart from the psychological effects of watching at least one of their own parents slowly die. In Zambia two-thirds of child prostitutes are AIDS orphans. Many suffer from persistent malnutrition and get little or no formal education so drift into becoming street children.

There are several types of migrating communities both in traditional societies of cattle herders and modern societies in which children grow up within a form of socialisation which is quite adequate by the standards of those groups. These societies such as the Romany one, have their own language and self-sustaining conventions which for both adults and children function both to exclude outsiders and to usefully tighten their own inclusiveness. It seems reasonable to suggest that in these circumstances the children are brought up to a reasonable standard of pro-social behaviour which does not necessarily clash with that of the surrounding society.

Some exclusive religious sects have had poor effects on the pro-social training of children when membership includes a repudiation of family ties and responsibility towards the families of converts. In the United States Father Divine movement children were accepted as members of the Kingdom but were often rejected latter. They suffered behavioural disorders due to social and emotional insecurity because of the neglect of their parents who were previously recognised by the movement. There were also problems as the children were deprived of the social enjoyments and social contacts outside the sect (Bender, 1940).

Most macro-societies accept that there are various types of communities within their boundaries which vary from what the majority of citizens might consider as having correct but not ideal behaviour. There are always going to be micro communities which are considered to be outside the orbit of political, social and economic acceptability the septic fringe communities of urban-industrial society.

The high density poverty stricken slums on the edges of Third World towns make the anti-social behaviour of children almost inevitable. These communities live in decayed housing, housing made of packing cases without sanitation or water seasonally either too hot or too cold, the pavement livers in Indian cities and those who live in concrete drain pipes during urban regeneration schemes as well as the squatters in abandoned housing.

All these communities have aspects of pro-social behaviour taught to their children which cannot be subject to complaint; the indulgence towards infants, but with abrupt late weaning at 2-3 years and obedience to their parents. They are all taught to hold hostility to a minimum but the children are above all under pressure to become self preserving adults as early as possible as their social environment is so obviously unreliable (Nydegger, F and C, 1963).

These communities are in practice isolated to a very large extent from the main-stream socialisation because their children are brought up to accept the advantages and obligations of what is often both geographical and social isolation. The "us" in this context within which children develop provides them with the advantages of conformity in the mutual support provided against the "them" of outsiders.

## Anti-social Behaviour in Bureaucratically Defined Communities

While most societies devote much ideological attention to the family as having primary responsibility for the pro-social behaviour of their children much of their waking lives are spent out side and beyond the control of even the most responsible of parents.

In economically well-developed societies children from an early age spend most of their waking lives for most of the year in communities which are both bureaucratically and geographically separate from the outside communities in which they live and of course from their homes. A different set of behaviour is expected of them and enforced as soon as they pass through its gates.

There is an intensification of this segregation of children from the surrounding society starting with pre-school nursery play schools, the day schools possibly involving the children for eight hours per day, then boarding schools with fixed terms divided by holidays, officially run homes for those whose parents have been ruled as incapable of caring for them and detention centres for children who have broken the law and received court sentences.

Some centralising states have special organisations for the indoctrination of children into a particular ideological framework such as the Young Pioneers in Communist Russia which did in fact stress obligations to and organise projects for the communities and their families in which the children lived.

In all these situations the child is socialised into pro-social behaviour which is related to a rule book taught by the staff and visible enough on notice-boards and from announcements at assemblies. The child soon learns that there are advantages and disadvantages in conformity to these rules but they also learn at the same time that their lives are slotted into time-tables by the sound of bells and that the whole process of education has many parallels to the conveyor belt in industry. The individual treatment of the child tends to be an exception to the mass process of passing large numbers of children through a graded system of uniformities; the syllabus dictated by the impersonality of examination boards and education ministries.

The boarding school in Western societies is the most obvious example in which control is administered round the clock by formal authorities but overall the commonest exposure would be in the military and for young people legal imprisonment or being taken into care. Particularly in developing societies a large number of citizens have had the experience of imprisonment for political reasons and for petty crimes such as the failure to pay basic "head" taxes. Perhaps unusually a British Colonial Office report on African prisons was headed by the comment about "the gift of civilisation" which presumably meant the imposition of regularity and impersonalised cleanliness.

But for children in increasing numbers the experience of schooling is that of a pattern of required behaving which is totally different to that of the primary group environment in which they have grown up. Much behaviour which is defined as anti-social by the school authorities would not receive much attention at home and the accumulation of transgressions heavily penalises individuals.

Noise is accepted only in specified areas and is at times penalised, punctuality throughout the day is an overriding requirement, sitting still for long periods in specified places and talking only when officially required to do so. So children through education become aware of a whole range of social requirements which while enabling learning would not appear to be an automatic part of learning, and would not relate to learning by emulation in the lives of the higher primates.

This is not to degrade the efforts of teachers to individualise their efforts as much as they can but small group research shows that any group going into double figures tends to become impersonal and to divide itself up into smaller more personal groupings. The system also depersonalises as subjects are taught by different teachers in different places and for different age groups; each child comes under a succession of teachers who may be liked or disliked or to whom they are indifferent; this encourages anti-social behaviour.

From this prolonged experience children also learn that there is an insider social system running parallel to and largely in opposition to the official one which has a different pattern of pro-social behaviour which they learn for their acceptance into the communion of their peers. This bilateral pattern of behaviour which they learn does not teach pro-social behaviour in more than abstract terms but nevertheless may teach valuable lessons in the ways that individualism can be maintained in institutions which would otherwise functionally override their personalities.

The pro-social behaviour marked out through the universalising educational systems of economically well off societies and which are usually emulated to various extents by other states, is a particular form of socialisation coming from particular historical and economic conditions.

It would seem to prepare children for distant idealised and opportunist possibilities for which may be as many as ninety per cent will fail to attain because they cannot reach the standards necessary for employment at a level above that of unskilled or semi-skilled jobs or because employment in hoped for fields are just not there and indeed probably never likely to be in terms of the numbers who aim to qualify for employment there.

Since children are educated en masse because it is accepted both politically and morally as a process that will benefit them while the children as they become adolescents are more interested in job opportunities and to have skills that they can use with some immediate hope of success rather than the abstractions of seemingly unusable learning in the fields of abstract subject learning.

This is a system which has a very short history in which learning is detached from hands on practice and in most societies known from history the main learning which is passed on to children has been from emulation and apprenticeships even for elite positions. The question of what use is this type of education for the generality of children is not a question for which an answer is provided; only such people as the Amish answer this for their long standing social system that they educate their children for the jobs in life which they are likely to do within the community and not for jobs that may or may not be available in the outside world. The Amish had to battle for many years in many states in the United States for the right to conduct their own educational system for their own needs in which a number of adults were sent to prison before it was accepted by official outsider bureaucrats that they were doing a good job in preparing their children for participating in a form of life which the majority continuing to find satisfying (Hostetler & Huntingdon, 1971; Hostetler, 1993; chapter 8).

Schooling may prepare a minority for satisfying roles or to take on their equivalents because their education has stimulated their intelligence. In newly independent countries in which the departure of expatriates from administrative and a variety of non-technical jobs, education paid off immediately but once this vacuum was filled, children were faced with waiting for the retirement of office holders who had been promoted at very young ages or to fill the posts in expanded bureaucracies which provided the prestige of position but low pay and the inevitability of having to moonlight or work part-time on family farms into order to get food. The enthusiasm of parents for education may well be fading fast and be passed on to their children when few employment opportunities exist for which there is harsh competition and the need for nepotism. The same job is requiring higher and higher qualifications as the educational related pyramid fills up from the top. This is a global phenomenon of which children become aware from talking with their peers and their older siblings.

Children are realists and become aware early that equality of opportunity is an illusion; schools and tuition are unequal, personal ability and intentions vary and opportunities at the end of education appear to be dictated by luck and economic needs. Tests and sports are competitive and divisive; these hurdles filter out many more than they filter in. They learn about inequalities from the behaviour of their siblings and from the treatment of the handicapped in their communities as well as a whole range of stereotypes into which they slot everyone in the outside world.

There is another aspect of childhood which teaches them not only that there is no equality but that they are in modern societies debarred legislatively from the opportunities of being useful and even from being required to be useful. They are subjected to segregation by adults not only in compulsory schooling but also in being debarred from employment. In societies which have not reached this level of economic success, children will work in their family homes and contribute to their families by getting work outside in towns and villages because there is no alternative to this practical and urgent necessity. This system seems to ignore the fact that every child are adults in due course will spend their lives in meaningful relationships in small primary groups for which the educational system provides no training at all.

It would seem therefore that these segregating educational systems make a muted contribution to the type of living that these children when grown up are likely to experience and if anything contributes significantly to the anomie felt by many older children who fail to achieve the opportunities for material success and choose therefore to filter into anti-social behaviour.

## Stress on Children in Urban Settings

It has not been established that urban life is by definition more stressful for adults, adolescents and children than any comparable life in rural environments; there are too many variables for any such clear cut distinction which is a commonplace assumption (Inkeles & Smith, 1974). Cities come in many varied forms and provide for individual experiences which provide for the excitements and variations which just do not occur in subsistence farming environments (Basham, 1978). Even contemporary Swedish farmers have described the monotony of agricultural work which may parallel office work but outside the office there is more going on.

Children who have lived all their lives in cities cannot be compared with those who have lived all their lives in rural settings as for a start they will have been socialised into different patterns of thinking and behaving which might even lead to stress. If they are the children of immigrants from what kind of backgrounds have they come and in many African situations children move from urban to rural and back again as their situations demand. Then there is the issue of the type of environment in to which these people move; living in a shanty town on the edge of Lima or on the pavements of Kolkata cannot be compared with a government provided flat in London. There is also the issue as to the extent in which family lives in rural and urban settings are distinctive; the main difference between an overcrowded house in Bangladesh and Birmingham is less heat and the stress reducing automatic provision of water and lighting.

We are looking at whether children are under different or the same forms of stress when they live in distinctly separate social environments or move from one to the other and under what conditions. Are they under stress or do they become socialised by habituation to the forms of living in towns which involve not so much crowding and higher human densities but the density of ethnic and social strangers, smaller families with well dispersed relatives who may even be in other countries and the specialised employment of their fathers who may be away for most of the day and the social isolation of their mothers.

Whether a child is under stress or rather has the adaptive ability to solve their problems by pro or anti-social behaviour depends on their psycho-social personality, the socio-cultural milieu in which they live, the external physical environment and their personal bio-chemistry (Howard & Scott, 1965). The grouping of children into categories prevents the recognition of the very personal ways in which children cope or fail to cope with the conditions under which they are more or less forced to live.

Parents and children moving to cities are either moving involuntarily as refugees from famine or warfare or voluntarily in some sort of planned change for economic betterment in which ordinarily the man precedes and creates a new domestic environment before the family arrives as would be the case of many Asians in Britain.

Alternatively in East Africa the mother remains on the farm and the father works in the town with the children divided between them as with the Haya Protestant clergyman who had the sons with him in the town for better educational opportunities. The daughters remained with his wife who worked the fields to provide him with the means to continue his urban ministry. Alternatively children move in and out of rural and urban environments wherever they may be more economically useful or self-reliant (Weisner, 1976).

Even the usual distinctions between rural and urban environments make changes in how families carry out child training in their pro-social behaviour necessary but there can never be clear cut differences. The availability of traditional child care practices in city living families will carry on whenever the grandparents are regularly involved in child care as their parents are working. At the same time there will be the opportunities to try out new patterns when step-mothers and fathers appear or younger siblings or step-siblings (Whiting, 1974).

Many cities contain pockets of traditionalism in which ethnic or tribal minorities live near to each other in ways which are self-supporting; tribal clusters in Nairobi, caste ones in Banaras or orthodox Muslim families in London in which the women rarely go out of doors and the shopping is done by the husband.

Sometimes there is an adequate social fit between quasi-traditional rural behaviour and the behavioural requirements for urban living. The Sukuma of Tanzania lead lives which have the general characteristics of urban-industrial living; self-reliance, exogamy, living as far away from others as possible and no particular reliance on relatives and affines.

Studies have shown that there are variations in the personalities of the Kenyan children whether they are living in the Nairobi city environment where they were less sociable and more often acted dominantly or aggressively towards their siblings (Weisner & Abbott, 1977) than rural ones.

It is not surprising that children react more clearly to the changes in their lives which come from urban living. The pastoral Guajiro of Venezuela who have come to live in the capital city working in competitive wage labour replacing their pastoral way of life in which their children were productively involved. Parents found that they were powerless to control their economic resources, the disintegration of the corporate descent groups so that the conjugal and mother-child family replacing the matrilocal extended ones. The mother now makes a less important economic contribution so that the rural socio-economic distinctions disappear in the more egalitarian urban culture and more importantly formal education replaces the acquisition of status through kinship and cattle (Watson, 1968).

While sociologists comments have certain uniformity in concentrating on urban density, complexity and mixed cultures concluding that children of necessity must have feelings of isolation and individualism, this may not be so. From a child's point of view cities may be relatively less complex and less demanding that rural life. It is an empirical question as to whether or not city size, complexity and heterogeneity as causes of stress even exist in children's minds (Weisner, 1981).

The main distinction between town and country is that children have few responsibilities which fit into the economic needs of their families which apply as much to a pig farmer in Kansas as it does to the Abaluhyia farmer in Kenya where children are useful. In cities they may be aware of their uselessness and the boredom of selfish individualism; voluntary chores which are not economically necessary and part-time work to give themselves more spending money.

Other variables such as the absence of siblings for regular child care because they are in school and the greater availability of mothers if they do not have paid work, since they do not have to prepare food for cooking, fetch water or firewood, make clear cut divisions impossible.

There is some indication that urban nuclear households are able to exert less pressure for obedience, more shared decision-making, more parent child especially mother-child interactions and more verbal interactions seeking or requesting behaviour from children (Whiting B.D. & J.W.M., 1975).

Children and adolescents in cities have no role other than dependency and their necessary and growing feelings of self-worth are further negated by their long-term subordination in schools as well as in Western societies where there are legal restrictions on their ability to get part-time and holiday work. Their growing feelings of self-importance and their legal subordination is a constant clash encouraging anti-social behaviour.

In cities children are early made aware of the dangerous differences between the home environment and the outside world. In rural situations this distinction is also clear but the unknown "other" is usually well beyond the social and geographical horizon. In cities the "other" is usually omnivorous and is more or less outside the front-door and this dangerous distinction is augmented by the stereotypes of appearance produced by gossip.

Lastly the subsistence farming family may no longer have a father in more or less permanent residence as the low prices for agricultural produce may lead to the absence of the men as migrant labourers leaving the mother to perform the roles of both parents. This is broadly similar to the urban setting where the father is away all week days and is only acting as a parental figure at nights, weekends and for family holidays.

## Behaviour and Reactions to Change

Merton's typology of reactions to change forms a useful framework for assessing the reactions of children to the change with which they are as a matter of course surrounded by the facts of biological and psychological development and alterations within the social environment in which they live (Merton,1957).

The majority of children conform to the broad patterns of behaviour which they learn from their socialisation and the minority who are upwardly mobile because of political and educational processes may still retain in other social areas the patterns of their natal environment. Education in developing countries probably provides the greatest strain on this tendency to conform but there are many young people who go through education as a form of ritualism, going through the processes of participation without seeing any point in it as it might not concern them, doing this because it is less stressful than developing any personal opposition to the processes in which they are involved. They are in education because this is what all other children are going through, a part of the conveyor belt of growing up.

Then there is the reaction of retreatism in which children and more particularly adolescents react to the strains of change by retreating into themselves. They do not turn up for school in large numbers in which they have the tacit agreement of their parents who do not want to be bothered as well as those who go into drink and drugs or become clinically depressed.

In the last two categories there are the revolutionaries who go into active opposition through becoming delinquents in active opposition to all forms of adult socialisation whether in education or the home. Finally there are the children and adolescents who try and alter the circumstances in which they are growing up by developing ambitions and possibly ways of behaviour which involve changes within the system but are not necessarily revolutionary. The difficult child may have sensible ideas behind their non-conformity.

Chapter-13

# Generational Relations and Pro-social Behaviour

Any consideration of the pro-social behaviour of children has to involve from the start the reciprocal behaviour of parents, the inevitable generation gap which is at its most extreme at birth and gradually narrows with increasing age; further that this is combined with the unity of alternate generations and the complications of classificatory relationships and adoption.

These considerations have to start with the basic biological fact that only the mother has a clear biological, observable and unavoidable social link with the baby which she produces. Of course there is a father in every case but who this individual is not known except by the conventions of the society in which a man is accepted as the father of a child; this is not based on any biological proof which has only become available recently and not even in some cases even on proof that the man had access to the woman producing the baby. Some societies are stated not to have understood physical paternity such as the Ananda of Central Australia (Reynolds & Tanner, 1995: 53) and the Tully River Blacks (Wade, 1968). According to Islamic rules a man can claim as legitimate a child born to his divorced wife up to four years after their separation if she has not remarried (Levy, 1069: 79-80). We have to accept that the relationship of the mother to her child is based on nature modified by nurture but that of the father is based on nurture and the only contribution from nature would be genetic traits of which very few are known with any certainty.

The relationship of parents to their children is polarised between that of subsistence societies in which children are material assets in the survival of their own families and in industrial societies in which they are material handicaps restricting the activities and well-being of their parents.

## Generational Relations in Subsistence Families

There is a traditional saying in many subsistence societies that if a guest stays more than a day he is given a spade and expected to help in their livelihood, and much the same applies to children as soon as they are older enough to walk. They are required to take a working part in what their families have to do in order to survive.

Most such societies have words for infant and child but the distinguishing features of those systems are that they are fractions of adulthood, not owning status that is independent. Leaving aside the biological urge to breed and the consequent successful breeding of children they are from the very start weighed up by their parents as potential material assets to their families; they are not seen as having any essential individuality apart from this.

Once the child is born particularly if the baby is a boy and the mother is now referred to as the mother of so and so since his birth has assured the continuation of his father's patrilineage. The daughter has no such status since she marries out and her children do not carry her family's name. The boy is initially seen as the potential supporter of his parents in their old age if only until he marries and segments off with his own family.

Whether the child is a boy or a girl, their births have created a linkage between her husband's and her own families; a larger circle of reciprocal support in times of difficulty as well as widening the sphere of social, economic and political influence.

If the child is a girl and reaches maturity, she will be assessed as a socially marketable commodity in which her assets can be used in negotiating a marriage which will be useful to her parents in which her education would raise her value. In most sub-Saharan societies she brings in bride-wealth payments from the groom's family which are distributed among her patrilineage. In India on the other hand the dowry which the bride has to bring with her if the marriage if aimed at enhancing her family's status and is the cause of much indebtedness. The fact that daughters are assessed in terms of the difficulties which they bring with them is also shown in both India and elsewhere is that sons are fed before daughters and are taken to doctors earlier. Overall with both boys and girls it is hoped that the expenditure for keeping these children up to their marriages will equal the return that their parents get from their work in home and farm; in economic terms there is a balance of payments.

## Generational Relationships in Urban-industrial Families

Even if the isolated nuclear family may not be quite so isolated as the phrase suggests, only in immigrant families are children likely to be born in families in which the mother has permanent built-in help. If there is a permanent relationship between the father and the mother, the arrival of a child means that the binary relationship which created the pregnancy is now a tertiary one in which the child has priority over that relationship; one is perhaps reminded of the sign in the back windows of some British cars that "a dog is not just for Christmas".

From the time of birth the child becomes an increasing handicap on the parents who no longer have any freedom of movement without special arrangements and even the sexual activities of the father and mother have to be modified by times when the child is not listening or is well asleep or out of the house. The clothing and feeding of the child is costly and there is little or no return for their parents as the child only occasionally and usually unwillingly helps in the running of the household.

While in the subsistence family the children help with the upkeep of their own families and there is an appreciable return from their work which replaces that which would have to be done by their parents, this is not so in urban-industrial societies. Incomes of wage earners are not related to their children so that the income for a couple is divided by two but with a child it has to be divided by three. Children are social and economic handicaps.

## Education and its Value to Parents

No traditional society has ever had an educational system or system of training which is not directly related to immediate social and economic needs of those directly involved, possibly only the Jews have historically effectively integrated status and religious education. The early schools in many countries particularly colonial ones were to provide junior clerks for the administration and latter to replace expatriates so that they could run their own countries. Education has started with a close relationship to possibilities of and needs for employment; it is in its foundation utilitarian and only recently has it come to be a "good thing" independent of what use it might be to those who were compulsorily educated.

So if children were useful in the home sending them to school was a handicap on their families overall productivity since very young children can fetch and carry, scare birds and take livestock to water; walking to school also takes up time which might have been productively used at home. Political independence advanced a few but in general education has not provided its much publicised advantages. So in many quasi-traditional subsistence societies, education has not been an asset to parents but has developed into a state created process by which children are encouraged to leave home and no longer contribute to the welfare of their families.

In developed societies in which education is compulsory and whatever the end results it gives mothers some relief from the need to constantly supervise and provide so that they can return to work. Overall education has not been a success since it is undertaken to get employment and it is not related to that nor provided it. Both parents and children have seen education as a means to social betterment and upward mobility; however has the upper grades fill up and depending on the expansion of their society, the more children become educated, the greater the demand for yet higher qualifications. It seems unlikely that any more than a few children being educated see it as a "good thing" if it does not directly help them to become independent of their parents.

It has not brought any relief to parents from the need to support their children except in their regular and episodic absence and they do not help in the house nor do they feel obligated to partially pay back to their parents the costs to them of their upbringing. The educational process does not make many parents feel that they have benefited from having children in the first place.

## Infanticide and the Value of Children to their Parents

If we accept that only in subsistence societies are children of value and that the sentimentality attached to parenthood has probably little significance in comparison to other factors, then we can see that infanticide is perhaps inevitable. Infanticide and abortion has to be seen as a reflection of how prospective parents evaluate the long-term value of their children.

Except in the case of the killing of the first-born children of wealthy Carthaginians (Weyl, 1968) which was done for religious reasons, the killing of their children is done by the parents except in the cases of deformed children who are killed at birth as was the case with the Sukuma of Tanzania.

The parents who kill their children are of course going against the nature of the biological urge to reproduce, so we have an aspect of nurture which is so strong as to overturn something which could be considered genetic as originally something coming from nature.

First there is the issue of straight forward survival. Eskimos have to survive throughout the year by the hunting skills of adult males and it seems that one adult male can keep two to three non-hunting adults alive. Women do not hunt but prepare food and clothing. So it is a straightforward question of reducing useless mouths who in the case of women would marry into other families, so girl babies were often killed. In a Netsilik Eskimo community circa 1920 (Rasmussen, 1931) 40 out of 108 babies were killed of which 38 were girls. Affection for children or its absence had nothing to do with it as girls do not grow into hunters. It was a straightforward question of survival foreseen over the future decades. One suspects that other hunting and gathering societies practice infanticide as a mother can only carry one child at a time as well as the fact that prolonged breast feeding has always limited the possibilities of conception by delaying the restarting of menstruation.

Then in Hindu India if the parents are of a high caste their daughters would have to marry men of an equivalent socio-religious status. If this would be difficult and to which there is the cost of marrying them off, so girls tend to get killed by their fathers (Dickermann, 1979) since these factors were also combined with subsistence farming. The 1852 Mysore census for the Thakoor sub-caste showed 10695 boys to 5865 girls (Pakrasi, 1970).

There is also the case of contemporary China which has a one child per urban family as an enforced rule which at first resulted in so much infanticide of girl babies to have led to a shortfall of millions of girls. This combined with the abortions from a pre-birth diagnosis of the baby's sex, has led to current estimates that some 23 million adult males will not be able to get wives.

There is also the belief in Japan that girls born in the Year of the Horse will make poor wives has led to increased numbers of abortions in 1966, 43.1 as against an estimated rate of 30.6 per 1000 births and neo-natal deaths from whatever cause in that year was 6.94 for boys and 7.78 for girls (Kaku, 1975a and b); a combination of purposive action and neglect.

Infanticide is less likely in Islamic societies in which it is religiously prohibited as in Christianity and Judaism, but their divisionary system of inheritance gives women property in their own right. So it does not make sense to kill them as babies and a lot more sense to marry within the family even to the extent of double cousin marriages so that inherited property stays within the family (Tanner, 1964).

Our conclusion must be that beyond the enduring relationships between mothers and their children, nurture has allowed the consistent killing of girls either in abortion or infanticide when it is in the economic and social interests of the parents and indeed the communities in which they live to do so.

## Illegitimacy and its Relationship to Value of Children

It seems likely that the attitude of parents to their illegitimate children and the adverse effects on such children stems in part from the limited rights which the former have over their offspring. Sukuma men in Tanzania are interested in getting control over illegitimate girl children as they would then have some access to the bride-wealth which might come with their marriages and indeed under urban slum conditions have a value for their mothers which boys do not have as servants and child prostitutes. A Sukuma Christian chief without sons kept his only daughter unmarried so that when she produced a son from a lover, he would be able to inherit his grandfather's position.

So we see that men see value in their children and the need to acknowledge their parentage because they have a legal title to them and this provides them with provable status and without this, fathers have no rights over or expectations from their offspring.

Surely if there was a genetic need for children as individuals there would be cross-cultural evidence of fathers supporting their illegitimate offspring but there is very little evidence of this. Almost universally these children have a morbidity and mortality far higher than that of legitimate ones (Berkman, 1969; Scurletis et al., 1969; Nodari and Pirovane, 1970). These rates only improve when National Health Services provide care based on the child and not its parentage. Well intentioned charitable institutions could do little to offset this mortality (Fortier, 1963) until the invention of vulcanised rubber allowed bottle feeding for abandoned babies.

In conclusion the assessment of adult attitudes to children tends to be twisted round the basic fact that all social scientists have been children and even if they have not had children themselves their relatives and friends have and perhaps more importantly there is usually a critical approach to the behaviour of both adults to their children and to the children themselves which they see around them on an irregular basis. They all start with the feeling verging on certainty that they know much about the subject.

Secondly these assessors of adult to child behaviour are a self-selected group of middle class intellectuals who have become part of a modern paradigm which expects that children should be treated with care and affection as individuals in their own right independent of what their parents may need or expect. In this view they are not to be treated as immature adults, commodities in their families whose potential is to be assessed in relation to the narrow needs of their particular adults who carry the cost of their upbringing.

The conclusions cross-culturally seem to be clear. In subsistence families children have few functions other than that of developing their contributions to their own and their families survival; an elasticity of function in a primary context. In families in which their income is from secondary sources not related to the efforts of family members and usually the only one earner, their children from start to finish are a social and economic handicap reducing the surpluses available to their progenitors for their own uses.

Parental love for their children may well be a modern ideology correlated to and a justification for their expense and may have no independent role. In time and motion terms the showing of affection by parents for their children and children for their parents must be extremely small even in early childhood and for children mainly to gain advantages for themselves.

Children result from biological acts which may not have had the intention of procreation and from this, children are produced which no doubt provide their parents with some psychological satisfactions, particularly their mothers. In modern individualised families they are a handicap on the real and potential activities of their parents and increasingly so until they go off to lead independent live without much concern for their parents unless it is in their material and psychological interests to do so.

Chapter-14

# THE TRANSITION IN MORAL DEVELOPMENT

## The Problem of Contemporary Pro-social Behaviour

Morality is behaviour related to other people, not other people in general but related to specific people. The need to behave in ways that are defined as moral relates overwhelmingly to those in the primary groups in which the individual is socially situated. It is this group and the individual which has to be examined as the basis for all behaviour which can be called moral.

A primary group can be defined as containing a number of people with whom the individual considers himself or herself to be emotionally and unavoidably close and from whom there is a mutual sense of emotional and material obligation. This is combined with a code of pro-social behaviour with which members feel it to be advantageous to comply and to socialise their children towards this end.

In subsistence quasi-traditional agricultural communities which predominate in contemporary societies, children and adolescents spend most of their lives in the one primary group composed of neighbours and relatives. If different social relationships can be seen as rings of association, then in these communities most of these rings coincide.

In urban-industrial contemporary societies children initially spend almost all their lives in a primary group which is usually smaller than the ones in subsistence communities. By the age of five years, excluding the time spend asleep, they are increasingly involved with secondary groups in which they have specialised sectionalised roles as in school forms, sports teams and peer groups. If we divide the time spent in this primary group in a normal week, this would be a small proportion of the total time in which children are awake. Most of their time will be spent with a sibling, slightly more with their mothers and minimally with the father. The primary group acts as a family only when the children are young and at weekends and during holidays. Parents pay for their children but there is minimal inter-familial participation.

Children are also in tertiary groups in which they have no more than touch and go relationships of no permanency at all. While in subsistence societies a child will know by sight and name virtually everyone they meet. In urban societies a child will know far fewer in a primary sense, hundreds by secondary association and a constantly varying thousands in a tertiary sense as they go to school, go shopping or indeed looking out of the bus or train window about whom they will socially know almost nothing. The rings of social behaviour do not coincide at all except that the individual child is the role holder in the centre of each ring in which different behaviour is usually expected. The child is made into a more isolated individual by the ephemeral nature of most of the social relationships through which the pass so quickly and so disconnectedly.

## The Basis of Moral Behaviour

The basis of moral or pro-social behaviour must surely be in a pattern of behaviour which in the feelings of the individual whether child, adolescent or adult that it pays off; they are socially, economically, politically, religiously or psychologically better off as a result of behaving pro-socially.

Every human interaction can be in some way viewed as driven by reciprocity, but the primary group predominates in all areas of interaction. In contemporary social life primary groups are constantly forming and reforming for a wide variety of reasons; individuals need the closeness of reciprocal relationships on which they can depend emotionally and materially. The generalities of social interactions with fellow citizens, inhabitants of the same village and town or worshippers in the same temple, church, synagogue or church are of little importance? It is a fundamental mistake to make sentiment predominate in assessing the inter-relationships of parents and children; it is a cultural delusion of urban-industrial societies.

The influence of kinship is often assumed to be paramount but who are kin is often a matter of social definition and propinquity, except for the mother-child one. All other primary relationships are the result of long developing processes in which within a culture there is an immediate and quasi-inherited perceived and theoretical advantage. For children who are what kin is a matter of social definition usually illustrated in linguistic terms and learning. It is only assumed to be natural after it has been socially created.

Within any primary group there are advantages from conforming to the pattern of behaviour which the group considers to be correct or at least a reasonable way to behaviour. Those that follow these codes of behaviour receive in return a range of benefits. There may be a few culture wide prohibitions or requirements but what these are is a matter for situational definition in the small groups in which it occurs. All children in all cultures are taught that it is wrong to steal but this is always conditioned by what is being stolen from whom and where. In East Africa cattle theft from a fellow tribesman is a moral wrong and from a neighbouring tribe almost a moral obligation.

Thus the basis within which pro-social behaviour can be identified and seen to function is the primary group. Beyond this self-sustaining and self-interested group abstract ideas of correct behaviour develop from which the returns are personal psychological ones and less frequently material.

There are few if any material returns for behaving well in the contemporary social environments in which both adults and children spend most of their time in secondary and tertiary groups. This may involve primary group members but not any need for them to exercise control over their children other than to admonish them when their behaviour becomes a matter of public comment and bureaucratic involvement. A child that steals and brings home the stolen goods is not likely to be effectively controlled by their primary group adults even if they do become aware of the thieving.

## The Family is not the Primary Group in which Pro-social Behaviour Pays off

What are the primary groups in which "good" behaviour pays off. Firstly there is the family but this is a very elastic term in which there may not be a single pattern of behavioural requirements; what constitutes the family will vary with the roles performed by individuals and this must vary again with age and innumerable situational circumstances; in this sense the family may be no more than an advertising gimmick and in fact it may involve both unitary and divisive ways of behaving. Cross-culturally many families are divided violently over inheritable property and status. The western tensions between adolescents and their parents is an obvious example of a primary group which may only function cohesively for some matters threatening the whole family but in everyday affairs there will be little agreement. When prestige and property have to be divided then siblings ignore any suggestions of primary group obligations.

The so-called isolated nuclear family has been found to be less isolated than what was originally thought theoretically, but it is not the most efficient and self-cohesive unit since it does not function as a single social form. Most of its members spend most of every day within other primary and secondary groups with which it is no more than vaguely interdependent. The family head depends on his work groupings, the children on school ones and the woman on neighbourhood groupings which she creates for herself.

Perhaps the family farm family might be the best example of a continuing group but much depends on the working relationships of the mother-in-law and daughter-in-law which in both India and China have tended to be stressful leading to significant suicide rates. In the former the daughter-in-law is regarded as a source of family income from her dowry payments and in the latter she is treated as a servant.

The Hindu joint family in which the sons and their wives live in the same house as the father would be a better example since all involved see the advantages of pro-social behaviour. However whether the wives share these views with their husbands cannot be certain since their own area of negotiable self-interest is only in the bedroom.

The family may function reasonably well as a primary group when the child is an infant but by the time of adolescence upwards the family disintegrates as a primary group; the daughters marry out and the sons set up their own households with unrelated women who have their own family agendas. Such families are only initially primary and then as always disintegrate into no more than a nostalgic memory.

In many societies the adolescents are usually in overtly or covertly antagonistic relationships with their parents basically because neither they nor the societies in which they live allow them to be treated as adults. Traditional subsistence and herding societies often accept them as junior adults with accepted communal functions so that this inter-generational hostility is less obvious and quite effectively contained. In modern societies at the same age young men and they are biologically just that cannot smoke drink or drive.

So overall the family as a primary group may exist for some of its members for some of the time, but it persists as a nostalgic memory or a romantic ideal and so as an effective socialiser towards and maintainer of the pro-social behaviour of young people has to be treated with some scepticism.

Kin in the primary group sense of long-term continuing obligations requiring particular patterns of pro-social behaviour may be in reality short-term and perhaps generally confined to rites of passage, religious and social rituals in which this disunity is marked off and restrained by special behaviour and costumes. So perhaps we can set aside kinship as the commonest form of primary groupings, because only in the mother-child relationship does it have any great social longevity, although be ideologically seen as the ideal form of group relationship.

## The Importance of Primary Group Membership for Everyone

Even though we have established that the family may not be as significant a primary group as might be supposed, it must remain the principal and enduring basis for moral and pro-social behaviour because it is so versatile and profitable for those involved. Further it is accepted that membership of these groups will always involve some conformity to their standards of pro-social behaviour and that there are situations in which these requirements overlap those of other groups. The terminological division between moral and pro-social behaviours is based on the fact that the latter have a pragmatic base conferring advantages on members. These turn into moral obligations when there is no longer any effective pragmatic basis for conformity.

Primary groups in which people find the most convenient and indeed necessary elements for reasonable social living and in which there are material as well as psychological benefits, take many forms outside the conceptual dominance that primary groups are predominantly families. Primary groups exist everywhere and in every type of social groupings and at every level of social, economic and political development.

Whether congeniality comes before their material usefulness, they are certainly interrelated. In any modern society there are bound to be large numbers of alternative social relationships and in this there is bound to be some choosing of the people with whom individuals want to associate as similar in some ways to themselves from which develop in time material needs and mutual obligations. So it would seem that in subsistence communities primary group memberships are provided for children and the fact that there is less migration in and out of such communities makes for the greater stability of such groupings. In urban and industrial communities where there is less permanency and more variety, children and adolescents are increasingly involved in choosing the primary groups in which they wish to be involved as individuals.

So in a modernised society an individual may be in several primary groups which only occupy segments of time and space; work, sport, hobbies and religion. Perhaps they should be classified as segmented part-time primary groups which do not usually have any overall control over or obligations over behaviour in more than one primary group at a time. Perhaps also these primary groupings are a feature of modern life which has a segmenting emotional and material effect over the lives of all individuals living in this type of variegated social environment.

Individuals may also prefer this scattering of obligations in place of the round the clock geographically restricted primary groups in societies which do not have these mixed and mobile groupings. The division in the types of primary groups may thus be between communities in which the members are relatively static and those in which the people are relatively mobile not only geographically but also in terms of employment and status.

## The Failure of Morality to be Socially Realistic

Morality fails to enthuse children, adolescents or indeed adults because it appears to concentrate on abstract relationships or situations which are not experienced in any personal individual way. This is recognised in the injunction to love ones neighbour as oneself. The neighbour is not everyone but someone next door; it is a reasonable requirement with a pay off based on the pragmatics of social and geographical nearness. It is revolutionary in the way that by implication it pushes out obligations beyond the primary or secondary groupings.

It is difficult to see any workable interpretation of this requirement that unites them to the inhabitants of Preston, Patna, Papeete and Paris; they do not even know where these places are in many cases and of course do not know each other. It is a ludicrous requirement within any known system of social pro-social behaviour.

Neither group nor individuals within such groups as these will see any moral or pro-social requirement to each other except that they are told by religious and political power-holders that they ought to be concerned when they have the surplus means in time and money to do something about this interpretation of neighbourliness.

This is no doubt a very worthy idea and fits in with the contemporary ideas of globalization and the global village, but such ideas do not help children to get on within their existing and future primary groups in which day in and day out they will spend their lives.

The morality taught to children is frequently designed to be worked out in the small groups in which all the children have a self-interest. This is because the idea of pay-offs for pro-social behaviour is not something that appeals to those who think and plan for the teaching of moral behaviour to children. It is perhaps too realistic in its understanding of how and why adults behave and distasteful to those who have an abstract and indeed moral framework for thinking about how they ought to behave. Yet ethologically "good" behaviour for continued living in a primary group must have a very long history indeed. Moral concern for those whom we do not know is politically motivated and supported by international charities.

Contemporary moral behaviour requirements have no relationship at all to what went on in earlier primary groups. No known groupings of the higher apes functions on the basis that behaviour to outsider individuals and groups has any dimension other than their own self-interests.

It must be very doubtful whether in any contemporary society the pro-social behaviour in primary groups is extended to all outsiders. Even those who devote their lives to ameliorating the misfortunes of others realise that their own survival necessitates "selfish" behaviour and the primary group of their fellow helpers has to have priority.

Amish children no doubt grow up with a preference for the children of outsider Amish families, but this would be based on a known and observable affinity, but it would be considerably weakened in relation to Amish children whom they have never seen before. Much the same would apply to highly specialised. Orthodox Jewish communities but not to all children of such groups to which it would not be possible to have any personalised sense of obligation; there would be far too many when personalised obligations cannot in reality be workable beyond very small numbers and almost within a visible radius.

The preference of Jews for Jews or whatever identifiable group is being considered as it might affect actual behaviour is not likely to cover any wide range of activities; it would be narrowly conceived and narrowly practised. Pro-social behaviour has always been filtered through the necessities of proximity.

Schools do not teach children that they should behave at home and contribute materially to their primary groups; in fact this is avoided by filling up time with home-work when they might be helping their parents materially. Behavioural requirements are very specifically related to the school environment and only peripherally related to the immediacies of outside life.

## Communal Behaviour as a Rarity

There can be little doubt that moral behaviour to and by people outside the primary groups in which they have their needs fulfilled, is not common and probably involved only a small number of people. While Afro-American and Latino adolescents are more often the subject of studies into drug-taking and delinquency, a number have been found to be committed to the needs of the wider community (Hart et al., 1995). Four contexts seem to correlate to this wider involvement; warm relationships with persons who themselves evidence moral character, opportunities to form and test moral commitments, discussion of commitments and their meaning for the individual and experiences that facilitate the sense of effectiveness and connection to the future.

This seems to be similar to what the Sukuma of Tanzania would understand to be the correct way to bring up their children; the difference being that in that culture this is the generally acceptable way to bring up children that does not require any special underlining. This is much more easily done there because the microcosm of required behaviour within the neighbourhood is a miniature of the larger surrounding macrocosm; a functional but in a way a coincidental unity. In contemporary urban-industrial societies this type of behaviour no doubt reflects what people think that should do but in fact is an unusual microcosm which does not form part of any macrocosmic cultural behaviour.

## Moral Behaviour in Relatively Static Communities

If we accept that all humans need close and restricted relationships for a variety of psychological, social, economic, political and religious reasons, their importance must depend on their salience. In a relatively static and stable community all relationships can be seen as within circles of personal significance. In a quasi-traditional society these circles of personal significance largely overlap in that they are within the same definition of neighbourhood; no one is likely to have important relationships with those who are outside a ten minute walking distance; peer groups, kin groups, working groups and play groups whether for communal purposes or working collectively on a sequence of farms would be composed of more or less the same people.

In a modern housing estate as was shown in the diagrams in Whyte's Organisation Man (Whyte, 1957) these concentric circles do not coincide so closely as the ten minute geographical area is larger because of cars, public transport and the telephone. They are still largely concentric for the women and children but more so at the lower end of the social scale. But Whyte's diagrams showed that for most voluntary activities geographical closeness was a dominant factor in who associated with whom. Overall even in modern societies a surprising number marry within this ten minute circle.

In this situation the significance of primary groups lies in their coincidence, a concentration of more or less the same people. Thus no one association will have the embellishments which comes from more egocentric isolation. Pro-social behaviour is established and reinforced by primary groups which cover a wide range of pay-offs.

## Moral Behaviour in Relatively Mobile Communities

The ideas dominating such communities will not be ones that relate to the needs of day to day existence as would be the case in subsistence communities whether in agriculture or slums. For most such communities the turn over is too high for the community to provide important primary groups; most individuals have lived in dozens of localities and may have had several jobs or relationships. Such people may have no idea that relates to a specific home locality.

Primary groups may be formed outside the circle of where people live and may relate to long-term advantages as in the juvenile gang which provide job opportunities and status change possibilities each of which will have their own pro-social requirements.

In modern societies, primary groups that contain man, woman and children may only exist for a low proportion of time probably only over weekends and family holidays. The fact that the man comes home in the evenings may renovate the primary group of husband and wife but largely exclude that of the children.

The husbands will have primary groupings at work founded on reciprocities and the passage of information and those of hobbies and sport provide further wider connections as well as status. The children's primary groups will be that of their peers and generally school and sports related. The wife will have a local group of women friends circulating round gossip groups in local houses and shops and also that their children share the same schools so that they meet there on a regular basis.

There is no feeling of community because it has no functional unity and above all because there is no immediate returns for thinking in those terms. It is possible that because these people lead segregated lives that each primary group has a more intense emotional significance than would be the case if the primary group had more wide ranging involvements.

## Conclusions

It would seem that in subsistence communities there is an on-going integration of pro-social behavioural requirements and pay-offs. Whether this can be described as morality must remain a question of definition as it would often have the support of ancestors and their power to sanction. But like Colgate's toothpaste advertising slogan these overarching primary groups provide a "ring of confidence".

In modern societies children are taught this same code of behaviour which functioned well enough in communities in which primary groups were integrated into much of all that was going on and it paid-off, but now this behaviour is classified as a moral requirement which is outside the primary groups which children, adolescents and adults create for their own reciprocating purposes, and provides no pay-offs. More over onto the relative simplicities of primary group pro-social behaviour have been added enormous quantities of legal requirements which the encroaching society has defined as having to be obeyed even if the individuals have no idea that such rules exist. Primary group pro-social behavioural requirements are known and followed or the delinquent is sanctioned into compliance or expelled.

The requirement to obey the state because by definition it exists for the benefit of its citizens and its rulings have been laid down by bureaucrats, is perhaps to fictionalise the requirements of morality. Pro-social behaviour is born in and remains principally effective in primary groups as it always has a functioning reciprocal basis and it is perhaps this that should be the basis of what is taught to and required of children.

# Bibliography

(The numbers in Boldfaces following each reference give the text page on which the article or book is cited)


Abbink, J. (2000). "Violence and the Crisis of Conciliation," *Africa*, 70 (4): 527-550. **107**

Abrahams, R & S. Bukurura (1933). "Party, Bureaucracy and Grass-roots Initiatives in a Socialist State. The Case of Sungusungu Vigilantes in Tanzania," (pp.92-100) in C.M. Hann (ed.), *Socialism, Ideals, Ideologies and Local Practice*. London: Routledge.

Abromovitch, R. *et al.* (1986). "Sibling and Peer Interaction: A Final Follow-up and a Comparison," *Child Development*, 57: 217-229.

Ainsworth, M & B.A. Wittig (1996). "Attachment and Exploration of One Year Olds in a Strange Situation," Canadian J. Psychiaty 107-137. **50**

Alber, E. (2003). "Denying Biological Parenthood. Fosterage in Northern Benin," *Ethnos*, 68 (4): 487-506. **68**

Anderson, E. (1984). "The Acquisition of Sociolinguistic Knowledge. Some Evidence from Children's Verbal Role-play," *Western Journal Speech Communication*, 48: 125-44. **84**

Anderson, J.R. (1983). *The Architecture of Cognition*. Cambridge, Mass : Harvard University Press. **81**

Andreski, S. (1964). *Elements of Comparative Sociology*. London: Weidenfeld & Nicolson.

Aronson, E. *et al.* (1994). *Social Psychology*. New York: Harper Collins.

Ashley-Montague, M.F. (1957). *The Reproductive Development of the Female with Special Reference to the Period of Adolescent Sterility*. New York: Julian Press.

Ashton, H. (1952). *The Basuto*. Oxford: Oxford University Press. **204**

Ballard, J.G. (1983). *The Empire of the Sun*. London: Harper Collins. **229**

Barker, R.G. & L.S. Barker (1961). "Behaviour Units for the Comparative Study of Cultures," (pp.457-476) in B. Kaplan (ed.), *Studying Personality Cross-culturally*. Evanston: Row & Peterson.

Barry, H.B. *et al.* (1957). "A Cross-cultural Survey of Some Sex Differences in Socialisation," *Journal of Abnormal Social Psychology*, 55: 337-342. **236**

Basham, W.R. (1978). *Urban Anthropology. The Cross-cultural Study of Complex Studies*. California: Mayfield, Palo Alto. **249**

Batibo, H. (1985). *Le Kisukuma (langue Bantu de Tanzania), Phonologie, Morphologie*. Paris: Editions Recherche sur les Civilisations. **89**

Batson,C.D. (1991) *The Altruism Question: Toward a Social-psychological Answer*. New Jersey: Erlbaum Assoc, Hillsdale.

Baston, C.D. *et.eal.* (1993). *Religion and the Individual. ASocial Psychological Perspective.* New York : Oxford University Press.

Baumrind, D. (1971). "Current Patterns of Parental Authority," *Developmental Psychology Monograph*, 4 (1); 1-103. **195**

Bayly, S. (1999). *Caste, Society and Politics in India from the 18th Century to the Modern Age*. Cambridge: Cambridge University Press.

Bender, L. *et al.* (1940). "Behaviour Problems in Children from the Homes of Followers of Father Divine," *Journal of Mental & Nervous Diseases*, 91: 460-272. **245**

Bercheid, E. *et al.* (1986). "Emotional Experience in Close Relationships. Some Implications for Child Development" (pp. 131-164 ) in W.W. Hartup & Z. Rubin (eds.), *Relationships and Development*. Hillsdale, New Jersey: Erlbaum. **188**

Berkman, P.L. (1969). "Spouseless motherhood, psychological stress and physical morhidity" J. Heath and Social Behaviour 10 : 323-24.

Bernand, C. & S. Gruzinski (1996). "Children of the Apocalypse: The Family in Meso-Americo and the Andes," (pp.161-215) in A. Bourguiere et al. (eds.), *A History of the Family*. Cambridge, Mass: Harvard University Press. **190**

Bernstein, B. (1975). *Class, Codes and Control*. London: Routledge & Kegan Paul. **75, 98, 199**

Berry, J.W. & J.A. Bennett (1992). "Cree Conceptions of Cognitive Competence," *International Journal of Psychology*, 27: 73-88. **110, 182**

Bleiler, E.F. (1963). *Essential Japanese Grammar*. New York: Dover. **110**

Bloom, A. (1981). *The Linguistic Shaping of Thought. A Study of the Impact of Language on Thinking in China and the West.* Hillsdale, New Jersey: Erlbaum. **91, 99**

Bluebond-Langner, M. (1978). *The Private Worlds of Dying Children*. Princeton, New Jersey: Princeton University Press. **137**

Bond, M.H. & M. Cheung (1984). "Experimenter Language Choice and Ethnic Affirmations by Chinese Trilinguals in Hong Kong," *International Journal of Intercultural Relations*, 8: 347-356. **99**

Boston, R. (1988). "Holy Terrors," *Church and State,* 44: 154-6.

Bouchard, T.J. (1994). "Genes, Environment and Personality," *Science*, 264: 1700-01. **9**

Bronfenbrenner, U. (1970). *Two Worlds of Childhood: US and USSR*. New York: Russell Sage Foundation.

Bugental, D.B. & J.J. Goodnow, (1997). "Socialization Processes," (pp. 389-462) in W. Damon & N. Eisenberg (eds.), *Handbook of Child Psychology*. New York: Wiley. **195**

Burton, M & L. Kirk. (1979). "Differences in Maasai Cognition of Personality and Social Identity," *American Anthropologist*, 81: 841-873. **93**

Buss, D.M. (1995). "Evolutionary psychology," *Psychological Inquiry*, 6: 1-30.

Calhoun, J.B. (1966). "The Role of Space in Animal Sociology," *Journal of Social Issues*, 22 (4): 46-58.

Call, K.T. *et al.* (1995). "Helpfulness and the Development of Competence in Adolescence," *Child Development*, 66: 129-138.

Caudill, W. & H. Weinstein (1974). "Maternal Care and Infant Behaviour in Japan and America," (pp. 225-276) in T.S. Lebra & W.P. Lebra (eds.), *Japanese Culture and Behaviour*. Honolulu: University of Hawaii Press.

Chandrasekhar, S. (1959). *Infant Mortality in India: 1901-55*. London: Allen & Unwin.

Clancy, P.M. (1986). "The Acquisition of Communicative Style in Japanese," (pp. 213-250) in B.B. Schieffelin & E. Ochs (eds.), *Language Socialization across Cultures*. Cambridge: Cambridge University Press.

Cohen, D & A. Gunz (2002). "As Seen by the Others. Perspectives on the Self in the Memories and Emotional Perceptions of Easterners and Westerners," *Psychological Science*, 13 (1): 55-59. **60, 182**

Cohen, D.B. (1999). *Strangers in the Nest. Do Parents Really Shape their Child's Personality, Intelligence or Character*. New York: Wiley. **9**

Comnitz, L. (1978). "Survival and Reciprocity. The Case of Urban Marginality in Mexico," (pp.181-207) in C.D. Laughlin & I.A.

Brady (eds.), *Extinction and Survival in Human Populations.* New York: Columbia University Press. **218**

Cory, H. (1953) Sukuma Law and Cusom, London. Oxford University, Press. **122**

Crow, B. (1992) 'Understanding Famine and Hunger' in T. Allen and A. Tnomds (eds) Poverty and Development in the 1990, Oxford. Oxford University Press. **122**

Dalrymple, W. (2002). *White Mughals. Love and Betrayal in 18th Century India.* London: Harper Collins. **111**

D'Andrade, R.G. (1981). "The Cultural Part of Cognition," *Cognitive Science*, 5: 180. **172**

Davis, K. (1947). "Final Note in a Case of Extreme Isolation," *American Journal of Sociology*, 50: 432-37. **64**

Dawkins, R. (1976). The Selfish Gene Oxford. Oxford University Press. **43**

——. (1995). *River out of Eden.* London: Weidenfeld & Nicolson. **218**

Deliege, R. (1999). *The Untouchables of India.* Berg: Oxford. **55**

Deregowski, J.B. (1970). "Effect of Cultural Value of Time upon Recall," *British Journal of Social & Clinical Psychology*, 9: 37-41. **114**

Dickermann, M. (1979). 'Famele infanticide reproductive trategies and social stratification; a preliminary model'. In Chagnon, N.A. and Irons, E. (eds). Evolutionary biology and human social behaviour; and anthropological perspective. Duxbury, Duxbury Press. **258**

Diener, E & C. Diener (1996). "Most People are Happy'," *Psychological Science*, 7: 181-186. **10**

Doi, L.T. (1962). "Amae: A Key Concept for Understanding Japanese Personality Structure," (pp.132-139) in R.J. Smith & R.K. Beardsley (eds.), *Japanese Culture.* London: Aldine. **159**

Du, S. (2003). *Chopsticks Only Work in Pairs. Gender Unity and Gender Equality among the Lahu of South-West China.* New York: Columbia University Press. **37**

Eckensberger, L.H. (1994). "Moral Development and its Measurement across Cultures," (pp.71-78) in J. Lonnrer & R. Malpass (eds.), *Psychology and Culture.* Boston: Allyn & Bacon. **229-30**

Eisenberg, N. (1996). "Caught in a Narrow Kantian Perception of Pro-social Development: Reactions to Campbell and Christopher's Critique of Moral Development Theory," *Developmental Review*, 16: 48-68.

Eisenberg, N & P.H. Mussen (1997). *The Roots of Pro-social Behaviour in Children*. Cambridge: Cambridge University Press.

Elwin, V. (1947). *The Muria and their Ghotul*. Bombay: Oxford University Press.

Ember, C. (1973). "Feminine Task Assignment and the Social Behaviour of Boys," *Ethos*, 1: 424-39. **193**

Engle, T.L. *et al.* (1943). "Attitude Differences between Amish and Non-Amish Attending the Same Schools," *Journal of Educational Psychology*, 34: 206-214. **238**

Evans-Pritchard, E.E. (1939). "Nuer Time-reckoning," *Africa*, 12 (2): 189-216. **115, 212**

Eveleth, P.B. (1986). "Timing of Menarche: Secular Trend and Popular Difference," (pp. 39-52) in J.B. Lancaster & B.A. Hamburg (eds.), *School-age Pregnancy and Parenthood*. New York: Aldine de Gruyter.

Falbo, T & D.F. Polit (1986). "Quantitative Research of the Only Child Literature: Research Evidence and Theory Development," *Psychological Bulletin*, 1000: 176-189. **14**

Falbo, T. & D.L. Poston (1993). "The Academic, Personality and Physical Outcomes of Only Children in China," *Child Development*, 64: 18-35. **14**

Farriss, N.M. (1995). "Remembering the Future, Anticipating the Past; History, Time and Cosmology among the Maya," in D.O. Hughes & T.R. Trautmann (eds.), *Times, Histories and Ethnologies*. Ann Arbor: University of Michigan Press. **211**

Feyisetan, B.J. (1990). "Post-partum Sexual Abstinence, Breast-feeding and Child Spacing among Yoruba Women in urban Nigeria," *Social Biology*, 37 (1-2): 110-117. **164**

Fischer, M.M.J. (1980). *Iran. From Religious Dispute to Revolution*. Cambridge, Mass: Harvard University Press.

Flack, J.C & F.B.M. de Waal (2000). "Any Animal Whatever. Darwinian Building Blocks of Morality in Monkeys and Apes," (pp.1-29) L.D. Katz, (ed.), *Evolutionary Origins of Morality*. Bowling Green, Ohio: Imprint Academic. **31**

Flaks, D.K. *et al.* (1995). "Lesbians Choosing Motherhood: A Comparative Study of Lesbian and Heterosexual Parents and their Children," *Developmental Psychology*, 31: 105-114. **13**

Foley, W.A. (1997). *Anthropological Linguistics*. Oxford: Blackwell. **104**

Fortes, M. (1938). "Social and Psychological Aspects of Education in Taleland," *Africa*, XI (4). **204**

Fortier, B. de la (1963). 'Les enfants trouves a l' hopital general de Montreal. 1754-1804'. Laval Medical 34; 442-53.35; 335-47.36; 551-9. **259**

Foucault, M. (1979). *Discipline and Punishment.* Harmondsworth: Penguin. **212**

Frazer, J. (1922/1963). *The Golden Bough. A Study in Magic and Religion.* New York: Macmillan. **183**

Frijda, N & G. Jahoda. (1966). "On the Scope and Methods of Cross-cultural Psychology," *International Journal of Psychology*, 1: 109-127.

Gaikwad, V.R. (1967). *The Anglo-Indians.* London: Asia Publishing House.

Gajdusek, D.C. (1973). "Kuru in the Hew Guinea Highlands," in J.D. Spillane (ed.), *Tropical Neurology.* Oxford: Oxford University Press. **172**

Gaskins, S. (1996). "How Mayan Parental Theories Come into Play," (pp. 345-363) in S. Markness & C.M. Super (eds.), *Parents' Cultural Belief Systems. Their Origins, Expression and Consequences.* New York: Guilford Press.

____. (1999). "Children's Daily Lives in a Mayan Village: A Case Study of Culturally Constructed Roles and Activities," (pp. 25-61) in A. Goncu (ed.), *Children's Engagement in the World. Socio-cultural Perspectives.* Cambridge: Cambridge University Press.

Geertz, C. (1973). "Deep Play. Notes on the Balinese Cockfight," in C. Geertz (ed.), *The Interpretation of Cultures.* New York: Basic Books. **169**

Gennep, A van. (1960). *The Rites of Passage.* London: Routledge and Kegan Paul.

Gernet, J. (1985). *China and the Christian Impact. A Conflict of Cultures.* Cambridge: Cambridge University Press. **181**

Giddens, A. (1991). *Sociology.* Cambridge: Polity Press. **210**

Glasse, R. (1967). "Cannibalism in the Kuru Region of New Guinea," *Transactions New York Academy of Sciences*, 29: 748-54. **171**

Glick, J. (1968). "Cognitive Style among the Kpelle," Paper read in American Educational Research Association, Annual Conference Chicago. **110**

Goffman, E. (1969). *The Presentation of Self in Everyday Life.* Harmondsworth: Penguin. **72**

Golding, W. (1954) *Lord of the Flies.* London. Faberand Faber. **11**

Goodall, J. (1986). *The Chimpanzees of Combe. Patterns of Behaviour.* Harvard: Belknap Press. **34**

Goody, E. (1970). "Kinship Fostering in Gonja. Deprivation or Advantage," (pp. 1-74) in P. Mayer (ed.), *Socialization. The Approach from Social Anthropology*. London: Tavistock. **184, 188**

Gray, R.F. (1963). *The Sonjo of Tanganyika*. London: Oxford University Press. **115, 212**

Guiora, A.Z. (1985). "The Psychodynamics of Bilingualism," American Psychological Association Conference, Los Angeles. **113**

Hall, E.T. (1966). *The Hidden Dimension*. New York: Doubleday. **109**

Hallowell, A.I. (1963). "Ojibwa World View and Disease," (pp. 258-315) in I. Galdston (ed.), *Man's Image in Medicine and Anthropology*. New York: International University Press.

Hannerz, U. (1992). *Cultural Complexity. Studies in the Social Organisation of Meaning*. New York: Columbia University Press. **173**

Harris, J.R. (1995). "Where is the Child's Environment? A Group Socialization Theory of Development," *Psychological Review*, 102: 458-489. **16**

____. (1998). *The Nurture Assumption. Why Children Turn Out the Way They Do?* London: Bloomsbury. **14, 17**

Hart. D et al. (1995). 'Moral Commitment inner-city Adolescents' (pp. 317-341) in A. Colby and W. Damon (eds) *Morality in everyday life developmental perspectives*. Cambridge. Cambridge University Press. **268**

Heine, S. *et al.* (1999). "Is There a Universal Need for Positive Self-regard?" *Psychological Review*, 106: 766-794. **182**

Hewlett, B.S. (1991). *Intimate Fathers*. Ann Arbor: University of Michigan Press. **13**

Hoban, B. (1994). "Recollections of 1950's childhood"; 338 in M. Tanner (ed.), *Ireland's Holy Wars. The Struggle for a Nation's Soul*. New Haven: Yale University Press. **239-40**

Hodges, J & B. Tizzard (1989). "IQ and Behavioural Adjustment of Ex-institutional Adolescents," *Journal of Child Psychology & Psychiatry*, 30: 53-98. **185**

Hoffman, M.L. (1982). "Development of Pro-social Motivation: Empathy and Guilt," (pp. 281-311) in N. Eisenberg (ed.), *The Development of Pro-social Behaviour*. New York: Academic Press.

____. (1984). "Empathy, Its Limitations, and Its Role in a Comprehensive Moral Theory," (pp. 283-302) in W.M. Kurtines

& J.L. Gewirtz (eds.), *Morality, Moral Behaviour, and Moral Development*. New York: Wiley.

Hostetler, J.A. (1993). *Amish Society*. Baltimore: John Hopkins Press. **248**

Hostetler, J.A. & G.E. Huntington. (1970). "The Hutterites. Fieldwork in a North American Communal Society," (pp.194-219) in G.D. Spindler (ed.), *Being an Anthropologist. Fieldwork in Eleven Cultures*. New York: Holt, Rinehart &Winston. **90, 177, 248**

____. (1971). *Amish Children. Education in the Family, School and Community*. Philadelphia: Harcourt Brace Jovanovich.

Howard, A & R.A. Scott. (1965). "A Proposed Framework for the Analysis of Stressing the Human Organism," *Behavioural Science*, 10: 141-160. **250**

Hsu, F.L.K. (1971). *Kinship and Culture*. New York: Aldine. **47-8**

Húmphrey, C & J, Laidlaw (1994). The Archetypal Actions of Ritual. A Theory of Ritual Illustrated by the Jain Rite of Worship. Oxford University, Oxford. **82**

Huxley, T.H. (1894). *Evolution and Ethics*. Princeton: Princeton University Press. **43**

Inkeles, A. & Smith, D.H. (1974). *Becoming Modern. Individual Change in Six Developing Countries*. Cambridge, Mass: Harvard University Press. **249**

Invernizzi, A. (2001). *Street Children in Africa, Asia and Eastern Europe*. Annotated Bibliography. Bonn: Deutsche Kommission Justicie et Pax. **240**

Iwao, S. (1993). *The Japanese Woman. Traditional Image and Changing Reality*. New York: Free Press. **104**

James, A. (1993). *Childhood Identities. Self and Social Relationships in the Experience of the Child*. Edinburgh: Edinburgh University Press.

James, A. (1993) *The Japanese Woman. Traditional Image and Changing Reality,* New York : Free Press.

James, A. *et al.* (1998). *Theorizing Childhood*. Cambridge : Polity Press. **138**

Jenks, C. (1998) 'Childhood and Social space. Examples from the United Kingdom'(pp. 91-109) D.K. Behera (ed) *Children and Childhold in our contemporary societies*, Delhi, Kamla-Raj. **165**

Jenness, D. (1935). *The Ojibwa Indians of Parry Island, Their Social and Religious Life*. Ottawa: Canadian Department of Mines.

Jing, J. (2000). *Feeding China's Little Emperors. Food, Children and Social Change*. Stanford, California: Stanford University Press.

Joshi, P.C. (1979). "Fieldwork Experience; Relived and Reconsidered," (pp.73-99) in M.N. Srinivas *et al.* (eds.), *The Fieldworker and the Field*. Delhi: Oxford University Press.

Kaku, K. (1975). 'Were girl babies scrified to a folk superstition in 1966 in Japan'. Annals Human Biology, 2; 391-3. **258**

——, (1975). "Increased Induced Abortion Rate in 1966. An Aspect of a Japanese Folk Superstition," *Annals Human Biology*, 2 : 111-115. **258**

Karmiloff-Smith, A. (1992). *Beyond Modularity. A Developmental Perspective on Cognitive Science*. Cambridge, Mass: MIT Press. **81**

Kaye, M.M. (2002). *Sun in the Morning*. London: Charnwood. **90**

Kelley, H.H. *et al.* (1983). *Close Relationships*. New York: Freeman. **188**

Kenyatta, J. (1939). *Facing Mount Kenya*. London: Secker & Warburg. **205**

Kindermann, T.A. (1993). "Natural Peer Groups as Contexts for Individual Development: The Case of Children's Motivation in School," *Developmental Psychology*, 29: 970-977. **17**

Kochanska, G. (2002). "Mutually Responsive Orientations between Mother and their Young Children: A Context for the Early Development of Conscience," *Current Directions in Psychological Science*, 11 (6):191-5. **76**

Kohlberg, L. (1969). "Stage and Sequence. The Cognitive Development Approach to Socialisation," (pp. 325-480) in D.A. Goslin (ed.), *Handbook of Socialisation Theory and Research*. New York: Rand McNally,

____. (1981). *The Philosophy of Moral Development. Moral States and the Idea of Justice*. San Francisco: Harper & Row.

Kolenda, P.M. (1968). "Region, Caste and Family Structure: A Comparative Study of the Indian Joint Family," (pp. 339-396) in M. Singer & B.S. Cohn (eds.), *Structure and Change in Indian Society*. Chicago: Aldine. **146**

Konner, M.J. (1972). "Aspects of the Developmental Ethology of a Foraging People," (pp. 285-304) in N.B. Jones (ed.), *Ethological Studies of Child Behaviour*. Cambridge: Cambridge University Press. **50**

Kumagai, A. (1981). "A Dissection of Intimacy. A Study of Bipolar Posturing in Japanese Social Interaction - Amaeru & Arayakasu-Indulgence & Deference," *Culture, Medicine and Psychiatry*, 5: 322-333. **91**

Kurado, S. (1984). "Interaction over Food among Pygmy Chimpanzee," (pp. 301-24) in R. Susman (ed.), *The Pygmy Chimpanzee*. New York: Plenum.

Laursen, B & W.A. Collins (1994). "Interpersonal Conflict During Adolescence," *Psychological Bulletin*, 115: 197-209.

Lazarus. R.S. (1968) 'Stress' International Encyclopedia Social Science. New York, Macmillan, 12 : 337-48. **126**

Leach, E.R. (1964). "Comments on Naroll's 'On Ethnic Unit Classification',". *Current Anthropology*, 5 (4): 299. **2**

Lerner. R.M. et al. (1993) Time, Process and the Diversity of Developmental Injectories in Human Life : A Developmental contextual Perspective (pp. 41-59) in G. Turkewitz and D.A. Devernny (eds.). *Developmental time and Timing*. New Jersey, Erlbaun. **26**

Lewis, O. (1959). *Five Families. Mexican Case Studies in the Culture of Poverty*. New York: Random House.

____. (1961). *The Children of Sanchez*. New York: Random House. **48**

____. (1966). *La Vida*. New York: Random House. **195**

LeVine, R.A. (1959). "Gusii Sex Offences. A Study in Social Control," *American Anthropologist*, 61: 965-990.

____. (1973). *Culture, Behaviour and Personality*. Chicago: Aldine. **174-5**

____. (2003). *Childhood Socialization. Comparative Studies of Parenting, Learning and Educational Change*. Hong Kong: University of Hong Kong. **103**

Levy, R. (1964). The social structure of Islam. Cambridge University Press, London. **254**

Lienhardt, G. (1951). *Divinity and Experience. The Religion of the Dinka*. Oxford: Clarendon Press. **181**

Linton, R. (1936). *The Study of Man*. New York: Appleton-Century.

Lomnitz, L. (1978). "Survival and Reciprocity. The Case of Urban Marginality in Mexico," (pp.181-207) in C.D. Laughlin and I.A. Brady (eds.), *Extinction and Survival in Human Populations*. New York: Columbia University Press. **156**

Loogman, A. (1965). *Swahili Grammar and Syntax*. Pittsburgh: Duquesne University Press. **109**

Lykken, D & A. Telligen (1996). "Happiness is a Stochastic Phenomenon," *Psychological Science*, 7: 186-189. **10**

Lynd, R.S. & H.M. Lynd (1956). *Middletown. A Study of Modern American Culture*. New York: Harcourt, Brace & World. **3**

Ma, H.K. & M.C. Leung (1992). "Effects of Age, Sex and Social Relationships on the Altruistic Behaviour of Chinese Children," *Journal of Genetic Psychology*, 153: 293-303

Maccoby, E.E. (1992). "The Role of the Parents in the Socialization of Children: An Historical Overview," *Developmental Psychology*, 28: 1006-1017. **12**

____. (1996). "Peer Conflict and Intra-family Conflict. Are There Conceptual Bridges?" *Merrill-Palmer Quarterly*. 42: 165-176.

____. (1999). "The Uniqueness of the Parent-child Relationship," in W.A. Collins & B. Laursen (eds.), *Relationship as Developmental Contexts*. Mahwah: Erlbaum. **188, 196**

Mahfouz, Naguib (1994). *Palace Walk*. Vol. I. Black Swan, London: The Cairo Trilogy. **197**

Maretski, T.W. & H. Maretski (1963). "Taira. An Okinawan Village," (pp.367-539) in B.B. Whiting(ed.), *Six Cultures. Studies in Child Rearing*. New York: Wiley. **234**

Maslow, A.H. (1987) *Motivation and Personality*, New York, Harper and Row. **5**

McCall, M. (1985) Environmental and Agricultural impact of Tanzania's Villagisation programme' in Clarke, J.I. *et al* (eds) *Population and Development Projects in Africa*, Cambridge, Cambridge University Press. **121**

McClelland, D.C. (1961). The Achieving Society. New York: Van Nostrand. **175**

____. (1981). "Child Rearing versus Ideology and Social Structure as Factors in Personality Development," (pp. 73-90) in R.H. Munroe *et al.* (eds.), *Handbook of Cross-cultural Human Development*. New York, Garland: STPM Press. **174**

McClelland, J.L. *et al.* (1986). "The Appeal of Parallel Distributive Processing," (pp. 2-44) in D.E. Rumelhart et al. (eds.), *Parallel Distributive Processing. 1. Foundations*. Cambridge, Mass: M.I.T. Press. **170**

McKusick, V.A. (1969). *Human Genetics*. New York: Prentice-Hall. **170**

McKusick, V.A. et al. (1965). "Dwarfism in the Amish and Cartilage-hair Hypoplasia," *Bulletin of Johns Hopkins Hospital*, 116: 285-326. **171**

Mead, M. (1963). *Sex and Temperament in Three Primitive Societies*. New York: Morrow. **59**

Meer, F. (1956) New lives for old, New York. Harper collins. **120**

____. (1976) *Race and Suicide in South Africa*, London. Routledge and Kegan Paul. **39**

Merton, R.K. (1957). *Social Theory and Social Structure*. Glencoe: Free Press. **253**

Miller, J.G. *et al.* (1990). "Perceptions of Social Responsibilities in India and the United States. Moral Imperatives or Personal Decisions," *Journal of Personality & Social Psychology*, 58: 33-47.

Miner, H. (1953). *The Primitive City of Timbuctoo*. Princeton: Princeton University Press.

Minturn, L & J.T. Hitchcock (1963). "The Rajputs of Khalapur, India," (pp.205-361) in B.B. Whiting (ed.), *Six Cultures. Studies in Child Rearing*. New York: Wiley. **235**

Mintz, S.W & E. Wolf (1950). "An Analysis of Ritual Co-parenthood (compadrazgo)," *Southwestern Journal of Anthropology*, 6: 341-68. **194**

Moore, J. (1984). "The Evolution of Reciprocal Sharing," *Ethology and Sociobiology*, 5: 5-14. **33**

Morgan, G.A. & H.M. Ricciuti. 1969. "Infants Responses to Strangers during the First Year," (pp. 253-271) in B.M. Fox (ed.), *Determinants of Infant Behaviour.* **50**

Mtshali, M. (1982). *Give Us a Break. Diaries of a Group of Soweto Children*. Braamfontein: Skotaville Press. **243**

Murase, T. (1974). "Naikan Therapy," (pp.388-397) in T.S. Lebra & W.P. Lebra (eds.), *Japanese Culture and Behaviour*. Honolulu: University of Hawaii Press. **91**

Musun-Miller, L. (1991). "Effects of Maternal Presence on Sibling Behaviour," *Journal of Applied Development Psychology*, 12: 145-147.

Newcombe, N.S. (2002). 'The Nativist-Empiricist Controversy in the context of Recent Research in Spatial and Quantitative Development,' *Psychological Science* 13(5) : 395-401. **127**

New York Times (2002) Father Steals Best. Crime in an American Family. **25**

Nodari, R. and Pirovane, G. (1970). 'Sulla mortalita infantile. Raffronte dei dati statistici referiti ai bambini nati nel matrimonio e fuori del matrimonio' Minerva Pediatrica. 22 : 1254-6 and 1449-51. **259**

Nydegger, W.F & C. Nydegger (1963). "Tarong: An Ilolos Barrio in the Philippines," (pp .695-867) in B.B. Whiting (ed.) *Six Cultures. Studies in Child Rearing*. New York Wiley. **245**

O'Malley, P. (1983). *The Uncivil War. Ireland Today*. Boston: Houghton Mifflin. **55**

Pakrasi, K.B. (1970). Female infanticide in India. Calcutta, Editions Indian. **258**

Panter-Brick, C. (2002). "Street Children, Human Rights and Public Health. A Critique and Future Directions," *Annual Review of Anthropology*, 147-171. **243**

Parker, J.G. (1995). "Peer Relations, Child Development and Adjustment: A Developmental Psychopathology Perspective," (pp. 96-161) in D. Cicchetti & D. Cohen (eds.), *Developmental Psychopathology*. New York: Wiley. **16**

Peteet, J. (1994). "Male Gender and Rituals of Resistance in the Palestinian Intifada: A Cultural Politics of Violence," *American Ethnologist*, 21 (1): 31-49. **4**

Plomin, R & D. Daniels (1987). Why are Children in the Same Family so Different from One Another?" *Behavioural and Brain Sciences*, 10: 1-50. **9**

Price, L. (1987). "Ecuadorian Illness Stories. Cultural Knowledge in Natural Discourse," (pp. 313-342) in D. Holland & N. Quinn (eds.), *Cultural Models in Language and Thought*. Cambridge: Cambridge University Press.

Qvortrup, J. (2005). 'The little's' and the prospects for generational childhood studies.

Rasmussen, K. (1931). *The Netsilik Eskimos. Report of the Fifth Thule Expedition, 1921-24*. Copenhagen: Gylendalske Boghandel. **145-6, 258**

Raum, O.F. (1940). Chagga childhood. A description of indigenous deucation in an East African tribe, Oxford, Oxford University Press. **49**

Redfield, R. (1956). *Peasant Society and Culture: An Anthropological Approach to Civilisation.* Chicago: Chicago University Press.

——.(1950) *A Village That Chose Progress*. Chicago, University of Chicago Press. **120**

Rehberg, H.R. & C.L. Richman (1989). "Pro-social Behaviour in Pre-school Children: A Look at the Interaction of Race, Gender and Family Composition," *International Journal of Behavioural Development*, 12: 385-401.

Reynolds, V. (1976). *The Biology of Human Action*. Reading: Freeman. **172**

Reynolds, V & R. Tanner (1995). *The Social Ecology of Religion*. New York: Oxford University Press. **177, 254**

Rice, D. (1992). *The Dragoon's Brood. Conversations with Young Chinese*. London: Harper-Collins. **201**

Richards, M.P.M. (1996). "The Childhood Environment and the Development of Sexuality," (pp. 183-205) in C.J.K. Kenney & S.J. Ulijaszek (eds.), *Long-term Consequences of Early Environment: Growth, Development and the Lifespan Developmental Perspective*. Cambridge: Cambridge University Press.

Robinson, J. A (1968) *Crisis International Encyclopaedea Social Science*. New York, MacMillan, 3: 510-514. **129**

Romney, K. & R. Romney (1963). "The Mixtecs of Juxtlahuaca, Mexico," (pp. 543-691) in B.B. Whiting (ed.), *Six Cultures. Studies in Child Rearing*. New York: Wiley. **234**

Rosaldo, M.Z. (1987). "Moral/Analytic Dilemmas Posed by the Intersection of Feminism and Social Science," (pp. 281-301) in P. Rabinow & W.M. Sullivan (eds.), *Interpretive Social Science*. Berkeley: University of California Press. **169**

Rosenthal, A.M. (1964). *Thirty-eight Witnesses*. New York: McGraw-Hill.

Rowe, D.C. (1994). *The Limits of Family Influence: Genes, Experience and Behaviour*. New York: Guilford Press.

Sapir, E. (1949). Selected Writings in Language, Culture and Personality. Berkeley: University of California Press. **86**

Scanlon,T. *et al.* (1998). "Street Children in Latin America," *British Journal of Sociology,* May, 1596-1600. **242**

Schaffer, H.R. (1977). *Mothering*. London: Open Books. **185-6**

Scheffelin, B.B. & E. Ochs. (1986). "Language Socialisation," *Annual Review of Anthropology*, 15: 163-191. **84**

Scurletis. T.D. *et al.* (1966). 'Trends in illegitimacy and associated mortality in North Carolina. 1957-66.' North Carolina Medical J. 10; 214-21. **259**

Schutz, A. (1967). *Collected Papers-I. The Problem of Social Reality*. The Hague: Martinus Nijhoff. **173**

Schwartzman, H.B. & L. Barbera (1976). "Children's Play in Africa and South America. A Review of Ethnographic Literature" (pp. 11-18) in D.F. Lancy & A.B. Tindall (eds.), *The Anthropological Study of Play*. Cornwall, New York: Leisure Press. **205**

Shah, J.H. (1959) Causes and Prevention of Suicide, Indian Conference of Social Work, Hyderabad. **39**

Shapira, A & Madsen, M.C. (1969). "Cooperative and Competitive Behaviour in Kibbutz and Urban Children in Israel," *Child Development*, 40: 609-617.

——. (1974). "Between- and within-group Cooperation and

Competition among Kibbutz and Non-kibbutz Children," *Developmental Psychology*, 10: 140-145.

Shoufani, M. (1988). Interview in Morocco Ministry of Education quoted by E.W. Fernea. "Childhood in the Muslim Middle East," (pp. 4) in E.W. Fernea (ed.), *Children in the Muslim Middle East*. Austin: University of Texas. **22**

Singa, S.D & K.P. Pothen (1982). *Slum Children of India*. New Delhi: Deep & Deep. **242**

Smetana, J.G. (1997). "Parenting and the Development of Social Knowledge Reconceptualised: A Social Domain Analysis," (pp.162-192) in J.E. Grusec & L. Kuczynski (eds.), *Parenting and Children's Internalising of Values*. New York: Wiley.

Smith, P.K. (1979). "How Many People Can a Young Child Feel Secure With?" *New Society*. 869: 504-6. **50**

Solberg, A. (1997). "Negotiating Childhood: Changing Construction of Age for Norwegian Children," (pp. 63-84) in A. James & A Prout (eds.), *Constructing and Deconstructing Childhood*. London: Falmer Press. **141**

Starrett, G. (1996). "The Margins of Print. Children's Religious Literature in Egypt," *Journal of Royal Anthropological Institute* (ns), 2: 117-139.

Steinberg, L.D. *et al.* (1982). "Effect of Working on Adolescent Development," *Developmental Psychology*, 18: 385-395.

Steiner, G. (1975). *After Babel. Aspects of Language and Translation*. London. Oxford University Press. **84**

____. (1989). *Real Presences*. London: Faber. **49, 85**

Stevenson, H.N.C. 1943. The Economics of the Central Chin Tribes. *Times of India*, Bombay. **88**

Stiles, H.R. (1869). *Bundling; Its Origins, Progress and Decline in America*. Albany: Munsell.

Swart-Kruger. J & D. Donald (1994). "Children of the South African Streets," (pp.107-121) in A. Dawes & D. Donald (eds.), *Childhood and Adversity. Psychological Perspectives*. Capetown: Philip. **243**

Tanner, R.E.S. (1964). "Cousin Marriage in the Afro-Arab Community in Mombasa, Kenya," *Africa*, 34 (2):127-139. **259**

____. (1967) *Transition in African Beliefs*. New York, Maryknoll. **47**

____. (1997). "Cognitive Development, Socialisation and Cognitive Mutations. A Critique and Elaboration of Boyer's Naturalness of Religion. A Case Study of the Sukuma of Tanzania," *Journal of Social Sciences*, 1 (2): 91-98. **10**

____. (2002). "Some Reflections on Being the Subject of Research into Memory. An Academic Critique of Methodology Applied to a Single Person," *Quality and Quality*, 36 (1): 81-91.

Tellegen, A. *et al.* (1988). "Personality Similarity in Twins Reared Together or Apart," *Journal of Personality & Social Psychology*, 54: 1031-1039. **9**

Tesson, G. et al. (1987). "The Social Rules that Children Use in their Interpersonal Relations," *Contribution to Human Development*, 18: 36-57.

Thomas, W.I. & D. Thomas (1928). "Situations Defined as Real are Real in their Consequences," (pp. 572) in G.P. Stone & H.A. Fabermass (eds.), *Social Psychology through Symbolic Interaction*. Waltham, Mass: Xerox College Publishing. **148**

Tietjen, A. (1986). "Pro-social Reasoning among Children and Adults in a Papua New Guinea Society," *Developmental Psychology*, 22: 861-868.

Triandis, H.C. (1994). *Culture and Social Behaviour*. New York: McGraw-Hill. **98**

____. (1995). *Individualism and Collectivism*. Boulder, Colorado: Westview. **159, 231-2**

Turnbull, C. 1973. *The Mountain People*. New York: Simon & Schuster. **5**

Turner, V. (1967). *The Forest of Symbols. Aspects of Ndembu Ritual*. Ithaca: Cornell University Press. **109**

____. (1968). *The Ritual Process. Structure and Anti-Structure*. London: Routledge and Kegan Paul.

Ueda, K. (1974). *Sixteen Sways to Avoid Saying 'No' in Japan. Patterns of Communication in and out of Japan*. Tokyo: ICU Communication Department. **91**

United Nations (1989). Convention on the Rights of the Child, United Nations. New York. **184**

Urban, G. (1996). Metaphysical Community the interplay of the senses and the intellect-Austin. University of Texas. **25**

Vandell, D.L. & M.D. Bailey (1993). "Conflicts between Siblings," (pp. 242-269) in C.U. Swantz & W.W. Hartup (eds.), *Conflict in Child and Adolescent*. Cambridge: Cambridge University Press. **218**

Varkevisser, C.M. (1973) Socialization in a changing society. Sukuma Childhood in Rural and Urban Mwanza, Tanzania. The Hague : Centre for the Study of Education in Developing Societies. **47**

Veale, A. *et al.* (2000). "Psychological Perspectives of 'Abandoned' or 'Abandoning' Street children," (pp.131-145) in C. Panter-Brick

& M.T. Smith (eds.), *Abandoned Children*. Cambridge: Cambridge University Press. **242**

De Waal, F.B.M. (1987). "Tension Regulation and Non-reproductive Functions of Sex among Captive Bonobos," *National Geographic Research*, 3: 318-35. **33**

____. (1989). "Dominance 'Style' and Primate Social Organisation," (pp. 243-63) in V. Standen & R.A. Foley (eds.), *Comparative Socio-ecology. The Behavioural Ecology of Humans and Other Mammals*. Oxford: Blackwell. **38**

____. (1997). "The Chimpanzee's Service Economy: Food for Grooming," *Evolution and Human Behaviour*, 18: 375-86. **33**

Wade, N. (1968) 'Virgin Birth and the Tully River Blacks'. New Society. 26 July. **254**

Wainryb, C. (1991). "Understanding Differences in Moral Judgements. The Role of Informational Assumptions," *Child Development*, 62: 840-851.

Watson, L.C. (1968). *Guajiro Personality and Urbanisation*. Los Angeles: Latin American Centre, University of California. **251**

Waugh. E (1953) *Brideshead Revisited*. Penguin, Harmondsworth.

Weber, M. (1951). *The Religion of China*. New York: Free Press. **182**

____. (1978). *Economy and Society. An Outline of Interpretive Sociology*. Berkeley: University of California Press. **74**

Weisner, T.S. (1981). "Cities, Stress and Children. A Review of Some Cross-cultural Questions," (pp.783-808) in A.H. Munro *et al.* (eds.), *Handbook of Cross-cultural Human Development*. New York: Garlandstrom Press. **252**

____. (1976). "Consequences of Rural-urban Migration for Families and Children in Kenya," *Kenya Education Review*, 2: 108-114. **251**

____. (1986). "Implementing New Relationship Styles in American Families," (pp.185-205) in W.W. Hartup & Z. Rubin (eds.), *Relationships and Development*. Hillsdale, New Jersey: Erlbaum. **13**

Weisner, T.S. & S. Abbott (1977). "Women, Modernity and Stress. Three Contrasting Contexts for Change in East Africa," *Journal of Anthropological Research*, 33: 421-451. **251**

Weisner, T & R. Gallimore. (1977). "My Brother's Keeper: Child and Sibling Care-taking," *Current Anthropology*, 18. **184**

Weisner, T.S. *et al.* (1983). "Putting Family Ideals into Practice: Pro-naturalism in Conventional and Non-conventional California Families," *Ethos*, 11: 278-304.

Weyl, N. (1968). "Some possible Religious Reflexivity and Transmission Frequency," *Social Anthropology*, 1: 91-103. **257**

Whitehouse, M. (2002). "Religious Reflexivity and Transmission Frequency," *Social Anthropology*, 1: 91-103. **82**

Whiting, B. (1974). "Folk Wisdom and Child Rearing," *Merrill-Palmer Quarterly of Behaviour and Development*, 20: 9-19. **251**

Whiting, B.B. & C.P. Edwards. (1988). *Children of Different Worlds. The Formation of Social Behaviour*. Cambridge, Mass: Harvard University Press. **51**

Whiting, B.B. & J.W.M. Whiting (1975). *Children of Six Cultures. A Psycho-social Analysis*. Cambridge, Mass: Harvard University Press. **64, 252**

Whyte, W. H. (1957). The Organisation Man. Anchor, New York. **269**

Wilmot, P & M. Young, (1957). *Family and Kinship in East London*. London: Routledge and Kegan Paul. **53, 142-3**

Wilson, E.O. (1975). *Sociobiology*. Cambridge, Mass: Harvard University Press. **6**

Wolf, M. (1975). "Women and Suicide in China," (pp.114-42) in M. Wolf & R. Witke (eds.), *Women in Chinese Society*. Stanford, California: Stanford University Press. **39**

Woodhead, M. (1997). "Psychology and the Cultural Construction of Children's Needs," (pp.63-84) in A. James & A. Prout (eds.), *Constructing and Reconstructing Childhood*. London: Falmer. **184**

Wrangham, R.W. (1975). The Behavioural Ecology of Chimpanzees in Gombe National Park, Tanzania. Unpublished Doctorial Dissertation, Cambridge University. **33**

Wright, L. (2004). "The Kingdom of Silence," *New Yorker*. January 5, 48-73. **222**

Youniss, J & J. Smollar. (1989). "Adolescents' Interpersonal Relationships in Social Context," (pp.300-316) in T.J. Berndt and G.W. Ladd (eds.), *Peer Relationships in Child Development*. New York: Wiley.

Yang, B. *et al.* (1995). "Only Children and Children with Siblings in the People's Republic of China: Levels of Fear, Anxiety and Depression," *Child Development*, 66: 1301-1311. **14**

# INDEX